HISTORY AROUND US

Schools Council History 13-16 Project

This project was set up in 1972 at the University of Leeds and continued there for five years with a Schools Council grant of £126,000.

Its main aim was to suggest suitable objectives for history teachers, and to promote the use of appropriate materials and ideas for their realisation. This involved a reconsideration of the nature of history and its relevance in secondary schools; the design of a syllabus framework which shows the uses that history may have in the education of adolescents; and the setting up of experimental 'O' level and C.S.E. examinations.

Project Team

David Sylvester (Director to 1975)
Tony Boddington (Director from 1975)
Gwenifer Griffiths (from 1975-1976)
William Harrison
John Mann (1974–1975)
Aileen Plummer
Denis Shemilt (Evaluator from 1974)
Peter Wenham (to 1974)

Schools Council History 13-16 Project

HISTORY AROUND US
Some guidelines for teachers

Holmes McDougall Edinburgh

Design and illustration by Graham D. Smith
Picture research by Procaudio Ltd.

Holmes McDougall
Allander House
137–141 Leith Walk
Edinburgh EH6 8NS

ISBN 0 7157 1554-2

© Schools Council Publications 1976. All Rights Reserved. No part of this publication may be reproduced, stored in a retrieval system, or transmitted, in any form or by any means, electronic, mechanical, photocopying, recording or otherwise, without the prior permission of the copyright owner.

Printed in Great Britain by
Holmes McDougall
Allander House
137–141 Leith Walk
Edinburgh EH6 8NS

CONTENTS

	Introduction	7
1	Prehistoric Britain	15
2	Roman Britain	25
3	Castles and fortified manor houses	47
4	Country houses	65
5	Church buildings and furnishings	83
6	Town development and domestic architecture	107
7	Industrial archaeology	129
8	The making of the rural landscape	153
9	Aspects of the history of the locality	169

ACKNOWLEDGEMENTS

We should like to thank the Schools Council History Project Trial School Teachers for their help with the preparation of sections of this booklet and in particular:

Roman Britain:
D. Greenwood, Ashington Grammar School, Northumberland. P. Jarman, Spurley Hey High School, Gorton, Manchester. Mrs. M. Toose Hatfield Girls' Grammar School, Hertfordshire.

Castles:
R. S. Bambrick, Bangor Boys' Secondary School, N. Ireland. C. Hirst and A. Upton, Cross Green School, Leeds, W. Yorkshire. J. Howe, Whitley Bay High School, Tyne and Wear. N. T. Malden, Bishop Vesey's Grammar School, Sutton Coldfield, Warwickshire.

Churches:
T. Scherb, Gosforth High School, Newcastle-upon-Tyne.

Town Development:
T. Carr, Richmond School, N. Yorkshire. G. Cooke, Hulme Grammar School, Oldham, Greater Manchester. Mrs. A. Eade, Cheadle Hulme County High School, Cheshire. D. Lunn, Bristol Grammar School, Avon. I. Plimmer, Gordano School, Portishead, Avon.

Industrial Archaeology:
A. Dunphy, Ellowes Hall School, Lower Gornal, Dudley, West Midlands. V. Kelly, Annadale Grammar School, Belfast, N. Ireland. W. Walker, S. Atkins, Chesterfield Grammar School, Derbyshire.

Aspects of the History of the Locality:
K. Burton, Nunthorpe Secondary School, Middlesbrough, Cleveland. G. Clarke, Lord William's School, Thame, Oxfordshire. S. Harber, Stockport School, Stockport, Cheshire. Miss E. Parkinson, Toothill Comprehensive School, Bingham, Nottinghamshire. J. F. Plummer, John Smeaton High School, Leeds, W. Yorkshire. J. Scott, Glossop School, Glossop, Derbyshire.

The authors and publishers are grateful to the following for permission to reproduce copyright material:

Routledge & Kegan Paul Ltd. for an extract from Joscelyne Finberg, *Exploring Villages*, page 7; Faber and Faber Ltd. for an extract from W. G. Hoskins, *Fieldwork in Local History*, page 7; a diagram from R. W. Brunskill, *Illustrated Handbook of Vernacular Architecture*, page 179; A. & C. Black Ltd. for an extract from Graham Webster, *The Imperial Roman Army*, page 33; author and Society of Antiquaries of London for extracts, maps, plans and photographs from the late Sir Mortimer Wheeler, *Maiden Castle: Dorset*, pages 38/43; editor and Eyre Methuen Ltd. for an extract from A. R. Myers (Ed.) *English Historical Documents*, VOL. IV, page 56; The Surtees Society for extracts and a photograph from its publications, pages 57/60, 102; an extract from 'The Close Rolls', transcript of a Crown-copyright record in the Public Record Office appears by permission of the Controller of H.M. Stationery Office, page 59; The Society for Promoting Christian Knowledge for a drawing from J. S. Fletcher, *The Story of English Towns: Pontefract*, page 60; The Historic Society of Lancashire and Cheshire for an extract from their 'Transactions', page 74; The Suffolk Institute of Archaeology for extracts from 'The Household Book of Dame Alice de Bryene' and 'The Account of William Burgh' pages 74/76; The University Press of Virginia for extracts from William Harrison, *The Description of England*, pages 77/78, 165; Gill and Macmillan Ltd. for an extract from Pamela Horn, *The Rise and Fall of the Victorian Servant*, page 80; B. T. Batsford Ltd. for plans from J. Charles Cox, *Parish Churches of England*, pages 88/90; The Thoresby Society for extracts from F. S. Colman, *History of Barwick-in-Elmet*, pages 96/97, 99/101, and from 'Aberford Parish Registers', pages 101/2; author and Methuen & Co. Ltd. for extracts from J. Charles Cox, *Churchwardens' Accounts from the Fourteenth to the Seventeenth Century*, pages 96/98; Chatto and Windus Ltd. for an extract from Cardinal Gasquet, *The Rule of St. Benedict*, page 103; for extracts from Geoffrey Chaucer's *Prologue to The Canterbury Tales*, trans. Nevill Coghill (Penguin Classics, 1960 edn.) pp. 23–25, 32, copyright © Nevill Coghill, 1951, 1958, 1960, reprinted by permission of Penguin Books Ltd. page 104; The University of Nottingham Press and the Literary executor for a map from Professor J. D. Chambers, *A Century of Nottingham History* 1851-1951, page 115; the maps appearing on page 118 are reproduced from the Local History Collection in Hull Central Library by kind permission of the Director of Leisure Services, Humberside County Council; David & Charles (Holdings) Ltd for extracts from Edward Baines, *History, Directory & Gazetteer of the County of York*, pages 120/121, 188/189 and J. Aikin, *A Description of the Country for 30 to 40 Miles Around Manchester*, pages 144/5; North Yorkshire Country Record Office, Northallerton for extracts from 'Richmond Borough Coucher books', page 125; Mr. Robert T. Clough for illustrations from *The Lead Smelting Mills of the Yorkshire Dales*, pages 142/143; Public Record Office of Northern Ireland for an extract from a 'Lagan Navigation Company minute book', page 146; Dudley Public Libraries for an extract from the 'Minutes' of a meeting about the Pensnett Railway, page 147; Manchester University Press for an extract from R. S. Fitton & A. P. Wadsworth, *The Strutts and the Arkwrights* 1758-1830, page 148; editor and Eyre & Spottiswoode (Publishers) Ltd. for an extract from Professor Dorothy Whitelock (Ed.), *English Historical Documents*, VOL. I, page 162; Essex Record Office for extracts from the 'Accounts of the Du Cane family', page 164; *The Guardian*, for an article by Peter Hildrew published November 29th, 1974, page 165; English Place Name Society for extracts from its volume 'The West Riding of Yorkshire', page 187; The Leeds City Art Galleries for the 'List of Rules', page 191.

The authors and publishers are grateful to the following for permission to reproduce photographs:

Crown copyright, reproduced with permission of the Controller of Her Majesty's Stationery Office, pages 8, 17, 18 (Bottom), 26 (Top and Middle left), 27 (Bottom left), 28, 48 (Bottom), 49, 50 (Top), 51 (Top) 70, 85 (Top left and right), 86, 87; Aerofilms Ltd. pages 9 (Top), 11 (Bottom), 18 (Top), 19, 26 (Bottom), 26/27 (Centre), 48 (Top), 50 (Bottom), 110 (Bottom), 154 (Top left), 155 (Top and Bottom left), 156 (Bottom), 157 (Bottom), 168, 173, 174 (Bottom), 175 (Bottom, 196 (Top); Radio Times Hulton Picture Library, pages 9 (Middle), 10 (Top), 11 (Top), 51 (Bottom), 84, 85 (Middle and Bottom left), 109 (Bottom), 110 (Top left), 111 (Top and Middle), 156 (Top), 174 (Top), 175 (Top), 196 (Bottom); National Monuments Record, pages 9 (Bottom), 64, 154 (Top and Middle left, Bottom right); Beamish, North of England Open Air Museum, pages 10 (Bottom), 134 (Top); Woodmansterne Ltd. pages 16 (Top), photo: Clive Friend FIIP, 27 (Top and Bottom left), photos: Clive Friend FIIP, Howard C. Moore; Ulster Museum, page 16 (Bottom); Janet and Colin Bord, pages 24, 46; The National Trust, pages 66 (Top), 67 (Top), 69 (Bottom), 133 (Middle); Photograph on page 67 (Bottom), by kind permission of the Marquess of Tavistock and the Trustees of the Bedford Estates; His Grace the Duke of Northumberland, K.G., P.C., F.R.S., pages 68, 69 (Top), K. Burton, Nunthorpe Secondary School, pages 85 (Bottom right), 109 (Top right), 155 (Bottom right); Hereford City Museums, page 109 (Middle left), photo: Hammonds; Nottingham Local Studies Library, page 110 (Middle right); Procaudio Ltd. page 111 (Bottom), photo: D. Wade; W. Walker, Chesterfield School, pages 130, 152; Philip Micheu, page 132 (Top left); Avoncroft Museum of Buildings, page 132 (Top right), 133 (Top left), photos: Colin Reiners; Ironbridge Gorge Museum Trust, page 132 (Bottom); Ulster Folk & Transport Museum, page 133 (Bottom); Higher Mill Museum, page 134 (Bottom); B. T. Batsford Ltd. page 154 (Bottom left); The Forestry Commission page 157 (Top).

INTRODUCTION

They come and they look, but how much do they see . . . ? The theme seems too familiar to arouse any real curiosity . . . if instead they could have put on a pair of spectacles which would have added an historical dimension to their vision how much more rewarding their looking would have been! If these visitors only knew they have before them a document on which is written the life story of a community.

Joscelyne Finberg, *Exploring Villages*

We live in a country that is richer than any other in the visible remains of the past . . . [but] . . . Most of us are visually illiterate. The material evidence of the past is all around us, if only we can construe the language it is speaking.

W. G. Hoskins, *Fieldwork in Local History*

Studying the history around us

Both authors comment on our lack of awareness of the visible evidence of the past which we 'see' around us every day. In this book we hope to provide some guidelines for teachers who want to prepare a course designed to help pupils study history by looking at their surroundings and identifying the remains of the past. Such a course could well be called 'Studying the history around us'. It involves the kind of work which is appropriate for pupils of a wide range of ages and abilities. Some teachers may use this approach to history with pupils in the ten to thirteen range, while others may prefer to include a one term course of *History Around Us* in their C.S.E. and G.C.E. 'O' level history syllabuses.

The visible remains of the past around us are many and varied but a number of major topics are immediately clear:

Prehistoric Britain
Roman Britain
Castles and fortified manor houses
Country houses
Church buildings and furnishings
Town development and domestic architecture
Industrial archaeology
Studies in the making of the rural landscape
Aspects of the history of the locality.

It is beyond the scope of this book to explore each of these themes in depth and so teachers who wish to pursue a particular topic further should consult specialist books. Suggestions for these are given in the Resources section at the end of each chapter.

The aims of the course

The character of the visible remains studied in these nine topics varies, but the aims are constant:

1. To make pupils aware that the visible remains of the past around us are as important a resource for our understanding of history as written documents.

2. To give pupils the knowledge, skills and techniques so they can:
a. identify the visible remains
b. study and interpret them
c. place them in their wider historical context.

3. To help pupils reconstruct the lives and purposes of people associated with historical sites at particular periods in the past.

4. To create an interest in and basis for further historical exploration of their environment which will continue beyond school.

Introduction

Stonehenge, Wiltshire

Hadrian's Wall, near Housesteads fort, Northumberland

Introduction

Shell keep castle; Caldicot, Gwent

Victorian country house; Thoresby Hall, Nottinghamshire

Norman church; St. John the Baptist, Adel, West Yorkshire

Introduction

Jacobean half timbered houses; Ludlow, Salop

Pithead winding gear; Blue Bell pit, Backworth, Tyne and Wear

Introduction

Withypool, Somerset: an interesting place for a village study

A street village; Barmby on the Marsh, Humberside

Introduction

The implications of the aims for methods and approaches

The aims have important implications for the approach to each topic as well as for teaching and learning methods:

1. It is important for teachers to explain this approach to history and its aims to pupils at the beginning of the course.

2. The starting point for each topic and the main emphasis throughout should be on visible evidence and its interpretation.

3. Fieldwork and visits to sites and museums are essential if pupils are to learn how to recognise and interpret the visible remains of the past around them.

4. Introductory sessions in school using maps, plans, filmstrips, slides and other material form an important part of the preparation for fieldwork and visits to sites. Pupils will then:

a. have an understanding of the general historical background
b. acquire the specialist vocabulary of the topic
c. learn to recognise the main features of the site to be studied
d. learn to read and use maps, plans, diagrams and guide books
e. learn some of the different skills involved in recording information — e.g. making maps, plans, diagrams, sketches, using a tape recorder, taking photographs and slides, completing record cards, surveying
f. begin to devise a framework of key questions about things to look for when exploring the visible remains of a period in the past.

5. During the visits and the classroom follow-up work some emphasis must be placed on the human associations of the site — how it reflects the needs, purposes and way of life of people in the past.

6. In order to find out about the people associated with different historical sites, pupils will:
a. study the visible remains
b. look at primary and secondary source material. Then they can combine the evidence to place the visible remains into general historical context.

7. Towards the end of the course we hope that some pupils will produce their own study of a site involving fieldwork and the use of relevant background source material.

Throughout this book we refer to a site visit. This does not imply that teachers should use only one site for study, they may prefer to use several.

Preparing the course

A successful course requires preparation. It would involve teachers in:

a. planning the course and its aims
b. selecting and visiting suitable sites for fieldwork
c. preparing assignment sheets for fieldwork and classroom investigation
d. collecting suitable background material, from both primary and secondary sources.

There are a number of people outside school who may be able to help with aspects of the course and its planning, e.g.

The organiser of the Schools Museum Service may provide: scale models of different sites such as castles, churches, Roman villas or Georgian houses, films and sets of slides showing different visible remains, historical costumes, information about history and museum trails.

The librarian in the local history library and the archivist in the local record office may offer advice about suitable background source material — both primary and secondary sources.

Museum curators and site custodians may give introductory talks and provide study facilities for visiting groups of pupils. Advance notice of such visits is essential.

The organiser of the Schools Library Loan Service may loan kits of background information books to the school for a term.

G.C.E. and C.S.E.

In some schools pupils may be studying *History Around Us* as part of a G.C.E. or C.S.E. history course. Some suggestions about course-work for teachers who wish to devise their own Mode 3 G.C.E. or C.S.E. syllabuses have been included with the guidelines for each topic. However teachers intending to adopt one of the courses

Introduction

listed below should contact the secretaries of the Examination Boards concerned for detailed information about the syllabus and course-work assessment scheme:

Schools Council History Project/Southern Universities Joint Board. G.C.E. 'O' level history syllabus.

Mode 1 C.S.E. history syllabus based on the Schools Council History Project course offered by your local C.S.E. board.

Schools Council History Project/Southern Regional Examinations Board. C.S.E. Mode 1 history syllabus.

Resources for studying the history around us

A Resources section has been included at the end of each chapter. Each section suggests useful books for teachers and pupils as well as filmstrips, slides and films.

Teachers may wish to purchase a cassette tape recorder and Polaroid camera for use during fieldwork.

Teachers may find further useful information in: Gwyneth Williams, *Guide to Illustrative Material for Use in Teaching History* (Historical Association, 1969 — revised edition in preparation)

General reference material

Educational Foundation for Visual Aids, *Audio Visual Aids Catalogue*, Part 2, 'History, Social History, Social Studies'
W. G. Hoskins, *Fieldwork in Local History*, (Faber, 1969)
T. H. Corfe (Ed.), *History in the Field*, (Blond Educational, 1970)
Robert Douch, *Local History and the Teacher*, (Routledge & Kegan Paul, 1967)
John Richardson, *Local Historian's Encyclopaedia*, (Historical Publications Ltd, 1974)
J. B. Harley and C. W. Phillips, *Historian's Guide to Ordnance Survey Maps*, (National Council for Social Service, 1965).

Teachers may also find this selection of addresses useful. All the publishers, film distributors, libraries, museums, etc. mentioned below are in the Resources section of a chapter in this book.

Attico Films, 27 Church Street, Wath-on-Dearne, Rotherham, South Yorkshire.
Bodleian Library, Assistant Librarian, Department of Western Manuscripts, Bodleian Library, Oxford.
Boulton Hawker Films Ltd., Hadleigh, Ipswich, Suffolk.
British Film Institute, 81 Dean Street, London, W.1
British Museum — now British Library; Photographic Service, British Library, Great Russell Street, London, W.C.2
British Transport Films, Melbury House, Melbury Terrace, London N.W.1
Contemporary Films Ltd., 55 Greek Street, London W1V 6DB
David and Charles (Publishers) Ltd, Newton Abbot, Devon
Department of the Environment, Clerk of Stationery, Department of the Environment, 11–13 Leathermarket Street, London, SE1 3HL
E.F.V.A. — Educational Foundation for Visual Aids: National Audio Visual Aids Library, 33 Queen Anne Street, London W1M OAL
Educational Productions — E.P., East Ardsley, Near Wakefield, Yorkshire
English Place Name Society, University College, Gower Street, London, W.1
Frank Graham (Publishers) Ltd, 6 Queen's Terrace, Newcastle-upon-Tyne, NE2 2PL
Gateway Educational Films Ltd, St Lawrence House, 29–31 Broad Street, Bristol, BS1 2HF
HMSO – orders by post, Government Bookshop, P.O. Box 569, London, SE1 9NN
HMSO — enquiries, for catalogues or information, HMSO, Atlantic House, Holborn Viaduct, London, EC1P 1BN

Agents for government publications outside London:
Leeds, Austick's Bookshop, 23 Cookridge Street
Leicester, The University Bookshop, Mayor's Walk
Liverpool, Parry Books Ltd, The University Bookshop, Alsop Building, Brownlow Hill
Maidstone, W. H. Smith & Son Ltd, 11 High Street
Middlesbrough, Boddy's Bookshop, 165 Linthorpe Road
Newcastle on Tyne, The Bible House, 14 Pilgrim Street; Thorne's Student Bookshop, 63–67 Percy Street
Northampton, C. B. Savage Ltd, 99–105 Kettering Road
Nottingham, Sisson & Parker Ltd, Wheeler Gate
Oxford, B. H. Blackwell Ltd. 50 and 51 Broad Street
Reading, William Smith (Booksellers) Ltd, 35–41 London Street

Introduction

Sheffield, W. Hartley Seed, 154–160 West Street
Southampton, John Adams Bookservice Ltd, 103 St. Mary Street
Stoke on Trent, Webberley Ltd, Percy Street, Hanley
Swansea, Uplands Bookshop Ltd, 4 Gwydr Square, Uplands; Singleton Bookshop Ltd, College House, Singleton Park
Wakefield, The Eagle Press, Wood Street
Wolverhampton, Bookland & Co. Ltd, 13 and 15 Lichfield Street

Hugh Baddeley Productions, filmstrip orders, Hugh Baddeley Productions, Educational Distribution Centre, 8 Brampton Road, St. Albans, Hertfordshire AL1 4P4
Hugh Baddeley Productions, film hire, 97 Moffats Lane, Brookmans Park, Hatfield, Hertfordshire AL9 7RP
John King (Films) Ltd, Film House, 71 East Street, Brighton, BN1 1NZ
Manchester Museum, The University, Oxford Road, Manchester M13 9PL
E. A. Meaden, Belton House, 53 Main Street, Loughborough, Leicestershire
Mills and Boon (Publishers), 17–19 Foley Street, London, W1A 1DR
Museum of Antiquities, The University, Newcastle upon Tyne, NE1 7RU
Nicholas Hunter Filmstrips, 40 Richmond Road, Oxford
Ordnance Survey — orders from the general public, from agents and local stockists
Ordnance Survey — trade orders, Director General, Ordnance Survey, Department 32, Romsey Road, Maybush, Southampton, SO9 4HD
Pictorial Charts Education Trust, 132-8 Uxbridge Road, London W.13
Pitkin Pictorials, 11 Wyfold Road, London, SW6 6SG
Public Record Office, Chancery Lane, London WC2 — telephone: 01 405 1041
Rank Audio Visual Ltd., P.O. Box 70, Great West Road, Brentford, Middlesex
Shire Publications, Cromwell House, Church Street, Princes Risborough, Aylesbury, Buckinghamshire HP17 9AJ
Slide Centre Ltd., Portman House, 17 Brodrick Road, London SW17 7DZ
Ulster Architectural Heritage Society, 30 College Gardens, Belfast, BT9 6BT
Ulster Museum, Ulster Museum, Botanic Gardens, Belfast, BT9 5AB
Visual Information Services Ltd, 12 Bridge Street, Hungerford, Berkshire
Visual Publications, 197 Kensington High Street, London W.8
Wayland (Publishers) Ltd. and Priory Press Ltd, 101 Grays Inn Road, London, WC1X 8TX
Woodmansterne Publications Ltd, Watford, WD1 8RD

1 PREHISTORIC BRITAIN

Some objectives and outcomes

We hope that by the time pupils finish their study of Prehistoric Britain they will:

1. have sufficient background knowledge about prehistoric people and their way of life to:
a. recognise different types of prehistoric remains
b. set them in their wider historical context.

2. have had practice at studying and interpreting:
a. several different types of prehistoric sites
b. different types of prehistoric objects to be found in museum collections.

3. have had practice at combining the study of visible remains and background material so they can:
a. reconstruct the lives
b. understand the purposes of the people who inhabited different types of prehistoric site.

4. have the knowledge, skills and enthusiasm to explore prehistoric remains and other aspects of their historical environment beyond school.

An approach

Teachers will wish to organise the course to suit the abilities of their pupils and to take account of the visible prehistoric remains in the locality of the school. We hope that the following suggestions will prove useful.

1. Introductory lessons

These could introduce pupils to the idea of prehistory and to the problems of studying people who have left no written record of their way of life. Some teachers may want their pupils to have some background knowledge about the evolution of man and/or the different chronological periods of prehistory — Palaeolithic, Mesolithic, Neolithic, etc.

2. The study of different types of sites

Following the introductory lessons teachers could divide the course into sections based on chronological periods. While studying each section pupils would acquire background information about the people and their way of life. This would be followed by investigations into the different types of visible evidence they left behind.
Prehistoric sites and artefacts would be studied by fieldwork and visits to museums, as well as by using slides, photographs, filmstrips and films. The local Schools Museum Service may provide examples of flint implements and models of different kinds of sites.

3. An outline of the course

a. Palaeolithic/Mesolithic people and their remains

Background lessons to find out about:
the climate and vegetation; the effect of these factors on the life style of Palaeolithic men
their way of life as hunters and food gatherers
the areas in which they settled and why they chose them.

The study of visible remains
their flint, stone and bone tools and implements
the rock shelters and caves in which they lived.

b. Neolithic people and their remains

Background lessons to find out about:
changes in climate and vegetation in Neolithic times
the introduction of agriculture and stockbreeding
the development of trading
improvements in tools and implements
the areas the farmers settled in
their reasons for choosing those particular areas
their way of life.

Neolithic tools of stone and flint c. 2700 – 1800 BC; Colchester and Essex Museum

Portal grave, c. 2500 BC; Ballyrennan, Co. Tyrone

Prehistoric Britain

Neolithic flint mines; Grimes Graves, Norfolk

Stonehenge, Wiltshire

Prehistoric Britain

Stone circle enclosing the later village; Avebury, Wiltshire

Bronze Age monument; Silbury Hill Wiltshire

Prehistoric Britain

Iron Age village; Chysauster, Cornwall

The study of Neolithic sites
These could be divided into three types. Teachers may want their pupils to look at only one example of each type of site but this will vary according to the locality of the school, e.g.

Homes and farms:
causeway camps, e.g. Windmill Hill, Wiltshire
hut circles and corn plots, e.g. Lough Gur, Limerick
villages, e.g. Scara Brae, Orkney.

Religious sites:
long barrows, chambered tombs, passage graves, henge monuments, e.g. Stonehenge phase one.

Trade and industrial sites:
trackways, e.g. Icknield way, flint mines, e.g. Grimes Graves, Suffolk.

c. Bronze Age people and their remains

Background lessons to find out about:
the introduction of metallurgical techniques
the effect of this new technology on the way of life
new burial practices
religion and the Druids
introduction of spinning and weaving
areas of settlement and the reasons for choosing them.

The study of Bronze Age sites
Teachers may want their pupils to study only one example of each type of site:

Homes and farms:
hut circles, strip lynchets and celtic square fields, e.g. Grassington Moor, North Yorkshire.

Religious sites:
round barrows, round cairns, single man burials —at first inhumation then cremation
stone circles e.g. Stonehenge phase two; standing stones; Llyn Cerig Bach, Anglesey and the finds connected with the Druids.

Trade and industrial sites:
copper and tin mines — often little remains as many sites have been used continuously ever since.

d. Iron Age people and their remains

Background lessons to find out about:
the introduction of iron
the increasing number of everyday objects,

weapons, tools, implements, horsetrappings, pottery, querns, coins, wheels,
religion and way of life
the areas of settlement and reasons for choosing them
the impact of the Roman occupation of Britain.

The study of Iron Age sites
Homes and farms:
hut circles and farm enclosures, e.g. Little Woodbury, Wiltshire
Belgic camps,
e.g. Wheathampstead, Hertfordshire
lake village, e.g. Glastonbury.

Hill forts:
e.g. Maiden Castle, Danebury Camp.

Religious sites:
cist burials in South East England;
cart burials in Yorkshire;
barrows, e.g. Danes Graves Nr. Driffield, Humberside.

4. Concluding lessons

These would draw the work together by discussing the visible evidence and asking the following questions:

What do we know about the changes in man's way of life between Palaeolithic and Iron Age times?
In what ways and for what reasons do the visible remains of Neolithic people differ from those of Iron Age people?

Pupils could prepare maps for their future reference showing different prehistoric sites:
a. within a day's travelling distance of home
b. in a different area of the country, one they might visit on holiday.

Studying sites: some questions and activities

The amount of help teachers give to pupils during fieldwork or classroom investigations, and the form it takes, will vary. All questions and activities should help pupils understand and interpret the visible remains at different types of site.
We hope the following suggestions will be useful.

1. Barrows and other tombs

Questions
What shape and size is the barrow or tomb?
What materials were used in its construction?
Judging from its shape, size and the building materials used how many people were involved in its construction and how long did it take to build?
How many people were buried inside? Were any grave goods found near them?
Were they cremated or interred?
What rank or status do you think the people in this grave had in their own community?
Are there any objects from the site in a nearby museum?
What do we know from both the barrow or tomb and the burial site about:
a. the kind of society which produced such monuments?
b. their religious beliefs?

Possible activities
Surveying work to record the shape and dimensions of the barrow or tomb.
Annotated maps to show and explain the location and distribution of different types of barrows or tombs.
Visits to a museum to observe objects found on this, or similar sites — the Schools Museum Service may provide objects for study in the classroom.
An illustrated account explaining how perhaps the barrow or tomb was built and who it was for.
An imaginative reconstruction of a burial ceremony explaining the ideas and beliefs of the people involved.

2. A ridgeway

Questions
Which route does the ridgeway take, and on what kind of land is it located?
Why was it located there?
Which areas of prehistoric settlement does it link?
Who might have used this ridgeway and why did they use it?
Did it continue to be used after prehistoric times? If so, by whom? If not, why not?
Is it linked to other ridgeways?

Possible activities
Production of an annotated sketch map showing the route taken by the ridgeway and the known areas of prehistoric settlement along its course.
An illustrated account explaining the purpose of the ridgeway and showing its relationship — if any, to other ridgeways.

3. A village or farming settlement

Questions
How many buildings were there in this settlement?

What shape and size were they?
What building materials were used in their construction?
How long do you think they took to build?
Do any signs of hearths survive?
Does any evidence of stock rearing or cultivation still survive?
Are there any signs of drainage or sanitation?
Are there any objects from this, or similar sites, in a nearby museum?
By studying the visible evidence what can we deduce about:
a. the size and type of community living here?
b. their way of life?

Possible activities
Surveying work to record:
a. the size and shape of individual buildings
b. layout of the settlement
c. location and extent of cattle pounds or field enclosures.

An illustrated account reconstructing daily life in the community.
An annotated sketch map showing the location of similar settlements.

4. A hill fort

Questions
What size and shape is the fort?
How many ramparts did it have?
How many entrances did it have and where were they located?
Where is the fort located?
Why was that particular site chosen?
Was it easy to defend?
Are there any signs of hut circles inside the hill fort?
From references in the works of Roman writers do we know the name of the tribe who inhabited this fort?
Do we know of any incidents in the history of the fort — either from the work of archaeologists or Roman writers, or both?
Are any objects from the fort in a nearby museum?
From the visible evidence, what do we know about the way of life led by the inhabitants of the fort?

Possible activities
Surveying work to record:
a. the size and shape of the hill fort and its ramparts
b. the location of entrances
c. the size and site of any hut circles.
Visit to a nearby museum to observe objects found on the site.

Annotated sketch map to show and explain the location of this and other forts in the area.
An illustrated account reconstructing life in the hill fort at a particular time.
(The Schools Council Integrated Studies Project has produced material about Danebury Camp which may be useful here. For full details see the Resources section at the end of the chapter.)
An illustrated account reconstructing a specific incident in the history of the hill fort.
(For material about the Roman attacks on Maiden Castle and Stanwick hill fort see Chapter 2, Roman Britain.)
Whenever possible pupils should observe and handle prehistoric tools and implements, and think about the way people made and used them. The local Schools Museum Service may help here.

The background source material

The only contemporary accounts about the prehistoric inhabitants of Britain were written by the Romans, Caesar and Tacitus. Pupils could read these for background information about life in Iron Age Britain. Paperback editions are readily available in libraries and bookshops. The following list of references may be useful:

Caesar *Gallic wars*:
1. Description of Britain and its Iron Age people — their appearance, coinage, food, marriage customs etc. Bk 5. Ch. 12–14.

2. Battle tactics of the Ancient Britons especially their use of chariots. Bk 4. Ch. 32–34.

3. Caesar's attack on Cassivellaunus' hill fort at Wheathampstead. Bk 5. Ch. 21.

4. General descriptions of Caesar's two campaigns in Britain mentioning tribal chiefs. Bk 4. Ch. 20–36 Bk 5. Ch. 8–11, 15–23.

Tacitus *Agricola*:
1. Description of Britain in the late Iron Age, its climate and crops. Ch. 10, 12.

2. Description of the Iron Age inhabitants of Britain. Ch. 11.

3. Description of their battle tactics. Ch. 12–13.

When studying most prehistoric sites pupils will have to read secondary accounts based on the work of archaeologists to find background information about the lives of prehistoric people.

Suggestions for guidebooks and books for pupils are in the Resources section.

Course work for G.C.E. and C.S.E. assessment

Some history teachers may wish to devise Mode 3 C.S.E. and G.C.E. 'O' level syllabuses which include work on *History Around Us: Prehistoric Britain*.

The following items of course work could be completed by pupils and submitted in a folder as part of their final assessment:

1. Descriptions of sites studied by fieldwork supported by maps, plans, sketches, photographs and any records or surveys.

2. Descriptions of sites studied in the classroom supported by relevant plans, maps and sketches.

3. Work setting one site in its historical context and relating it to other sites:

e.g. an illustrated account describing the route and purpose of a trackway such as the Icknield Way, to include an annotated sketch map showing the location and explaining the purpose of other trackways.

e.g. an illustrated account to show the structure, purpose and location of a Neolithic passage grave, including a comparison between Bronze Age burial mounds, Iron Age burial mounds and Neolithic graves.

e.g. an illustrated account comparing the visible remains of Palaeolithic and Iron Age people with their geographical location.

4. An imaginative reconstruction of:

either: an incident in the history of a site,
e.g. Caesar's attack on the camp at Wheathampstead,
e.g. Vespasian's attack on Maiden Castle.

or: life on a site at a particular time,
e.g. Lough Gur, Limerick in Neolithic times.

or: a study of the connection between a group of people in prehistoric times and a particular site,
e.g. description of the building of Stonehenge and the kind of society which produced such a monument,
e.g. the Druids and Anglesey, Llyn Cerig Bach.

Resources

Some of the books on this list are out of print. You should be able to obtain copies from your local library or from the Schools Library Loan Service. Resources are listed by order of importance, within each section.

Teachers' books

Eric S. Wood, *Field Guide to Archaeology in Britain*, (Collins, 1975)

Ordnance Survey, *Field Archaeology in Great Britain*, (HMSO, 1974)

Islay Doncaster, *Finding the History Around Us*, (Basil Blackwell, 1956)

Lloyd Laing, *The Archaeology of Late Celtic Britain and Ireland*, (Methuen, 1975)

Colin Renfrew (Ed.), *British Prehistory*, (Duckworth, 1974)

Joseph Raftery, *Prehistoric Ireland*, (Batsford, 1951)

Guide books to sites

For sites in England and Wales, write to HMSO; for sites in Northern Ireland write to the Ulster Museum, Belfast.

Material for pupils dealing with visible evidence

Schools Council Integrated Studies Project, *Unit 1: Exploration Man: 4 Finding out about the remote past: An Iron Age Hill Fort*, (O.U.P. 1974)

Jane R. Osborn, *Stone Age to Iron Age*, 'Focus on History Series', (Longman, 1968)

Islay Doncaster, *Life in Prehistoric Times*, 'Evidence in Pictures Series' (Longman, 1962)

Books for pupils giving background information

B. Green & A. Sorrell, *Prehistoric Britain*, (Lutterworth, 1968)

Robin Place, *Prehistoric Britain*, 'Then and There Series', (Longman, 1970)

M. & C. H. B. Quennell, *The Old Stone Age*, 'Everyday Life in Prehistoric Times', (Carousel Transworld, 1971)

M. & C. H. B. Quennell, *The New Stone Age*, 'Everyday Life in Prehistoric Times', (Carousel Transworld, 1971)

Michael Hyndman, *People before History*, Books 1 - 5, (Allen & Unwin, 1974)

Reference books for pupils

G. S. Hawkins & J. B. White, *Stonehenge Decoded*, (Fontana/Collins, 1970)

Kenneth Oakley, *Man the Toolmaker*, (British Museum, Natural History, 1963)

Maps and Charts

Ordnance Survey, *Map of Ancient Britain*
Ordnance Survey, *Map of Southern Britain in the Iron Age*
Patrick Gordon, *The Unfolding Past*, Time Charts Nos. 1, 2, 3 (O.U.P. 1975)

Slides

Sets about prehistoric sites from:

The Department of the Environment
Woodmansterne Limited
Avoncroft Museum of Building
Ulster Museum, Belfast

Filmstrips

Some are out of print but may be available from Teachers' Centres.

Stonehenge, colour, Rank 1965
Early Britain, 'Part 1: The People, their tools and their homes', 'Part 2: Burial, Avebury and Stonehenge', black and white, Visual Information Services Ltd, 1953
Prehistoric Mounds and Standing Stones, 'The English Scene', black and white, Tartan — distributed by John King

Films

Digging Up Man, 16 mm, colour, 15 mins. available from Rank Film Library
This film is designed to accompany Schools Council Integrated Studies material on an Iron Age hill fort.
Who were the British? 'The Immigrants' 16 mm, black and white, 25 mins. Anglia Television, 1966 — distributed by Rank
Who were the British? 'The Believers', 16 mm, black and white, 25 mins. Anglia Television, 1966 — distributed by Rank
Stonehenge, 16 mm, black and white, 18 mins. Gateway, 1955
The Beginnings of History, 16 mm, black and white, 55 mins. Ministry of Education Visual Unit, 1949 — distributed by E.F.V.A.
Mist of Time, 16 mm, colour, 26 mins. Aengus Films and Radio Telefís Éireann, 1969 — distributed by Contemporary Films.

The Ridgeway, near Uffington, Oxfordshire; a prehistoric trackway

2 ROMAN BRITAIN

Some objectives and outcomes

We hope that by the time pupils finish their study of Roman Britain they will:

1. have sufficient background knowledge about the Romans and their conquest of Britain to:
a. recognise different types of Roman remains
b. set them in their wider historical context.

2. have practised studying and interpreting:
a. several different types of Roman sites
b. different types of Roman objects found in museums and on site.

3. have had practice at combining the study of visible remains and background material so they can:
a. reconstruct the lives
b. understand the purposes of the people who inhabited different types of Roman site.

4. have the knowledge, skills and enthusiasm to explore Roman remains in Britain and other aspects of their historical environment beyond school.

An approach

Teachers will wish to organise the course to suit the abilities of their pupils and to take account of the visible Roman remains in the locality of the school. We hope that the following suggestions will prove useful.

1. Introductory lessons

These could be based on maps and suitable filmstrips — see Resources section, at the end of this chapter. They would introduce pupils to essential background information about Roman Britain:
e.g. a brief outline of the Roman Conquest of Britain, its purpose and progress:
a. in the lowland areas
b. in the highland areas
c. in their own particular area,
e.g. a list of the main types of Roman remains and objects which can be seen 'in the field' or in museums.

2. The study of different types of site

Pupils could study several different types of site and their visible remains by fieldwork, museum visits and by using slides and filmstrips. The local Schools Museum Service may provide artefacts and models of different kinds of site.

The sequence and number of sites studied will vary from school to school. Teachers could select examples from the following categories:

a. Military fortifications

Sites
Hadrian's Wall with its milecastles, vallum, military way, forts, civilian settlements, religious shrines, temples, etc. (Housesteads fort or Vindolanda fort and civilian settlement are good examples).
An individual fort, e.g. Manchester, Chester, Ribchester, Melandra, York.
A Saxon shore fort, e.g. Reculver, Richborough, Dover.

Museums
Vindolanda and Housesteads on Hadrian's Wall
Grosvenor Museum, Chester
Yorkshire Museum, York
Colchester Museum
Manchester Museum.

b. Roman roads

Watling Street, near Verulamium
Blackstone Edge, near Manchester
Wheeldale Moor, North Yorkshire.
For other local examples see Ivan Margary, *Roman Roads in Britain*, full details in the Resources section at the end of this chapter.

Roman Britain

Roman baths; Vindolanda, Hadrian's Wall, Northumberland

Mosaic decoration on dining room floor; Lullingstone, Roman villa, Kent

Roman road; north of Richmond, North Yorkshire

Roman fort; Vindolanda, Hadrian's Wall, Northumberland

Roman Britain

Roman beaker; Colchester and Essex Museum

Roman amphitheatre; Caerleon, Gwent

Tombstone of Centurion Legion XX; Colchester and Essex Museum

Roman Britain

A Roman fort of the Saxon shore; Richborough Castle, Kent

Latrines; Housesteads fort, Hadrian's Wall, Northumberland

c. Battlegrounds

Places associated with battles between the Roman army and the Ancient Britons:
Maiden Castle, Dorset
Stanwick hill fort, North Yorkshire
Mons Graupius in the North of Scotland.

d. Towns

Sites
York: A 'colonia' — a town for retired veterans
Verulamium: A 'municipium' — a self governing native town whose inhabitants were granted Roman citizenship
Bath: a 'spa' — health resort near mineral springs
Silchester: a tribal capital.

Museums
Castle Museum, Colchester
Silchester Collection, Reading Museum
Verulamium Museum
Grosvenor Museum, Chester
The London Museum
Corinium Museum, Cirencester.

e. Roman villas

Sites
Lullingstone, Kent
Chedworth and Woodchester, Gloucester
Fishbourne and Bignor, West Sussex
Low Ham, Somerset
Lockleys, near Welwyn
Park Street, St. Albans.

Museums
The County Museum, Aylesbury has a collection of finds from Latimer and Hambledon.

f. Mines and industries

Goldmines: Dolaucothi, Dyfed
Lead and silver mines: Mendips, Somerset
Greenhow Hill, Nr. Pateley Bridge, North Yorkshire
Iron mines: Sussex, the Forest of Dean.

3. Concluding lessons

These would draw the work on Roman Britain together by investigating the withdrawal of the Romans from Britain and the subsequent fate of Roman sites. This would provide an explanation for the condition of Roman remains as we see them today.
Pupils could prepare maps or lists for their future reference showing different Roman sites:
a. within a day's travelling distance of their home
b. in a different area of the country, one they might visit on holiday.

Studying sites: some questions and activities

The amount of help teachers give to pupils during fieldwork or classroom investigations and the form it takes will vary. All questions and activities should help pupils recognise, understand and interpret the visible remains. We hope the following suggestions will be useful.

1. Military fortifications

a. Hadrian's wall, including the vallum and military way

General questions
When was it built?
Where did the wall begin and end?
What were its different military components?
What do these and its location tell us about the strategic purpose of the wall and the fighting tactics of the soldiers?
What evidence is there about the way the wall was built and the people who built it?
When was it abandoned and what happened to it afterwards?

Questions on a section of the wall:
How wide is it?
How high is it?
Is the wall the same thickness from top to bottom?
What are the differences between the building stones used for the outside faces and the core?
Comment on the siting of the wall. How has the wall taken full advantage of natural features?
Are there any specially marked stones which could be mason's marks or centurial stones?

Possible activities
Annotated maps showing the military components of the wall and explaining its strategic importance.
Diagrams showing the fighting tactics adopted by soldiers on the wall.
An illustrated account describing building techniques.
An imaginative reconstruction of a soldier's turn of watch on the wall.

b. Forts

Individual forts, e.g. Chester or forts on Hadrian's Wall.

Questions
What size is the fort?
How thick are the walls?
Why was the fort sited here? Does it command a river crossing? Does it control a gap in the highland? Does it guard a roadway? Other reasons?

Are there any roadways leading from the fort?
Had the gateways single or double doors?
Had the gateways been blocked? If so, why?
Are there any interval towers or ditches visible?
What can be seen of the road system within the fort?
What features of the headquarters building can be identified?
Do any buildings have hypocausts and buttresses?
What does the site and the layout of the buildings tell us about the military function of the fort?
What do we know about the daily routine of the soldiers in the fort from:
a. its plan and buildings?
b. its location?
c. objects and artefacts in the museum?

Are there any inscriptions, tombstones or other types of evidence to tell us which legion inhabited the fort at a particular time?
Are there any traces on site or in a museum, of a civilian settlement near the fort? If so, what can we tell about the life of the soldiers and civilians from this evidence?
Are there any traces of religious shrines used by the soldiers? If so what do these tell us about their religious beliefs and practices?

Possible activities
Annotated plans of the fort which explain:
a. its tactical significance
b. the function of all the buildings.
Description of the civilian settlement and the life of its inhabitants, including plans of buildings and sketches of objects discovered.
Plan of a religious shrine or temple, e.g. the Mithraeum at Carrawburgh, and a description of the religious practices associated with it including sketches of altars and statues.
An imaginative reconstruction of the daily routine in a fort including plans of individual buildings and drawings of objects and artefacts discovered.

For details of visual aids and pamphlets on Vindolanda and Chester see Resources section at the end of this chapter.

2. Roman roads

Questions
Why was it built and what was it used for?
What route was chosen for this road and why?
How was it constructed and why were those particular methods used?
Who built the road?
Did it continue to be used after the Romans had left? If so, why?
Why was it abandoned and when?

Possible activities
The production of an annotated sketch map showing the route of a road:
a. over a particular stretch of country
b. over its whole length including all features such as highland, valleys, rivers, marsh, British hill forts, Roman forts, etc. which determined the course of road.
The production of diagrams showing the construction of the road.
A sketch map of the main Roman roads in Britain in use today.

3. Battlegrounds

Questions
Who fought at this site and when?
Why did the Romans decide to attack this particular site?
At which point did they make their assault?
Why did they choose that particular point?
Does any visible or archaeological evidence remain to tell us about the course of the battle?

Possible activities
Battlegrounds contain little visible evidence which can be interpreted by pupils unaided.
The battles at Maiden Castle, Stanwick and Mons Graupius provide excellent class-room detective exercises. These could include:
a. background information about Roman siege and battle tactics, to help pupils interpret the visible and archaeological evidence on site
b. information about the site and the battle from excavation reports, aerial photographs and contemporary Roman descriptions.

By combining these 'finds' and 'clues' pupils could reconstruct the course of the battle. For sources relating to the battles at Maiden Castle and Mons Graupius see the section which follows on background source material; for archaeological reports on Stanwick see Resources section, at the end of this chapter.

4. Towns

Questions
Why did a town grow up in this particular place at this time?
How was the town laid out and what types of building did it have?
What evidence of the street plan, buildings, or walls can we see today?
What do the plan and buildings tell us about the life of its citizens?
Did this town continue to be occupied after the Roman withdrawal? If so, why? If not, why not?

Possible activities
A town plan labelling all the buildings and explaining their different uses.
Annotated sketch maps to show the site of a town and reasons for its growth.
Drawings and plans of specific buildings, e.g. baths, temples, forum, theatre, together with descriptions of daily events in each building.
A map or written account listing and describing other types of town.
An imaginative reconstruction based on primary and secondary source material describing a specific incident in the history of a town, e.g. Boudicca's sacking of Colchester and St. Albans.

5. Roman villas

Questions
Where was the villa sited and why?
What were its boundaries?
What was the layout of the buildings?
What do the boundaries and the layout of the building tell us about:
a. the function of the villa?
b. the daily life and routine of its inhabitants?

What happened to the villa after the Roman withdrawal?
What evidence of the villa and its inhabitants can be seen today either on the ground or in the museum?

Possible activities
Annotated sketch map showing the site of villa and explaining its function.
Plan of the buildings explaining their different uses.
Imaginative reconstruction of a typical working day on a villa including drawings of typical objects and artefacts used.
Sketch map showing the location of other Roman villas in different parts of the country.

6. Mines and industries

Questions
Where is the mine sited and why?
What mineral was being worked or extracted?
Why did the Romans need this mineral?
How was it transported?
Where was it going?
Who mined or worked the mineral and under what kind of conditions did they work and live?

Possible activities
Plan of mine workings.
Annotated sketch map to show the location of the workings, the method of transport, the route and the destination of the mineral.

Some background source material

Types of primary sources

Narrative primary sources relating specifically to Roman Britain are few. Much of the work of historians for this period has been concerned with the skilful interpretation of visible remains — using archaeological evidence, inscriptions and references from Roman writers. Teachers may find that they have to rely on secondary sources, based on the work of archaeologists such as Sheppard Frere and Sir Ian Richmond for background information. For details, see Resources section at the end of this chapter.
There are some primary sources which pupils can use to help them interpret the visible remains of the Romans in Britain:

a. Extracts from the works of Roman writers

e.g. Caesar, *Gallic Wars*; Tacitus, *Annals* and *Agricola*; Virgil, *Georgics*. Full details are given in the Resources section at the end of this chapter.

b. Evidence from archaeological reports

The text of archaeological reports is often too technical for pupils to use though the diagrams can be helpful. Extracts from the following reports could be used by some pupils:
Geoffrey Meates' report on his excavation of Lullingstone Roman villa.
Professor Barry Cunliffe's report on his excavations at Fishbourne Roman villa.
Sir Mortimer Wheeler's reports of his excavations at Maiden Castle, Dorset, and Stanwick hill fort, North Yorkshire.
The report on the 'Deansgate dig' — the Roman fort at Manchester, by Professor Barri Jones and Dr. John Wild.
See the Resources section at the end of this chapter for full details.

c. Inscriptions

Inscriptions form an important part of the source material available to help us interpret the visible remains of Hadrian's wall. Transcriptions of most of the inscriptions found so far in Roman Britain have been reproduced in A. R. Burn, *The Romans in Britain*.
In this book the inscriptions are conveniently grouped under headings such as 'Life on Hadrian's wall', 'Life in Roman Towns', etc.

d. Objects and artefacts

These can be seen in many museums. Line drawing of all types of objects can also be found in the British Museum, *Guide to the Antiquities of Roman Britain*.

As translations of the Roman writers and inscriptions are easy to find extracts from them have not been reproduced in this book.

References for background information from primary sources

This list of references provides background information for the study of visible remains. For references from Caesar, see the section on background source material in Chapter 1.

a. The rebellion of Boudicca and the sacking of Verulamium and Colchester

Tacitus, *Agricola* 4–16
Tacitus, *Annals* XIV 29–39

b. The Governorship of Agricola

His campaigns A.D. 77-62: *Agricola* 18-28
for a discussion of the visible evidence about his marching camps: Sheppard Frere, *Britannia*
The battle of Mons Graupius, *Agricola* 29–40

An example of the use of sources

The Roman attack on Maiden Castle A.D. 43-46: a study in evidence

Background information about Roman siege and battle tactics in general

Sources 1·2 and 2·2 provide pupils with information about some of the battle tactics which the Romans may have used when attacking Maiden Castle and the ways in which the besieged inhabitants may have defended themselves.

Evidence relating to the attack on Maiden Castle in A.D. 43-46

Sources 3·2 and 4·2 provide evidence which suggests that it may have been attacked by Vespasian in his campaigns in A.D. 43-46.

Sources 5·2 and 6·2 suggest that it was probably the eastern end which was attacked since this had few defensive ditches.

Source 7·2 provides the archaeological evidence for a battle at the eastern end. Note the evidence provided on the plan of the east entrance — this suggest the Britons may have attacked the Romans using sling stones which were hurled from firing platforms.

Source 8·2 gives Sir Mortimer Wheeler's imaginative reconstruction of the battle. This could be used by pupils to check their own conclusions. Though most of the evidence has been reproduced from Sir Mortimer Wheeler's report published by the Society of Antiquaries, some items can be seen in the HMSO, *Guide to Maiden Castle*.

Roman Britain

Source 1·2 *The Roman siege of Jotapata*

This account describes an incident in the Roman war against the Jews in Palestine which began in 66 A.D. It is adapted from the account produced by Josephus (A.D. 37-100) a Jewish priest and historian who wrote a history of the Jewish war.

Jotapata was built on a precipice with steep valleys on every side but the north, where a wall had been built to prevent easy access, and it was on this side that Vespasian pitched his camp. After several days Vespasian decided to prosecute the siege with vigour and he caused a bank of earth and wood to be built up against the wall. Though the soldiers working on the bank were protected by hurdles, they were greatly impeded by the huge stones and darts aimed at them by the Jews. Vespasian then set 160 siege machines to work to dislodge the enemy from the walls by aiming stones and lances at them. Josephus, the leader of the Jews, decided to build the wall higher at this point, and he was able to do this by having a screen made of the raw hides of newly killed oxen strung along the top of the wall to protect the workmen. The hides broke the impact of Roman stones and darts, and being moist, they quenched the fire missiles...

Vespasian now brought in the battering ram, and at the very first stroke the wall was shaken and a terrible clamour was raised by the people within the city. Josephus tried to defeat the ram by ordering sacks to be filled with chaff and lowering them down over the wall so that they would receive the strokes of the battering ram; as fast as the Romans moved the great engine, so the Jews moved the sacks of chaff to that new place. In the end the Romans contrived to cut the sacks from off the ropes and so continued their battering of the wall. Three parties of the Jews then rushed out of the gates and set fire to the protective hurdles and skins on the ram. While this was taking place a Jew, renowned for his strength, cast a huge stone down from the wall and on to the ram and broke off the head of the engine.

About this time Vespasian was wounded in the foot and the Romans were so incensed that they renewed their attack on the city, and all the night through continued their bombardment with great stones and other missiles which brought havoc upon the besieged Jews. By morning the wall had yielded to the battering of the ram. The trumpets of the several Roman Legions sounded, the army gave a terrible shout and their darts flew so fast that they intercepted the light of day. However, Josephus's men stopped their ears at the sounds and covered their bodies against the darts. Then, while the Roman archers paused to reload, they charged out through the breech, and heavy fighting ensued. Then the Romans attempted to scale the un-breached part of the wall, and the soldiers were joined side to side with their shields so that they could not easily be broken. But Josephus caused scalding oil to be poured down upon them so that it burnt the Romans, and as the men were cooped up in their helmets and breast-plates, they could not get free of the burning oil and so they were beaten back.

By the forty-seventh day of the siege a deserter went to Vespasian and told him how few were left in the city and how weak they were. He also told how the Jews, worn out by their constant fighting and vigilance, usually slept during the last watch of the night and that this was the hour to attack the city. And so at the appointed hour the Roman army marched silently to the wall, cut the throats of the watch and entered the city without waking the sleeping Jews. So quickly and quietly did the Romans enter the city that the Jews were taken by surprise. The Romans, remembering all that they had suffered at the hands of the Jews, drove many of them down the precipice and slew all the multitude that appeared openly, but the women and infants, who numbered 1,200, they took into slavery... In all about 40,000 were slain at the siege of Jotapata. Vespasian gave the order that the city should be entirely demolished and all the fortifications burnt down, but there were few left to care.

Graham Webster, *The Imperial Roman Army of the first and second centuries* A.D., (A. & C. Black, 1969) pp. 243-5.

Source 2·2 *Scenes from Trajan's Column in Rome showing Roman siege and battle tactics*

Illustrations from Giovanni Giacomo de Rossi, *Colonna Traiana,* (1673 edition)

Roman infantrymen advancing towards the walls of a town in tortoise formation with shields overhead, to the front and sides to protect themselves against missiles and sling stones

Roman Britain

Roman soldiers giving the infantrymen covering fire with a ballista — a kind of automatic gun which fired bolts

Roman Britain

Roman soldiers with ladders for scaling walls and ramparts

Roman soldiers setting fire to the buildings and/or gate near the entrance of a fort or town. This may have been to provide a smoke shield for the assault. Alternatively the building may have been burned after the attack.

Roman Britain

Source 3·2 *An account of the campaigns of Vespasian, who later became Emperor Vespasian, in southern Britain in* A.D. 43-46

> When Claudius was Emperor, Vespasian was sent to Germany as lieutenant of a legion and from there he was posted to Britain. He fought 30 battles with the enemy conquering two great tribes and over 20 hill towns, in addition to the Isle of Wight. This campaign was partly under the conduct of Aulus Plautius, lieutenant to the consul and in part of Claudius himself.

adapted from J. C. Rolfe, *The Lives of the Caesars*, (The Loeb Classical Library, Heinemann, 1914) Book 8, Ch. 4

Source 4·2 *Map showing Iron Age hill towns in the area of southern Britain to the west of the Isle of Wight* A.D. 43-6

Sir Mortimer Wheeler, *Maiden Castle: Dorset*, (Society of Antiquaries Research Report. No. 12, 1943) p. 16, fig. 2

Roman Britain

Source 5·2 *Aerial photograph showing Maiden Castle today from the western end—in* A.D. 43-6 *the inner ramparts would have had pallisades*

Sir Mortimer Wheeler, *Maiden Castle: Dorset*, (Society of Antiquaries Research Report No. 12, 1943) plate LXXIV

Source 6·2 *Plan showing the defence system of ditches and ramparts at Maiden Castle in* A.D. 43-6

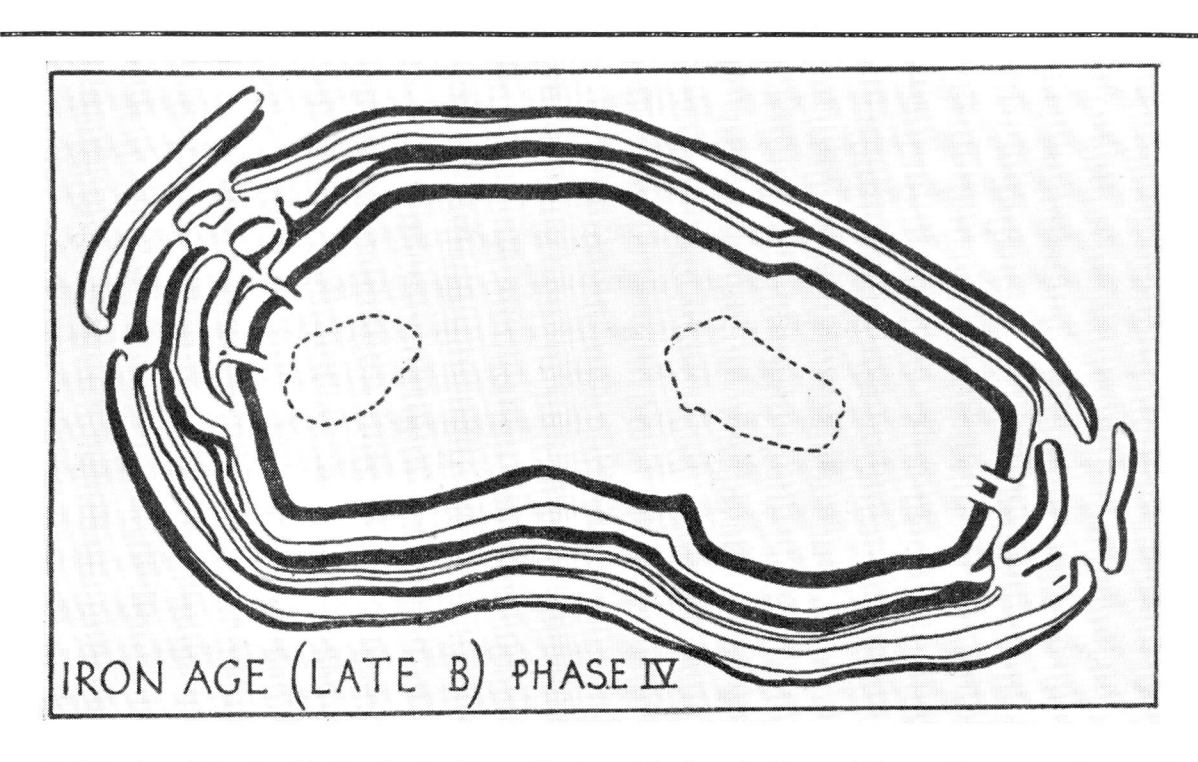

Sir Mortimer Wheeler, *Maiden Castle: Dorset* (Society of Antiquaries Research Report No. 12, 1943) p. 17, fig. 3

Source 7·2 *Extracts from Sir Mortimer Wheeler's report of excavations carried out at the eastern end of Maiden Castle in 1942-3*

First, scattered over the eastern end of Maiden Castle, mostly in and about the eastern entrance were found upwards of a dozen iron arrow-heads of two types: a type with pyramidal point, and the simple flat-bladed type with turn-over socket... Arrow-heads occurred at no other Iron Age level, but both types are common on Roman military sites where ballistae but no hand-bows are to be inferred. There, then, in the relatively small area uncovered, are the vestiges of the bombardment.

Secondly, the half moon bay close outside the portals of the eastern entrance was covered with a thick layer of ash associated with the post-holes of three or more circular huts. In and immediately below this ash were quantities of late Belgic [Iron Age] pottery. In the surface of the ash was similar pottery with scraps of pre-Flavian Samian [pottery]. There are the burnt Belgic huts, covered by the trodden vestiges of the continued post-conquest occupation for which more tangible evidence will be offered shortly.

Thirdly, into this ash a series of graves had been roughly cut, and into them had been thrown, in all manner of attitudes — crouched, extended, on the back, on the side, on the face, even sitting up — thirty-eight skeletons of men and women, young and old; sometimes two persons were huddled together in the same grave. In ten cases extensive cuts were present on the skull, some on the top, some on the front, some on the back. In another case, one of the arrow-heads, already described was found actually embedded in a vertebra (pl. LVIII, A), having entered the body from the front below the heart. The victim had been finished off with a cut on the head...

Plate LVIII, A

War cemetery: skeleton P7A, showing iron arrow-head embedded in a vertebra

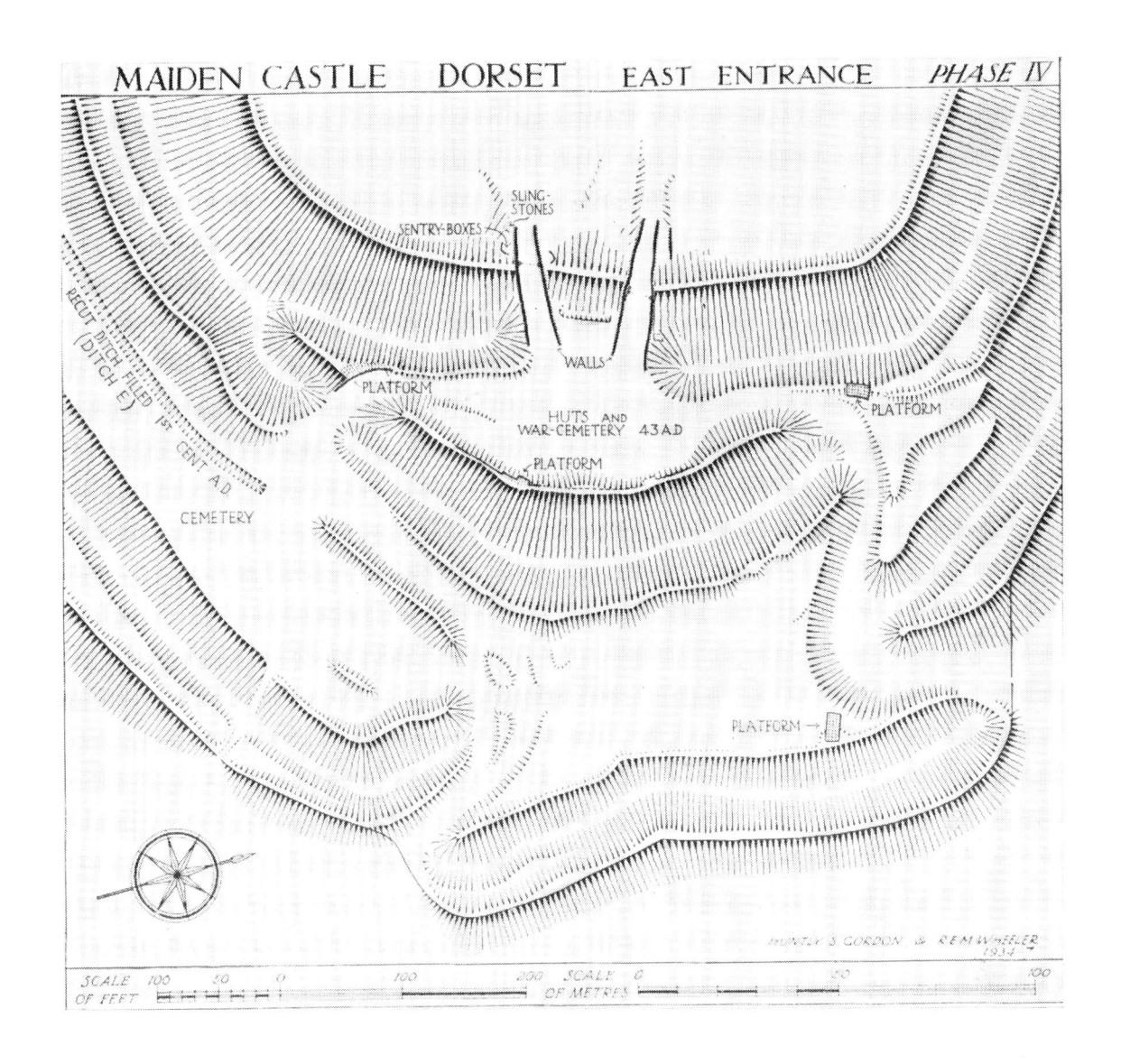

Maiden Castle, Dorset, East Entrance, 43-6 A.D.

Yet another skull had been pierced by an implement of square section, probably a ballista-bolt. The last two and some of the sword-cuts were doubtless battle-wounds; but one skull, which had received no less than nine savage cuts suggests the fury of massacre rather than the tumult of battle — a man does not stay to kill his enemy eight or nine times in the mêlée; and the neck of another skeleton had been dislocated, probably by hanging. Nevertheless, the dead had been buried by their friends for most of them were accompanied by bowls or, in one case, a mug for the traditional food and drink. More notable in two cases the dead held joints of lamb in their hands — joints chosen carefully as young and succulent. Many of the dead still wore their gear; armlets of iron or shale, an iron finger-ring, and in three cases bronze toe-rings, representing a custom not previously, it seems, observed in prehistoric Britain but reminiscent of the Moslem habit of wearing toe-rings as ornaments or as preventives or cures of disease. One man lay in a double grave with an iron battle-axe, a knife and, strangely, a bronze ear-pick across his chest.

The date of the cemetery was indicated by a variety of evidence. Most obvious is the Roman arrow-head embedded in the vertebra, but other associated relics point to the same conclusion. The seventeen pots put into the graves at the time of burial are all 'Romano-Belgic overlap' [late Iron Age 43-6 A.D. approx.]

One grave, moreover, contained a late British coin, and though it was impossible to say safely whether the coin was inserted at the interment or was incorporated in the loose ash into which the grave was cut, at least it was dropped within a very short time of the event.

There, then, is the climax of the more human side of the story of conquest. But on the structural side the evidence for that event and for its sequel is no less vivid. On the top-most Belgic road-metal, in both portals of the eastern entrance, excavation revealed the tumbled stones from the massive walls that had formerly flanked the entrance. Here and there the fallen stones lay overlapping, like a collapsed pack of cards, in the sequence in which they had formerly stood as a vertical wall. With them was no cascade of rampart-earth such as might have implied a fall through subsidence; the walls had been deliberately pulled down and no attempt had been made to replace them. But that was not all. Over the debris in each portal a new road had been built, metalled like the Belgic roads now buried beneath them. The new roads partially covered the surviving bases of the flanking walls, showing that the condition of these today is identical with their condition at the time of the road-building and confirming the permanence of the structural ruin. No provision of any kind was made in the new scheme for a gate; not a single post-hole was associated with the new road, and indeed the mutilated rampart-ends would have provided a poor setting for a fixed barrier. The implications of all this are evident. The entrance had been systematically 'slighted' and its military value reduced permanently to a minimum; but traffic through it did not cease, no interval occurred in the continuity of the occupation.

Sir Mortimer Wheeler, *Maiden Castle: Dorset,* (Society of Antiquaries Research Report, No. 12, 1943) pp. 62-4

Source 8·2 *Sir Mortimer Wheeler's imaginative reconstruction of the Roman attack on Maiden Castle* A.D. 43-6.

And so we reach the Roman invasion of A.D. 43. That part of the army of conquest wherewith we are concerned in Dorset had as its nucleus the Second Augustan Legion, whose commander, at any rate in the earlier campaigns, was the future Emperor Vespasian. Precisely how soon the invaders reached Maiden Castle can only be guessed, but by A.D. 47 the Roman arms had reached the Severn, and Dorset must already have been overrun. Suetonius affirms that Vespasian reduced 'two very formidable tribes and over twenty towns (oppida), together with the Isle of Wight', and it cannot be doubted that, whether or not the Durotriges (as is likely enough) were one of the tribes in question, the conquest of the Wessex hill-fort system is implied in the general statement. Nor is it improbable that, with the hints provided by the mention of the Isle of Wight and by the archaeological evidence for the subsequent presence of the Second Legion near Seaton in eastern Devon, a main line advance lay through Dorset roughly along the route subsequently followed by the Roman road to Exeter. From that road to-day the traveller regards the terraced ramparts of the western entrance of Maiden Castle; and it requires no great effort of the imagination to conjure up the ghost of Vespasian himself, here confronted with the greatest of his 'twenty towns'. Indeed, something less than imagination is now required to reconstruct the main sequence of events at the storming of Maiden Castle, for the excavation of the eastern entrance has yielded tangible evidence of it. With only a little amplification it may be reconstructed as follows.

Approaching from the direction of the Isle of Wight, Vespasian's legion may be supposed to have crossed the River Frome at the only easy crossing hereabout — where Roman and modern Dorchester were subsequently to come into being. Before the advancing troops some 2 miles away, the sevenfold ramparts of the western gates of . . . [Maiden Castle] towered above the cornfields which probably swept up to the fringe of the defences. Whether any sort of assault was attempted upon these gates we do not at present know; their excessive strength makes it more likely that, leaving a guard upon them, Vespasian moved his main attack to the somewhat less formidable eastern end. What happened there is plain to read. First, the regiment of artillery, which normally accompanied a legion on campaign, was ordered into action, and put down a barrage of iron-shod ballista-arrows over the eastern part of the site. Following this barrage, the infantry

> advanced up the slope, cutting its way from rampart to rampart, tower to tower. In the innermost bay of the entrance, close outside the actual gates, a number of huts had recently been built; these were now set alight, and under the rising clouds of smoke the gates were stormed and the position carried. But resistance had been obstinate and the fury of the attackers was roused. For a space, confusion and massacre dominated the scene. Men and women, young and old, were savagely cut down, before the legionaries were called to heel and the work of systematic destruction began. That work included the uprooting of some at least of the timbers which revetted the fighting-platform on the summit of the main rampart; but above all it consisted of the demolition of the gates and the overthrow of the high stone walls which flanked the two portals. The walls were now reduced to the lowly and ruinous state in which they were discovered by the excavators nearly nineteen centuries later.
>
> That night, when the fires of the legion shone out (we may imagine) in orderly lines across the valley, the survivors crept forth from their broken stronghold and, in the darkness buried their dead as nearly as might be outside their tumbled gates, in that place where the ashes of their burned huts lay warm and thick upon the ground. The task was carried out anxiously and hastily and without order, but, even so, from few graves were omitted those tributes of food and drink which were the proper and traditional perquisites of the dead. At daylight on the morrow, the legion moved westward to fresh conquest, doubtless taking with it the usual levy of hostages from the vanquished.
>
> Thereafter, salving what they could of their crops and herds, the disarmed townsfolk made shift to put their house in order. Forbidden to refortify their gates, they built new roadways across the sprawling ruins, between gateless ramparts that were already fast assuming the blunted profiles that are theirs to-day. And so, for some two decades, a demilitarized Maiden Castle retained its inhabitants, or at least a nucleus of them. Just so long did it take the Roman authorities to adjust the old order to the new, to prepare new towns for old. And then finally, on some day towards the close of the sixties of the century, the town was ceremonially abandoned, its remaining walls were formally 'slighted', and Maiden Castle lapsed into the landscape amongst the farm-lands of Roman Dorchester.

Sir Mortimer Wheeler, *Maiden Castle: Dorset*, (Society of Antiquaries Research Report, No. 12, 1943) pp. 61-2

Course work for G.C.E. and C.S.E. assessment

Some history teachers may wish to devise Mode 3 C.S.E. and G.C.E. 'O' level syllabuses which include work on *History Around Us: Roman Britain*.
The following items of course work could be completed by pupils and submitted in a folder as part of their final assessment:

1. Descriptions of sites visited, supported by maps, plans, sketches, photographs and any records or surveys.

2. Descriptions of other sites studied in the classroom, supported by plans, maps, sketches, etc.

3. Work setting a site in its historical context:
e.g. a written account explaining how, when and why the Romans came to Britain, outlining the stages of their conquest and relating them to the visible remains.
e.g. an annotated map of Hadrian's wall showing its military components, explaining its strategic significance and its relationship to the national road and defence system, including a brief description of the men who built it.
e.g. an annotated map or an illustrated account showing the route of a Roman road, or a section of it, and explaining the factors which influenced the Romans when building and siting roads, the purpose of the road and its relationship to the national road system.
e.g. an illustrated account of the foundation and growth of a town explaining the reasons for its foundation, including annotated maps to show its position in relation to roads, forts, and geographical features, and showing the distribution of the main types of towns in Roman Britain.
e.g. a written account explaining when and why the Romans left Britain, relating their departure to the fate of visible remains such as towns, villas and military fortifications.

4. An imaginative reconstruction of:
either: a specific incident in the history of a site,
e.g. Boudicca's sacking of Verulamium,
e.g. The Roman attack on Maiden Castle,
e.g. The battle of Mons Graupius.

or: life on a site during a particular period,
e.g. life at Lullingstone Roman villa in the fourth century A.D.,
e.g. life at Verulamium in the second century A.D.,
e.g. life at Vindolanda at a particular time.

or: a study of the connection between a historical personality or family and a site,
e.g. Agricola, Boudicca, Cogidubnus and Fishbourne.

Resources

Some of the books on this list are out of print. You should be able to obtain copies from your local library or from the Schools Library Loan Service.
Resources are listed by order of importance, within each section.

Teachers' books

Ordnance Survey, *Field Archaeology in Great Britain*, (HMSO, 1974)
Eric S. Wood, *Field Guide to Archaeology in Britain*, (Collins, 1975)
Sheppard S. Frere, *Britannia, History of Roman Britain*, (Cardinal, 1974)
Joan Liversidge, *Britain in the Roman Empire*, (Cardinal/Sphere, 1973)
Sir Ian Richmond, *Roman Britain*, 'Pelican History of England', (Penguin, 1970)
Keith Branigan, *Town and Country: Verulamium and the Roman Chilterns*, (Spurbooks, 1973)
Sir Mortimer Wheeler, *Stanwick Fortifications*, (Society of Antiquaries, London, 1954)
E. H. Jones, Michael Hayhoe & Beryl Jones (Eds.), *Roman Britain*, 'Themes Series', (Routledge & Kegan Paul, 1972)

Guide books to sites

HMSO, *Roman sites in England and Wales*
T. H. Rowland, *A Short Guide to the Roman Wall*, (Frank Graham, 1973)

Books for pupils dealing with visible evidence

G. I. F. Tingay, *From Caesar to the Saxons*, (Longman, 1969)
R. J. Mitchell, *Roman Britain*, 'Focus on History Series', (Longman, 1973)
Peter Hodge, *The Roman House*, 'Aspects of Roman Life Series', (Longman, 1975)
Peter Hodge, *Roman Towns*, 'Aspects of Roman Life Series', (Longman 1972)
B. Cunliffe, *The Romans: Aquae Sulis*, 'History Patch Series', (Ginn, 1971)
J. & D. Clarke, *The Romans: Camulodunum*, 'History Patch Series', (Ginn, 1971)
J. Wacher, *The Romans: Corinium*, 'History Patch Series', (Ginn, 1971)
D. F. Petch, *The Romans: Deva Victrix*, 'History Patch Series', (Ginn, 1971)
L. P. Wenham, *The Romans: Eboracum*, 'History Patch Series', (Ginn, 1971)
P. R. V. Marsden, *The Romans: Londinium*, 'History Patch Series' (Ginn, 1971)
A. McWhirr, *The Romans: Verulamium*, 'History Patch Series', (Ginn, 1971)
Elizabeth Blank, *The Romans: Ratae Coritanorum*, 'History Patch Series', (Ginn, 1971)
G. D. B. Jones & J. P. Wild, *The Deansgate Dig*, (Manchester Museum, 1973)
Brian Dobson & David Breeze, *The Building of Hadrian's Wall*, (Frank Graham, 1970)
Brian Dobson & David Breeze, *The Army of Hadrian's Wall*, (Frank Graham, 1972)
Ronald Embleton (Ed.), *Hadrian's Wall Reconstructed*, (Frank Graham, 1974)
Robin Birley, *Housesteads Roman Fort*, (Frank Graham, 1973)
Robin Birley, *Vindolanda: Roman Fort and Civilian Settlement*, (Frank Graham, 1973)
Robin Birley, *Discoveries at Vindolanda*, (Frank Graham, 1973)
Robin Birley, *Vindolanda*, (Frank Graham, 1974)
Robin Birley, *Civilians on the Roman Frontier*, (Frank Graham, 1974)
T. H. Rowland, *Dere Street: A Roman Road North*, (Frank Graham, 1974)
DOE, *The Roman Forts of the Saxon Shore*, (HMSO, 1964)

Books for pupils giving background information

G. I. F. Tingay, *From Caesar to the Saxons*, (Longman, 1969)
Joan Liversidge, *Roman Britain*, 'Then and There Series', (Longman, 1958)
M. & C. H. B. Quennell, *Everyday Life in Roman Times*, (Carousel/Transworld, 1972)
Lady Aileen Fox & Alan Sorrell, *Roman Britain*, (Lutterworth, 1961)
Graham Webster, *The Roman Army*, (Grosvenor Museum, Chester, 1973)
Peter Hodge, *Roman Family Life*, 'Aspects of Roman Life Series', (Longman, 1974)
David Birt, *Caesar's Invasions*, 'Longman History Units: Roman and Dark Age Britain', (Longman, 1976)
David Birt, *Roman Conquest of Britain*, 'Longman History Units: Roman and Dark Age Britain', (Longman, 1976)

David Birt, *The Roman Army in Britain*, 'Longman History Units: Roman and Dark Age Britain', (Longman, 1976)
David Birt, *Hadrian's Wall*, 'Longman History Units: Roman and Dark Age Britain', (Longman, 1976)
David Birt, *A Roman Town*, 'Longman History Units: Roman and Dark Age Britain', (Longman, 1976)
David Birt, *The Saxon Invasions*, 'Longman History Units: Roman and Dark Age Britain', (Longman, 1976)

Reference books

Anthony Birley, *Life in Roman Britain*, (Batsford, 1965)
Ivan D. Margary, *Roman Roads in Britain*, (J. Baker, 1973)
Barry Cunliffe, *Fishbourne: A Roman Palace and its Garden*, 'New Aspects of Antiquity Series', (Thames & Hudson, 1971)
Keith Branigan, *Town and Country: Archaeology of Verulamium and the Roman Chilterns*, (Spurbooks, 1973)
G. W. Meates, *Lullingstone Roman Villa*, (Heinemann, 1955)
HMSO, *Eboracum: Roman York*, Royal Commission on Historic Monuments Report, 1962.
Yorkshire Architectural and Archaeological Society, *Roman York from A.D. 71*, A handbook for visitors, (Sessions Book Trust, Ebor Press, York, 1971)

Primary source material giving background information about visible remains

Tacitus, *Agricola & Germania*, 'Penguin Classics Series', (Penguin, 1970)
Tacitus, *Annals*, 'Penguin Classics Series', (Penguin, 1975)
Caesar, *Conquest of Gaul*, 'Penguin Classics Series', (Penguin, 1970)
Virgil, *Eclogues & Georgics & Aeneid*, (O.U.P. 1966)
A. R. Burn, *The Romans in Britain: An Anthology of Inscriptions*, (Basil Blackwell, 1969)
British Museum, *Guide to the Antiquities of Roman Britain*, (1958)

Maps and Charts

Ordnance Survey, *Roman Britain*
Ordnance Survey, *Hadrian's Wall*
Ordnance Survey, *The Antonine Wall*
Warburton's *Map of the Roman Wall* (facsimile), (Frank Graham)
Frank Graham, *Charts of the Roman Wall: South Gate, Housesteads*
Frank Graham, *Charts of the Roman Wall: Mansio or Inn, Vindolanda*
Frank Graham, *Charts of the Roman Wall: Latrines at Housesteads*
Frank Graham, *The Roman Wall Reconstructed*, (12 colour paintings with text)

Slides

These can be purchased from the following organisations:
Verulamium, The Director, Verulamium Museum St. Michael's Street, St. Albans, Hertfordshire.
Vindolanda, Cameo Books, 6 Ryndleside, Oakes, Huddersfield, HD3 3Q3; Mr. Robin Birley, Vindolanda Trust, Bardon Mill, Hexham, Northumberland.
Hadrian's Wall, Museum of Antiquities, The University, Newcastle upon Tyne NE1 7RU; The Department of the Environment.
Lullingstone, The Department of the Environment.
Aldborough, The Department of the Environment.
Caerleon, The Department of the Environment.
Richborough, The Department of the Environment.
Roman soldiers/religion/daily life, Woodmansterne Ltd.
Colchester, Woodmansterne Ltd.
Mildenhall Treasure, British Museum.
Roman Chester, The Curator, Grosvenor Museum, Chester.

Filmstrips

Roman Britain: The Towns, colour, Hugh Baddeley Productions
Roman Britain: Fortifications, colour, Hugh Baddeley Productions
Roman St. Albans, Verulamium Museum, St. Michael's St., St Albans, Hertfordshire
Life in Roman Britain, 'Background to the Classics Series', black and white, Longman/Common Ground
The Roman Army, 'Background to the Classics Series', black and white, Longman/Common Ground
Roman Conquest of Britain, 'Background to the Classics Series', black and white, Longman/Common Ground
Bignor Roman Villa, colour, Visual Information Services, 1970
Boadicea, colour, Visual Publications, 1956
Hadrian's Wall, colour, Visual Information Services, 1969

Roman Britain

Films

Roman Britain: The Towns, 16 mm, colour, 15 mins. Hugh Baddeley Productions, 1973

Roman Britain: Fortifications, 16 mm, colour, 14 mins, Hugh Baddeley Productions, 1973

Roman Villa at Cox Green, 16 mm, black and white, 19 mins. British Film Institute, 1968

The Roman Wall, 16 mm, colour, 16 mins, Gateway, 1950

Who were the British? 5. The Builders, 16 mm. black and white, 25 mins. Anglia Television, 1967 — distributed by Rank

The Romans in Britain, 16 mm, colour, 20 mins. Boulton-Hawker, 1961

Fosse Way, near Sharnford, Leicestershire; a Roman road

3 CASTLES AND FORTIFIED MANOR HOUSES

Some outcomes and objectives

We hope that by the time pupils finish their study of castles they will:

1. have sufficient background knowledge about castles to recognise different types of castles in various parts of the country.

2. have had practice at using guide books to help them observe, record and interpret the visible evidence about:
a. the siting of castles
b. the layout and development of castles
c. different types of castle defences
d. different types of domestic accommodation in castles.

3. have had practice at combining the study of visible remains and background material so they can:
a. reconstruct the lives
b. understand the purposes of the people who inhabited, defended and attacked castles.

4. have the knowledge, skills and enthusiasm to explore castles and other aspects of their historical environment beyond school.

An approach

Teachers will wish to organise the course to suit the abilities of their pupils and to take account of the visible remains of castles in the locality of the schools. We hope that the following approaches will prove useful:

APPROACH 1

1. Introductory lessons

These lessons can be based on filmstrips, slides and maps and introduce pupils to the essential background information about castles, e.g.

a. Norman Conquest

the reasons for building castles and for their particular location.

b. the siting of castles

factors which influenced the choice of site — the need for a defensible position, proximity of natural defensive features, e.g. cliffs and rivers, control of routeways, etc.

c. the layout of castles

factors which influenced their design — defence and attack — hence curtain walls, sally ports, towers, drawbridges, moats, etc; shelter for a large number of people and animals; the ability to be self supporting for a long period of time — hence the baileys, wells, keeps, etc.

The siting and design of castles could be studied using plans of actual castles and the $2\frac{1}{2}$ inch Ordnance Survey map sections which show their geographical position. Alternatively teachers could design a simple simulation exercise about the siting of a castle.

The class would divide into groups or pairs and imagine they are Edward I or William the Conqueror and his castle builders with a particular strategic defence problem to solve. They would draw up a list of priorities to be considered when siting and planning their castle. Then they would be given an outline map of an area — real or imaginary, showing different features: hills, rivers, marshes, cliffs, routeways, etc. and choose a site

Castles and fortified manor houses

Motte and bailey castle; Eynsford, Kent

Stone keep castle; Rochester, Kent

Castles and fortified manor houses

Stone keep castle; Launceston, Cornwall

Multitower and curtain wall castle; Framlingham, Suffolk

Stone keep castle; Conisbrough, South Yorkshire

Castles and fortified manor houses

Concentric castle; Beaumaris, Anglesey, Gwynedd

Courtyard castle; Bodiam, East Sussex

Castles and fortified manor houses

Tudor castle; Deal, Kent

Fortified manor house; Stokesay, Salop

Castles and fortified manor houses

for their castle. Finally they would prepare ground plans of their castle to fit the shape of the site and the needs of the inhabitants.

If a real castle is chosen compare the results with the actual design and site at the end of the exercise.

d. The development of castles and their defences

The following types of castles, their defences and domestic accommodation could be studied using books, filmstrips and slides, see Resources section at the end of this chapter for full details.

Motte and bailey castles, eleventh and twelfth century
e.g. Pickering, Elsdon, Berkhamstead.

Stone keep castles, twelfth and thirteenth century
Square keeps: Rochester, Castle Rising, Tower of London, Corfe, Sherbourne, Pevensey, Portchester, Castle Headingham
Shell keeps: Restormel, Launceston, Windsor, Arundel, Lincoln, Lewes
Development of rounded keeps: Conisbrough, Caldicot, Orford, Carisbrook, Chilham.

Multitower and curtain wall castles, thirteenth century
The development of a stone curtain wall with square towers, later with rounded towers; the development of other defensive features — barbicans, machicolations, bartizans, murderholes, etc.
e.g. Dover, Framlingham, Caerlaverock.

Concentric castles, thirteenth century
Castles with two or three rings of defences getting higher towards the centre of the site,
e.g. Beaumaris, Rhuddlan, Harlech.

Four square or courtyard castles, fourteenth and fifteenth century
four ranges of buildings around a courtyard,
e.g. Bodiam.

Tudor castles and Martello towers
Often star shaped or clover leaf shaped,
e.g. Deal, Walmer, St. Mawes, Pendennis, Cowes.

Fortified manor houses
e.g. Little Wenham Hall, Suffolk, Stokesay Castle, Salop.

2. Visits to castles

Pupils could visit two or three different types of castles to study and record their plans, sites, defences and domestic accommodation in detail.

Follow up work would involve:
a. setting castles in their historical context
b. the imaginative reconstruction of:
either: life in a castle at a particular period,
or: a specific incident in a castle's history,
or: the study of a historical personality or family associated with a castle.

3. Concluding lessons

These could explain the state of castles as we see them today by investigating:
When and why castles ceased to be built.
The civil war and the deliberate destruction or slighting of many castles.

Follow up work could include:
The study of one particular castle, its role in the civil war and its subsequent fate,
e.g. Farnham, Skipton, Donnington, Pontefract.
An annotated map or maps designed for pupils' future reference showing the location of different types of castle:
a. within a day's travel of school
b. in a different area of the country, one they might visit on holiday
c. a map showing the distribution of castles in England, Wales, Scotland or Ireland.

APPROACH 2

A brief introduction followed by units of work centring round visits to different types of castle.

Introductory lessons:
the Norman Conquest and the reasons for castle building,
the siting of castles and the factors involved,
the layout of castles and the factors involved.

Unit 1

Background work on motte and bailey castles, their defences and domestic accommodation, together with a visit and/or slide lessons.
Activities:
recording and sketching,
discussion of the factors which influenced the building of these castles especially speed,
researching information about the person or family who first built or lived in the castle.

Castles and fortified manor houses

Unit 2

Background work on keep castles, their defences and domestic accommodation, together with a visit and/or slide lessons.
Activities:
recording and sketching,
discussion of the reasons behind the development of these castles,
imaginative reconstruction of life in the castle at this time.

Unit 3

Background work on multi-tower castles together with a visit and slide lessons.
Activities:
recording and sketching,
discussion of the reasons for the development of strong curtain walls, round towers, and other defensive features with special attention to firing angles,
the problems involved in defending a multi-tower castle — illustrated by a reconstruction of a specific incident.

Unit 4

Background work on concentric castles together with a visit and slide lessons
Activities:
recording and sketching,
discussion of the reasons for the development of this design,
discussion of the problems of attacking such a castle, e.g. by mining or siege engines, frontal gate attack, or attack at one point, followed by a reconstruction of a particular method of attack.

Unit 5

Background work on courtyard castles together with a visit and slide lessons,
Activities:
recording and sketching,
discussion of the reasons for their development and a comparison with other types of castle,
an illustrated account setting a castle in its historical context and relating it to other type of castles.

Unit 6

Background work on fortified manor houses together with a visit and slide lessons.
Activities:
recording and sketching,
discussion of why and when castles ceased to be built,
an illustrated account explaining the changes in castle design between 1070 and 1500.

Unit 7

Background work on Tudor castles and Martello towers together with a visit and slide lessons.
Activities:
recording and sketching,
discussion of the reasons for building this type of castle,
an annotated map of Britain and the continent showing the distribution of the castles and explaining their strategic purpose.

Concluding lessons:
The fate of castles, the civil war and the deliberate destruction or 'slighting' of many castles.
Follow up work:
a study of the fate of a specific castle and its role in the civil war:
e.g. Farnham, Skipton, Donnington, Pontefract.
Annotated maps showing different types of castle:
a. near school
b. in a different part of the country, one they might visit on holiday.

Studying sites: questions and activities

The amount of help teachers give to pupils doing fieldwork or classroom investigations and the form it takes will vary. All questions and activities should help pupils observe, understand and interpret the visible remains.

Castles and fortified manor houses

During a first visit teachers could provide detailed guidelines indicating what pupils should look for. During later visits many pupils will do their own recording and sketching work. Some of the following questions may be useful for teachers drawing up survey sheets.

Background questions

These questions can be answered in the classroom, using maps and plans, before a visit to the castle.

1. What kind of castle is this? Look at a plan.

2. The strategic purpose:
Was the castle commissioned by the king or a baron?
Was it part of the national or local defence plan?
Was it the base for a military campaign or merely a refuge?

3. The site:
What natural features have the builders used to strengthen its position? (e.g. water, cliffs, hills, etc.)
Does the castle dominate any routeways? What building materials were used for the castle?
Are there any stone quarries nearby which might have provided building materials?

Questions at the site

1. The military features of the castle

The approaches
Is there a dry or water-filled moat? How big is it?
Is there a curtain wall?
Has it round or squared towers?

Entrances and exits
Is there a barbican?
Did the gateway house a drawbridge? Is there any signs of the means of raising it? Is there any sign of a counterpoise pit for the drawbridge?
Were there double doors? Was there a portcullis? Which was the outer defence? How was the portcullis raised?
What means of attack were there against the besiegers at the gatehouse. How effective were they? e.g. fields of fire for arrow slits, guard rooms, machicolations, posterns, sally ports.

The walls and wall towers
How high and thick are they? Was there a walkway?
Is there a crenellated parapet? Were there bartizans?
Were rooms or staircases built into the walls? Do the battlements give good shelter to the soldiers and a good field of fire?
Are there signs of later improvements to the walls? e.g. flanking towers, artillery batteries, etc.
If there are flanking towers, are they round or square? Is the base splayed out at the bottom or straight?
How many arrow slits are there in each tower? Are they on more than one floor? What shape are they? Do they differ from tower to tower?
Did the towers have any other defences? Do you think the towers could have held out under attack independently?
Do the towers cover the wall and each other?
Did any of the towers have domestic accommodation?

2. The living quarters of the castle

Were these in a keep or gatehouse or were they along the sides of a courtyard castle?
Is there a Lord's hall?
Is there a solar and aumbry or store cupboard for valuables?
Are there any garderobes?
Where are the kitchen, pantries, cellars?
Where was the water supply?
How was sewage disposed of?
How many windows were there, how big and what shape were they?
Were they glazed or unglazed?
How many fireplaces can you find?
Is there a chapel?
How much privacy was there and who was it for?
How comfortable were the rooms: consider the heating, lighting and ventilation?

3. The development of the castle

In what way, if any, did the castle change and develop?
Is there any evidence of 'slighting' — deliberate destruction?
Is this a typical or unusual castle?

4. The people

Who built the castle?
When was the castle last lived in?
Are there any family crests which record ownership of the castle?
Who owned the castle in the past and who owns it now?
Did the castle play a part in any famous historical event?
Have the castle or its inhabitants left traces in the nearby town or village, e.g. in the names of the streets or in plaques in the local church?

Castles and fortified manor houses

Activities

After a group discussion about the site, teachers may allow pupils to explore the castle, sketching and recording at their own pace. A book of guidelines with spaces for drawings and comments may be easier for some pupils to handle than separate sheets of paper.

Some background source material

Types of primary source material

Certain mediaeval English and French chronicles have accounts of attacks and other incidents in the history of some castles. Chancery papers, e.g. Close Rolls, may provide information about certain events in a castle's history such as building and rebuilding.

Primary source material giving background information about life in a local castle during a particular period may be found in the local history section of the local reference library. For example, 'The Household Books', accounts and inventories of the great lords are often published by local record societies, e.g. Surtees Society for Northumberland. These can be used to create a picture of life in a castle at a particular time.

Local 'Histories' may contain extracts from eye-witness accounts of sieges, particularly during the civil war. Some castles may have printed extracts from documents relating to their history, e.g. Skipton Castle, see Resources section at the end of this chapter.

Teachers may have difficulty in finding suitable primary source material about castles. Pupils will have to use the available secondary source material.

Some examples of primary source material

Source 1·3 *An extract from the Anglo-Saxon Chronicle (A.D. 1137) describing how the barons used their castles to oppress the people*

When the King Stephen came to England, he held his council at Oxford; where he seized the Bishop Roger of Sarum, and Alexander, Bishop of Lincoln, and the chancellor Roger, his nephew; and threw all into prison till they gave up their castles. When the traitors understood that he was a mild man, and soft, and good, and no justice executed, then did all wonder. They had done him homage, and sworn oaths, but they no truth maintained. They were all forsworn, and forgetful of their troth; for every rich man built his castles, which they held against him: and they filled the land full of castles. They cruelly oppressed the wretched men of the land with castle-works; and when the castles were made, they filled them with devils and evil men. They took those whom they supposed to have any goods, both by night and by day, labouring men and women, and threw them into prison for their gold and silver, and inflicted on them unutterable tortures; for never were any martyrs so tortured as they were. Some they hanged up by the feet, and smoked them with foul smoke; and some by thumbs, or by the head, and hung coats of mail on their feet. They tied knotted strings about their heads, and twisted them till the pains went to their brains. They put them into dungeons, wherein were adders, and snakes, and toads; and so destroyed them. Some they placed in a crucet-house; that is, in a chest that was short and narrow, and not deep; wherein they put sharp stones, and so thrust the man therein, that they broke all the limbs ... Many thousand they wore out with hunger. I neither can, nor may I tell all the wounds and all the pains which they inflicted on wretched men in this land.

Rev. James Ingram (trans.), *Anglo-Saxon Chronicle*, Everyman edn., (J. M. Dent, 1912)

Source 2·3 *An extract from Roger of Wendover's chronicle describing King John's attack on Rochester Castle Kent in 1215*

He [King John] did not allow the besieged any rest day or night. For, as well as the stones hurled from the catapults and slings and the missiles of the crossbow men and archers, frequent attacks were made by the knights and their followers. When some were tired, other fresh ones took their place in the attack, which allowed the besieged no rest ... The siege lasted many days owing to the great bravery and boldness of the besieged, who hurled stone for stone and weapon for weapon ... on the enemy.

At last the King used miners. Many of the royal troops had been killed and he saw his siege engines were useless. Soon the miners threw down a great part of the walls. The food of the besieged also began to fail and they had to eat horses and even their costly chargers.

> The soldiers of the king rushed into breaches and forced the besiegers to leave the castle walls and enter into the keep ... The king then used his miners against the keep and after much difficulty they broke through the walls ... At last, not a scrap of food remaining ... all the garrison left the castle and surrendered to the king. They were nearly all unhurt, except for one knight who had been killed by an arrow ...

J. A. Giles (trans.), *Roger of Wendover's Flowers of History*, VOL II (Henry G. Bohn, 1849)

Source 3·3 *List of furnishings and articles commonly found in the Lord's Hall in the fifteenth century*
(from an English vocabulary made for the use of teachers in schools in the fifteenth century)

A board [i.e. a moveable table top]
A trestle [probably a pair of trestles for the board to rest on]
A bench cover [often worked in tapestry, painted cloth, or woven as a carpet if the owner could afford it, as means of display and of brightening the look of the bench]
A dorsal [this was a chair back cover and was also an impressive piece of tapestry, carpet, or painted cloth if the owner could afford it]
A mat
A table dormant [a permanent table, as distinguished from a trestle table, less common than trestle tables, and usually round]
A basin
A wash basin
A fire
A hearth
A brand
A yule-log
An andiron
A long settle
A chair
A pair of tongs
A bench
A stool
A cushion
Wood for the fire
A pair of bellows
A screen

A. R. Myers (Ed.), *English Historical Documents*, VOL IV, (Eyre and Spottiswoode, 1969) pp. 1145-6

Source 4·3 *Extracts from the inventory of Sir John Fastolf's possessions at Caistor Castle, 1459*

The Coke is Chambour
Item, j. feder bedde. Item, j. bolster. Item, ij. schetys.
Item, j. redde coverlyte of rosys and blood houndys hedys.

The Maister is Chambre
In primis, j. fedderbedde. Item, j. donge of fyne blewe.
Item, j. bolster. Item, ij. blankettys of fustians.
Item, j. payre of schetis. Item, j. purpeynt.
Item, j. hangyd bedde of arras. Item, j. testour. Item, j. selour
Item, j. coveryng.
Item, iij. curtaynes of grene worsted.
Item, j. bankeur of tapestre warke.
Item, iij. peces hangyng of grene worsted.
Item, j. banker hangyng tapestry worke. Item, j. cobbord clothe.
Item, ij. staundyng aundyris. Item, j. feddefflok.

Item, j. chafern of laten. Item, j. payre of tongys.
Item, j. payre of bellewes. Item, j. litell paylet. Item, ij. blankettys.
Item, j. payre of schetys. Item, j. coverlet.
Item, vj. white cosschynes. Item. ij. lytell bellys.
Item, j. foldyng table. Item, j. longe chayre. Item, j. grene chayre.
Item, j. hangyng candylstyk of laton.

The Yeomen is Chambur for Straungers
In primis, iiij. fether beddys. Item, iij. bolsterys.
Item, v. blankettys. Item, iiij. payre of schetys.
Item, j. coverlet of grene warke.
Item, ij. coverynges of white, grene, and blewe.
Item, ij. hangyng clothys of the same.

James Gairdner (Ed.), *The Paston Letters*, VOL III, (Chatto and Windus, 1904) pp. 182-5

Source 5·3 *Extracts from the Household Books of Lord William Howard of Naworth Castle*

NAWARD 1622

My Lord's Expenses.

(Inter alia) To Mr. Pryse for drawing a pedegree, lii^s.vi^d.
Grogeram to make my Lord a sute and taffety, vii£. ii^s.
For iii hatts and trimming others, l^s. To Lownes for
iii bookes, 5 Junii, xliv^s. A ryding sute for my
Lord, 13 Junii, iv£.ix^s. Stockins, silk and woosted,
15 Julii, iii£ix^s. Base [baize] to make a gown, 18
Nov., xlviii^s.vi^d. 2 little silver candellsticks,
xxii^s. To Mr. Hix the apothecary, iv£.iv^s. 4 pair of
mingled hose, 4 Decemb., xxxviii^s. . . .
Total of my Lord's parcells, cclxxi£.xxiii^d.
Wages Paid to Servants. cxlvii£.iv^s.iv^d.

My Ladies' Expenses, etc.

(Inter alia) Sept. 14. Sent to Mrs. Mary by W. Grayme, v^s.
Green ginger for her, vii^d. 30. A pair of Jarsey
stockins for Mrs. Aletheia bought by W. Grayme, iv^s.
Nov. 1. Gloves for Mrs. Lucye, iv^d.
To David Bell for making their coates
ii^s.x^d. To my Lady to give away, xi^s. To David
Bell making a gown for Mrs. Mary, another for Mrs.
Dorothy, and other woorke for my Lady, vii^s.vi^d.
5 yards of dubble base [baize] for Mrs. Marye,
xxii^s.vi^d. Decemb. 7. pair of stockins for Mr. Cotten's
children, iv^s.

Hopps

Octob. 19. One quarter of a hundred of new English
hopps bought at Newcastell, by W. Grame, at St. Luke's
fair, xxvii^s.vi^d.

Stabell Charges

(Inter alia) Dec. 9. Shoing my Lady's dubble gelding, xii^d.
Shoing Gray Ducket, iv^d. Janu. 18. Horsbread for Mr.
Howard brought from Newcastell, ii^s. July 14. Shoing
Gray Ducket and Gray Hasset, xviii^d.

Extraordinary payments

(Inter alia) Oct. 14. To a pore boy dighting the privies 6 times, xii^d. Nov. 17. Shoes for Mr. Dickes' soon, ii^s. July 20. Paid to Thomas Bell for the diet of v soldiers sent by Mr. Charles, for v dayes, xi^s. Paid to him for a sheet, and for burying a poor man that died in the Maynes-field, vii^s. 31 Charges of burying W. Newton's wyfe, xv^d.

Fuell

(Inter alia) Felling a tree in the parke for to burn, vi^d. 5 Feb. — iii loades of wood at London, 8 Junii xxvii^s. More for Scottish coale, ix^s. Feb. 6. v quarters of charcoale, vii^s. Apr. 15. To the collier for 28 quarters of coles, viii^s.ii^d.

Rewards and given to the Poor

(Inter alia) Sept. 3. To Simon Henderson leading greyhounds for Mr. Thomas, xii^d. 24. To Chr. Hoodles fetching my Ladie's dog from Thornthwate, xii^d. Octobr. 1. To a man bringing 2 fatt capons from Mr. Maior of Carlyle xii^d. 14. To a piper, iv^d. To a cornetor, ii^s. 15. To Mr. John Vaux his man of Catterlan, bringing 12 plovers, xviii^d. Novemb. 1. For bringing a glasse of water from Mr. Maior, vi^d. 12. To Widdow Brown by my Ladie's commandement, v^s. 17. To the players of Penreth, iii^s. To the poor, 2 Nov. vii^s.iv^d.

Fresh Acaites

From the 21st to the 28th Decemb.
inprimis egs, ii^s.ii^d. Rabbets, xii^d., and for Thornthwate, xii^d. 17 plovers, v^s.viii^d. 9 woodcocks, iii^s. A wild mallerd, vi^d. 2 partriges, xii^d. 2 pigeons, iii^d. Egs, iv^s.iii^d. 3 hens, xv^d. 4 capons, ii^s.iv^d. 2 hares, xii^d.
A woodcock, iii^d. 7 chickins, xvi^d. A hen, iv^d. A goose, viii^d, 4 killins, iv^s. A bodlin, vi^d. Flukes, vi^d. Fee, xii^d. Cheeses, viii^d. Egs, xx^d. 2 hens, x^d. iii chickins, ix^d. Egs, xvi^d. 9 cods, ix^s. 3 bodlins, xvi^d.
12 codlins, xiv^d. Flukes, ii^s.iv^d. 2 sea pyes, v^d. Fee, xii^d. Total, lv^s.

Salt and salt store

(Inter alia) August 6. For v pecks of salt, at xx^d. a peck, viii^s.iv^d. Decemb. 17. vi pecks of salt viii^s. Apr. 18. To Jo. Hoodles for iii pecks of salt, viii^s. 22. iii pecks d. of salt, vii^s.x^d. 27. A stone and a hallf, and half a quarter, of salt butter, by Mr. Radcliffe, vii^s.ix^d.

Grane of all Sorts

(Inter alia) Octob. 7. ii bushells of oates for the London horses, vi^s. Feb. 7. To John Bell for xx bushells of wheat, xiii^d. Total, cxix£.x^s.viii^d.

Wine

Octob. 19. ix gallons and a quart of sack at iii^s.ii^d. bought at Newcastell by Wm. Grame, xxix^s.iii^d. 18 quarts and a pinte of wine, claret, bought at Carlyle, xii^s.iv^d. 2 bottles of sack bought ther, xxi^s.

The Publications of the Surtees Society, VOL. LXVII, (1877)

Castles and fortified manor houses

Source 6·3 *An order from King Edward II to the Keeper of Pickering Castle, 1323*

Order to John de Kilvington, keeper of the Castle and honour of Pickering, to cause to be newly constructed a barbican before the Castle gate with a stone wall and a gate with a drawbridge in the same, and beyond the gate a new chamber, a new postern gate by the King's Tower and a roof to a chamber near the small hall; to cover with thin flags that roof and the roof of the small kitchen, to remove the old roof of the King's prison and to make an entirely new roof covered with lead, and to thoroughly point, both within and without, the walls of the Castle and tower, and to clean out and enlarge the Castle ditch. All this is to be done out of the issues of the honor as the King has enjoyed him by word of mouth, and the expense incurred therein when duly proved will be allowed him in his accounts. Pickering, 10 Aug., 1323.

The Close Rolls, 17 Edward II, M. 39, reproduced in the publications of the *North Riding Record Society*, VOL II, new series (1895) pp. 255-6

Source 7·3 *Extracts from "A journal of the first and second sieges of Pontefract Castle 1644-5 by Nathan Drake, a gentleman volunteer therein"*

The First Siege against Pontefract Castle, Dec. 1644.
28 *February*
The besiegers fired Elizabeth Cattell's house . . . and that day the besieged shot 4 cannon into the market place . . . After that the enemy was weary with bursting their gunnes with battery of the castle upward towards heaven and see that they could not prevail that way, then they came to be partners with Guydo Faulkes to dive downwards to the divell, to undermine us and to blow us up by their sevrall mines . . . But we perceiving theire intentions, we answered them at theire owne weapons and myned as fast as they, sinkinge in severall places within the castle and from thence and allso without the Castle Walles . . . and so have prevented all their plots.

The Second Siege against Pontefract Castle March 1645
From the 1st of March to the 10th theire was but little done in Pontefract Castle but fencing in of provision and other necessaryes for the use of the castle.
May 15th
This day was the souldyers set on worke to fill up a filthy pond which was in the Castleyeard and clensed all the Castleyeard, which was a very good worke to clense the castle from many noysome smelles.
May 27th
There was little shooting all that day but Joshua Walker killed one of the enemyes who taking a pipe of tobackoe in the lane by the primrose cloase . . . There was a poor little wench was keeping of a cow under Swillington tower was shot into the thigh by the enemy, but not killed.
. . . Captain Joshua Walker with his about 20 snaphaunces [guns] went out through the howses on the south side of the church . . . where they met all the cattell with the Sandall brave souldyers, who delivered them to him and then went all back again into and castle . . And then our drummes beate a retreat for all of our men to . . . retire to the castle . . . Thus having (by Godes assistance) releeved the castle to our great comforth we made boane fires up on the towers of the castle and played our cannon from the Kinge's tower into Mrs. Oates house in the markitt place . . .

The Publications of the Surtees Society, VOL XXXVII, (1861) pp. 14, 38, 46, 47

Castles and fortified manor houses

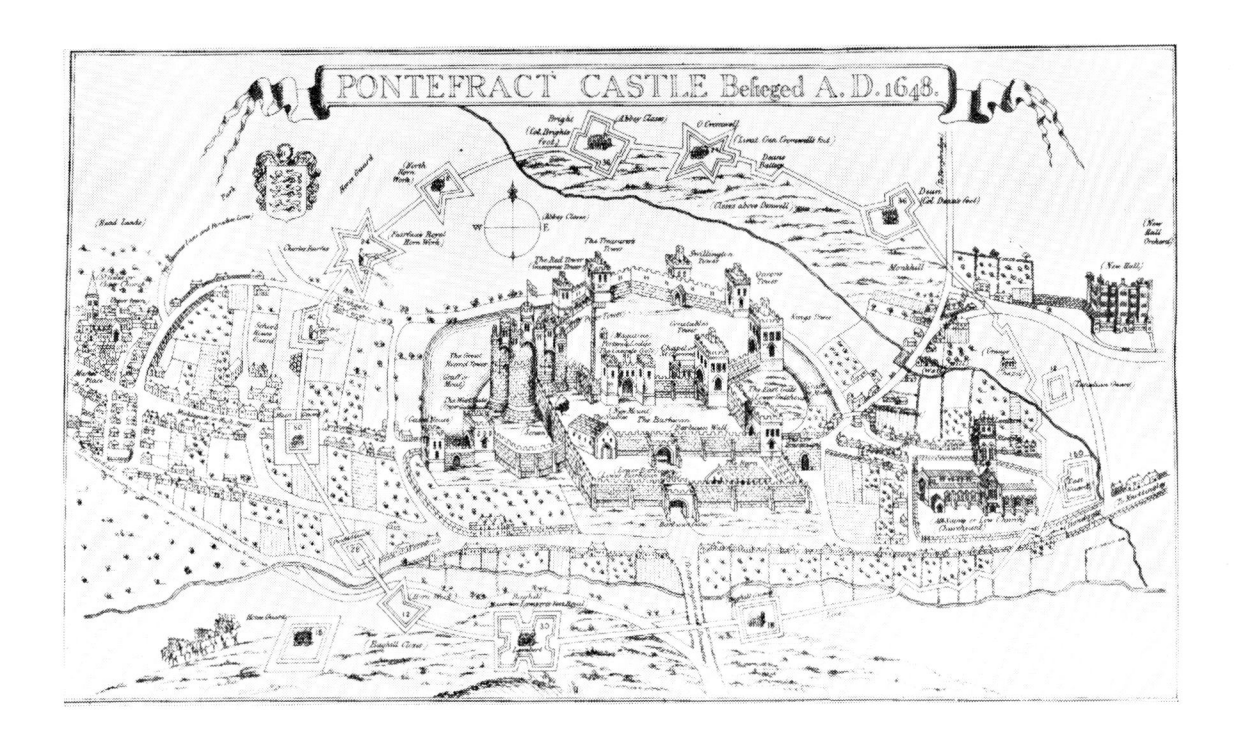

Source 8·3 *A plan showing the siege of Pontefract Castle in 1648*

The Publications of the Surtees Society, VOL. XXXVII (1861)

Source 9·3 *An old drawing of Pontefract Castle showing the castle before it was 'slighted' at the end of the civil war*

from a drawing in possession of the Society of Antiquaries, London; reproduced in J. S. Fletcher, *The Story of English Towns; Pontefract*, (S.P.C.K., 1920) p. 38

Castles and fortified manor houses

Source 10·3 *A petition drawn up at a town meeting in the Pontefract Moot Hall in March 1649 requesting the demolition of Pontefract Castle*

> To the supreme authority of England, the Co'mons assembled in Parliament. The humble peticon of the Major, Aldermen and all well-affected Inhabitants of the Towne of Pontefract. Humbly sheweth — That the Town of Pontefract since the beginning of these unhappy warres hath beene greatly impoverished and depopulated through the setting and continueing a Garrison in that Castle w'ch hath occaconed two severall tedious and chargeable Leagures to the great effusion of much pretious blood, the utter ruinating of no lesse than 200 dwellinghouses and upwards (whose confused heapes are lively and speaking Monuments of the Enemies' cruelty and yo' Peticoners' misery), the incredible decay of tradeing and commerce, the unavoidable hinderance and interrupcon of Tillage, the totall undoing of many well-affected p'sons and families, the sad devastacon of the place of publiq: worshipp amongst us. All w'ch damages sustenied by yo' poore Peticoners amounts unto the full value of 40,000li and upwards, yet hath God through his blessinge upon the unwearied paines of o'r forces there, once more opened a doore of hope for o'Recovery of that Garrison. May it therefore please yo' Hono'rs seriously to consider the sadd desolacons of o'poore Towne, the past and p'sent pressures, yea unsupportable burthens of yo' poore Peticoners by means of the said Garrison, And to appoint the same (immediately upon the Rendicon), to be wholly razed downe and demolished. And further to allott so much of the materialls of Lead and Timber towards the repaireing of o' place of publiq: worship and reedifijng of an habitacon for a Minister as shall amount unto 1,000li. That so the true causeof o' former miseries and future fears being removed. Yo' Peticoners may both be incouraged and inabled to serve yo' hono'rs in all yo' just and equitable comaunds w'th their lives and fortunes. And yo' Peticoners shall daily pray etc. Signed in the name and by the consent of the Aldermen and all the well-affected in the Towne of Pontefract, By me,
>
> EDWARD FIELDE, Major

L. Padgett, *Chronicles of Old Pontefract*, (Oswald Holmes at The Advertiser Office, Pontefract, 1905) pp. 166-177

Course work for G.C.E. and C.S.E. assessment

Some history teachers may wish to devise Mode 3 C.S.E. and G.C.E. 'O' level syllabuses which include work on *History Around Us: Castles and fortified manor houses*. The following items of course work could be completed by pupils and submitted in a folder as part of their final assessment:

1. Description of a castle visited supported by maps, plans, sketches, photographs and any records or surveys.

2. Descriptions of other castles studied by classroom investigation together with relevant maps, plans, sketches, etc.

3. Work setting one site in its historical context and relating it to other sites.

The work may be structured to answer particular questions. The example below attempts to set Warkworth Castle, Northumberland, into its historical context:

What type of castle is Warkworth?
When was it founded and by whom?

What was the extent of the castle when it was first built?
Is this typical or unusual for the period?
When was the castle recovered from the Scots by the English? How was this done, and why?
The castle was considerably altered in about 1400. In what ways was its military and domestic accommodation improved?
Why do you think the castle was altered at this time?
When did the Percys first own Warkworth?
What signs are there that they considered the castle important?
Describe the connection of Warkworth Castle with the problems of Henry IV.
Explain why Warkworth rapidly decayed after 1570.
Compare Warkworth with two other castles in terms of design and strategic importance.

4. Work involving the imaginative reconstruction of:

either: a specific incident in the history of a castle, e.g. the siege of Farnham Castle.

or: life in a castle at a particular period, e.g. Naworth in 1622 or Warkworth Castle in 1500.
Pupils could choose to write about a day in the life of one particular person who may have lived in the castle such as the Lord or Steward. They would have to ensure that their descriptions fitted in with the castle buildings at that time. For instance if the Steward was preparing for a banquet in the keep where would he go to? What cooking would be going on and where were the kitchens? Where would he get water, wine, beer, butter, etc.?

or: the study of a historical personality or family and its connections with a castle,
e.g. Lady Anne Clifford who restored many castles after the civil war,
e.g. Richard II and Pontefract Castle,
e.g. the Percy Family and Warkworth Castle.

Resources

Some of the books on this list are out of print. You should be able to obtain copies from your local library or from the Schools Library Loan Service.
Resources are listed by order of importance, within each section.

Teachers' books

W. Douglas Simpson, *Castles in Britain*, (Batsford, 1960)
Department of the Environment, *An Introduction to the Castles of England and Wales*, (HMSO, 1973)
Islay Doncaster, *Finding the History Around Us*, (Basil Blackwell, 1956) Ch. 3
Derek Frank Renn, *Norman Castles in Britain*, (J. Baker, 1973)
T. H. Corfe (Ed.), *History in the Field*, (Blond Educational, 1970) see 'Castles and Abbeys' in Part I, the regional guide in Part 2

Reference books for teachers and pupils

Wakefield Historical Society, *Sandal Castle*, (1965)
Philip Warner, *Medieval Castle: Life in a Fortress in Peace and War*, (J. Baker, 1971)
G. C. Williamson, *Lady Anne Clifford*, 'Local History Series', (Educational Productions, 1968)
J. L. Illingworth, *Yorkshire's Ruined Castles*, 'Country History Reprints', (Educational Productions, 1970)

Guide books

These are available for a wide range of castles, either from the site or from HMSO.

Books for pupils

John Kinross, *Castles in England and Wales*, 'Discovering Books Series,' (Shire Publications, 1973)
Henry Pluckrose, *Castles*, 'On Location Series', (Mills & Boon, 1973)
Marjorie Reeves, *The Medieval Castle*, 'Then and There Series,' (Longman, 1963)
Hugh Gregor, *Castles in Britain*, 'History Picture Topics', (Macmillan, 1972)
R. J. Unstead, *Castles*, 'Junior Reference Books', (A. & C. Black, 1970)
David Birt & Jon Nichol, *The Castle*, 'Longman History Units: The Middle Ages', (Longman, 1976)
Alan Sorrell, *British Castles*, (Batsford, 1974)
HMSO, *Yorkshire Castles*, (1973)
Frank Graham (Publishers), *No. 1 Mediaeval Castles of Northumberland*, 'Northern History Pamphlets'
Frank Graham (Publishers), *No. 22 Castles of the Northumberland Coast*, 'Northern History Pamphlets'
Frank Graham (Publishers), *No. 21 Castles and Walls of Newcastle*, 'Northern History Pamphlets'
Frank Graham (Publishers), *No. 24 Northumbrian Castles*, 'Northern History Pamphlets'
Frank Graham (Publishers), *No. 31 Northumbrian Castles*, 'Northern History Pamphlets'

Primary source material

This gives background information about castles.

Staffordshire Education Department, *Stafford Castle*, 'Local History Source Book'

James Gairdner (Ed.), *The Paston Letters*, Vol. III (Chatto & Windus, 1904) Caistor Castle

Skipton Castle, North Yorkshire; a number of information sheets and extracts from primary source material are available.

Building Accounts of Tattershall Castle, (1434–1472), (Lincoln Record Society, Vol. 55, 1960)

Slides

Slides of different types of castles can be purchased from:

The Department of the Environment

Museum of Antiquities, The University, Newcastle upon Tyne, NE1 7RU.

The Norman Conquest as illustrated in the Bayeux Tapestry, a slide set (Slide Centre Ltd.)

Models

Many Schools Museum Services have models of castles for loan to schools.

Filmstrips

Some are out of print, but may be available from Teachers' Centres or through the E.F.V.A.

The Castle, colour, Longman/Common Ground

Let's Visit Britain's Castles, black and white, Daily Mail, 1947 — distributed by E.F.V.A.

The Story of the Castle, black and white, British Transport, 1956

Films

Mediaeval Castle, 16 mm, black and white, 18 mins. G. B. Instructional, 1950 — distributed by Rank

Let's Look at Castles, 16 mm, colour, 18 mins. Attico Films, 1968

Castles: Defence and Siege Warfare, three 8 mm cassette films, colour, Attico Films, 1970

Castles and fortified manor houses

A fortified manor house; Little Wenham Hall, Suffolk

4 COUNTRY HOUSES

Some objectives and outcomes

We hope that by the time pupils finish their study of country houses they will:

1. have sufficient background knowledge to recognise different styles of country houses in various parts of the country.

2. have had practice at observing, recording, and interpreting the visible evidence of:
a. the architecture of the country houses
b. their interior plan and design
c. their furnishings and decorations
d. their gardens and parks.

3. have had practice at combining the study of visible evidence and background material so they can
a. reconstruct lives
b. understand the purposes of the people who lived in country houses at particular periods in the past.

4. have the knowledge, skills and enthusiasm to explore country houses and other aspects of their historical environment beyond school.

An approach

Teachers will wish to organise the course to suit the abilities of their pupils and to take account of the number and type of country houses in the locality of the school. We hope that the following suggestions will prove useful.

1. Introductory lessons

These could introduce pupils to the background knowledge necessary for the study of country houses and include discussion of:
a. the reasons for the end of castle building
b. the definition of a country house 'a house built for show and comfort, with no thought of defence',
W. G. Hoskins *English Landscapes*, p. 65

c. 'The Great Rebuilding' in the early sixteenth century, the reasons why people began to build country houses at this time:
e.g. the dissolution of the monasteries, the Reformation—releasing money and building materials previously given to the church;
increasing wealth from trade and the desire to invest this in land and houses 'for show and comfort' away from towns and villages;
the influence of the great houses built by the ministers of the Tudor monarchs at Burghley and Hampton.

2. The study of different types of country house

Most houses will be studied in the classroom using guide books, slides, filmstrips, primary and secondary source material. One or two visits should however be made to different types of country house so that pupils can observe, record, and interpret the visible evidence for themselves. N.B. Some pupils may study all types, but for average or less able pupils it may be better to group c, d, e and f, together under one heading, e.g. 'eighteenth century classical style houses'.

a. A Tudor Country House

e.g. Woollaton Hall, Nottinghamshire; Longleat, Wiltshire; Montacute, Somerset; Hardwick Hall, Derbyshire; Burghley House, Northamptonshire; Fritwell Manor, Oxfordshire; Studley Priory, Oxfordshire; Sutton Place, Surrey; The Vyne, Hampshire; Speke Hall, Merseyside; Little Moreton Hall, Cheshire.

b. A Jacobean Country House circa 1600-1660

e.g. Burton Agnes Hall, Humberside; Aston Hall, West Midlands; Castle Ashby, Northamptonshire; Knole, Kent; Raynham Hall, Norfolk; Thorpe Hall, Northamptonshire; Chastleton Hall, Oxfordshire; Grimshaw Hall, Warwickshire; Bramshill House, Hampshire; Balls Park, Hertfordshire; Hatfield House, Hertfordshire;

Country houses

Tudor country house; Hardwick Hall, Derbyshire

Jacobean mansion; Aston Hall, by permission of the Birmingham Museum and Art Gallery

Country houses

Queen Anne country house; Mompesson, Salisbury, Wiltshire

Palladian-style house; Woburn Abbey, Bedfordshire

A Robert Adam interior; The Long Gallery, Syon House, London

Charlton House, London; Blickling Hall, Norfolk; Bateman's, East Sussex; Wilton House, Wiltshire.

c. A late Stuart and Queen Anne Classical Style Country House

e.g. Chatsworth House, Derbyshire; Belton House, Lincolnshire; Stoneleigh Abbey, Warwickshire; Blenheim Palace, Oxfordshire; Seaton Delaval, Northumberland; Castle Howard, North Yorkshire; Chicheley Hall, Buckinghamshire; Easton Neston House, Northamptonshire; Eltham Palace, London; Hanbury Hall, Hereford and Worcester; Honington Hall, Warwickshire; Peckover House, Cambridgeshire; Petworth House, West Sussex.

d. A Palladian Style House circa 1720-1760

e.g. Holkham Hall, Norfolk; Stourhead, Wiltshire; Lyme Park, Greater Manchester; Houghton Hall, Norfolk; Clandon Park, Surrey; Ditchley Park, Oxfordshire; Edgcote, Oxfordshire;

Country houses

The East Front, Syon House; the exterior is substantially as it was in the 16th century, while the interior was redesigned after 1762

A Regency-style house; Polesden Lacey, Dorking, Surrey

A Victorian country house; Osborne House, Isle of Wight

Nostell Priory, West Yorkshire; Woburn Abbey, Bedfordshire; Wrotham Park, Hertfordshire.

e. An Adam House circa 1760-1790

e.g. Syon House, London; Kenwood House, London; Kedleston Hall, Derbyshire; Osterley Park, London; Saltram Park, Devon; Croome Court, Hereford and Worcester; Denton Hall, North Yorkshire; Harewood House, West Yorkshire; Hatchlands, Surrey; Heaton Hall, Greater Manchester; Newby Hall, North Yorkshire; Woodall Park, Herefordshire.

f. A Regency Country House circa 1790-1830

e.g. Althorp, Northamptonshire; Ashridge House, Hertfordshire; Dodington, Avon; Moggerhanger, Bedfordshire; Southill, Bedfordshire; Tyringham, Buckinghamshire.

g. A Victorian Country House — Gothic Revival

e.g. Cliveden, Buckinghamshire; Harlaxton Manor, Lincolnshire; Scarisbrick Hall, Lancashire; Alton Towers, Staffordshire; Balmoral, Aberdeenshire; Highclere Castle, Hampshire; Osborne House, Isle of Wight; Kelham Hall, Nottinghamshire; Knebworth House, Hertfordshire; Hughenden Manor; Buckinghamshire; Thoresby Hall, Nottinghamshire; Waddesdon Manor, Buckinghamshire; Wightwick Manor, West Midlands; Capesthorne Hall, Cheshire; Bryanston House, Dorset.

3. Concluding lessons

These could explain the present state of country houses. Many are being destroyed year by year. Others on private lands, owned by National Trust or city councils are opened to the public to provide funds for their upkeep. Few remain as country homes for noble families. Some pupils could look at the fate of their local 'Hall' and perhaps investigate the effect of the economic and social changes which followed the First World War.

Studying sites: some questions and activities

The amount of help teachers give to pupils during visits or classroom investigations and the form it takes will vary. All questions and activities

should help pupils to observe, understand and interpret the visible evidence. Teachers may find it useful to divide the study of each house, or type of house, into three sections:
1. the house
2. the gardens and park
3. the people.

Questions

1. The house

Outside

What is the house built of, and where did the building materials come from?

What is the style of the house — its windows, doors, roof, etc.?

What shape is the house, i.e. square, E-shaped, etc.?

Has it been altered or extended at any time?

Inside

How many rooms does the house have and how are they arranged?

What was each room used for? Which members of the household used it?

Are the ceilings decorated? If so, describe the designs and colours used.

What material are the fireplaces made of, what shape are they, and how are they decorated?

Which items of furniture does each type of room have?

What type of material is the furniture made from? Is all the furniture of a similar style?

Do any of the pieces have similar decorative motifs?

2. The gardens and park

How are the gardens, grounds and parklands laid out?

What other buildings are in the grounds? Were they separate from, or attached to, the house — e.g. stables, lodges, summerhouses, etc.?

3. The people

Who designed:
a. the house?
b. the furniture?
c. the gardens and grounds?
Who owned it when it was built?
Why did people have their houses:
a. designed and built
b. furnished in this style at this particular time?
Why did people have their gardens and parks laid out in this way at this particular time?
What do we know about the owner of the house, his family, and their daily lives from:
a. the exterior of the house?
b. the rooms and their layout?
c. the furnishings of the rooms, including portraits?
d. the gardens and grounds?
What do we know about the number and type of servants required by the family and the pattern of their daily lives from:
a. the situation of the house?
b. the situation and furnishings of the servants quarters?
c. the layout of the other rooms of the house?
d. the furniture?
e. the garden and grounds?
In what way was the daily life of the family, and servants in this house different from those who lived in an earlier style of house?
Did any important events take place in this house? Is any famous historical personality connected with the house?

Activities

For each type of house studied, pupils may produce a selection from the following items of work;

1. The house

An illustrated description, annotated sketches or photographs of the front of the house and its different features showing the architectural style and explaining the historical context.

Annotated plans of each floor, or wing, of the house showing the layout of the different rooms, and their functions.

Photographs, sketches or descriptions of different pieces of furniture and furnishings, with notes commenting on the materials used, the style, and design.

2. The gardens and park

An illustrated description or annotated plan of the gardens and grounds, explaining the purpose of different features e.g. ha-has, Doric temples, lodges, ice houses.

3. The people

Brief notes about the architect, cabinet maker, landscape gardener and owner of the house — where this information is known or easily accessible.

A short account explaining when and why the original owners had the house built, e.g. with materials and wealth from a monastery? With wealth acquired from trade?

A short illustrated account explaining why the

owners had their houses and gardens designed and furnished in one style at a particular period. An imaginative reconstruction of a typical day in the life of:
a. a member of the owner's family
b. a servant in the house.

A short study of a historical personality or family and its connections with a house, e.g. Bess of Hardwick, Robert Adam, John Churchill, the Parkers of Saltram.

A description, or reconstruction of events, or an incident in the history of the house.

Background source material

Teachers in some areas will find background primary source material about country houses easily, while teachers in other areas may have difficulty in doing so. We hope teachers will find the following list useful.

Different types of primary sources

1. Plans of the houses

These are available in the guidebooks for each house, or in family papers — see below.

2. Maps of the grounds and estate

The relevant section of the 25 inch Ordnance Survey plan first edition — circa 1860 onwards according to area, for the house and estate provides a clear basis for pupils to work from — see Source 1·4. Family papers often include estate plans — see below.

3. Family papers and inventories

Some have been deposited in local record offices. For example, some of the family papers belonging to the Gascoigne family who owned the house shown in Source 1·4 are in the archive library at Sheepscar in Leeds. Others may still be in the possession of the family. Some family papers have already been published by local record societies — particularly inventories and household accounts. Local record society volumes are usually available in reference or local history libraries.

Source 2·4 is an extract from an inventory of Speke Hall in 1624. Source 3·4 gives extracts from the *Household Book* of Dame Alice de Bryene of Acton Hall, Suffolk for October 1412. These give us an interesting picture of Dame Alice eating with her household in the great hall. They provide points of contrast with country houses from Elizabethan times onwards, showing the changes in design and life style which took place. Source 4·4, the Steward's accounts for Acton Hall, give us a good impression of the amount of thought and planning given to the running of such a household.

Extracts from the papers of several families from great country houses have been incorporated into books which tell the story of the house and the family at a particular time. For full details of these see the Resources section, at the end of this chapter.

4. Contemporary accounts and travellers' descriptions

Useful extracts describing the design and furnishings of country houses, their gardens, and the life style of their inhabitants can be found in:
a. William Harrison, *The Description of England*, there are chapters on food and diet, apparel and attire, parks and warrens, gardens and orchard, also on "the Manner of Building and Furniture of our houses" — see Source 5·4.
b. C. Morris (Ed.), *The Journeys of Celia Fiennes;* includes many descriptions of 'country seats',
c. Arthur Young, *A six months' tour through the North of England interspersed with descriptions of the seats of the nobility and gentry* 1771 — see Source 6·4,
Arthur Young, *A six week's tour through the southern counties of England and Wales, interspersed with accounts of the seats of the nobility and gentry* 1768,
Arthur Young, *A tour in Ireland* 1776–1779.
d. Many of Jane Austen's novels,
e.g. *Emma, Mansfield Park, Pride and Prejudice, Northanger Abbey* contain much useful and interesting information on country houses and the lives of their inhabitants.

Country houses

Source 1.4 *Extract from the 1908 edition 25 inch Ordnance Survey plan of the area around Parlington Hall, near Aberford, West Yorkshire*

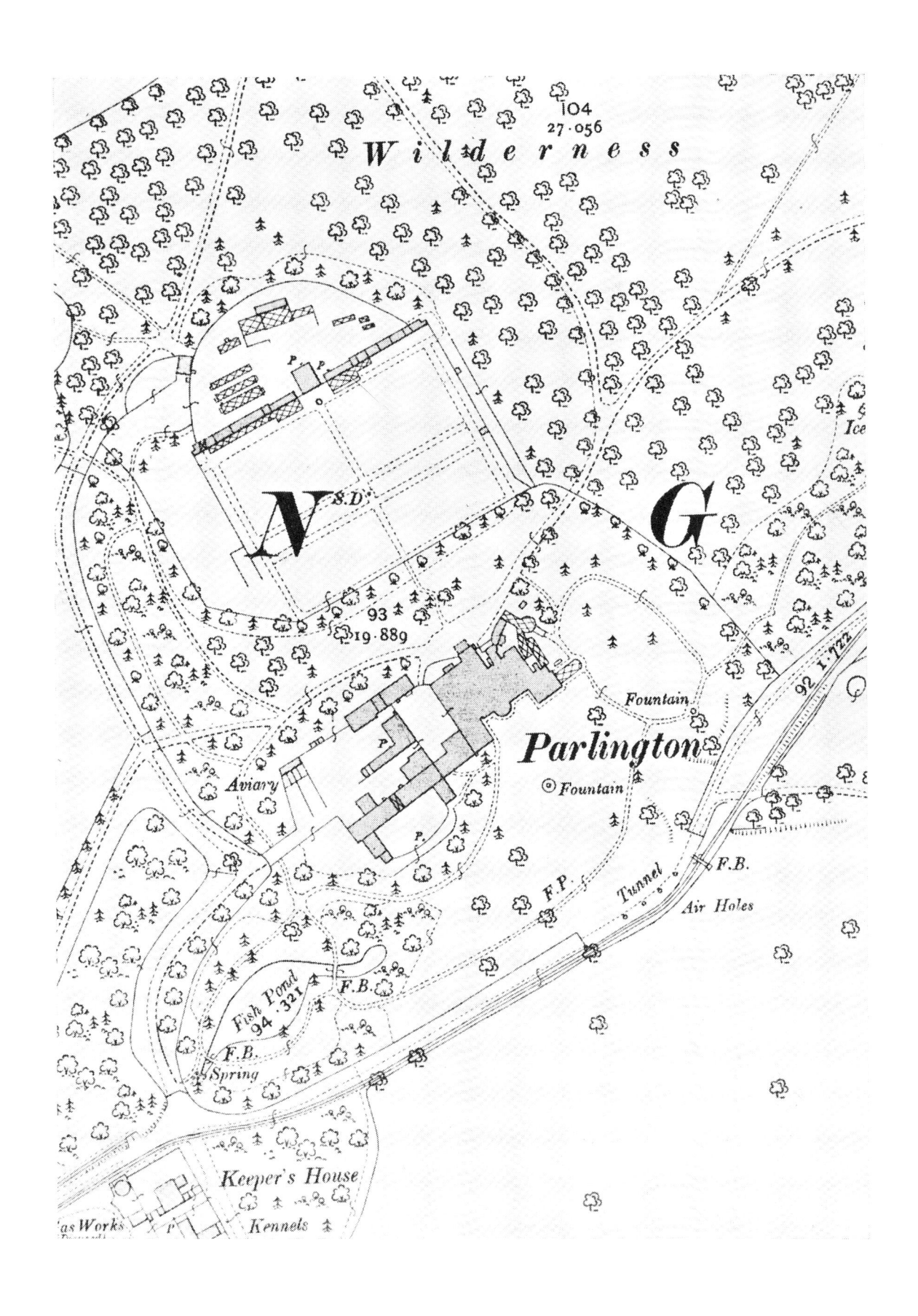

Source 2·4 *An extract from household inventory for Speke Hall, near Liverpool for 1624*

In the Great Parlour
Inprimis the King's armes cutt in woodd, hanging on the wall	xxx^s
Item one long drawing table	liii^{s}iii^d
Item one greene carpett for the table	xl^s
Item ii formes couered with greene & fringed	xiii^{s}iv^d
Item xxiv stooles couered with greene & fringed	v^{ii}x^s
Item iii chayres couered with greene & fringed with greene silk	xxx^s
Item ii little chayres couered alyke & fringed	x^s
Item one square table with a greene carpett fringed	xxviii^s
Item one cubbord with a greene carpett fringed	xx^s
Item one iron grate	v^s
Item ii greene curtens for the windowe	xx^s
Item vi quishens of Arras work	xl^s
Summa	xx^{li}xix^{s}viii^d

The Transactions of the Historic Society of Lancashire and Cheshire VOLS, 96, 97, (1945-6)

Source 3·4 *Extracts from the Household Book of Dame Alice de Bryene of Acton Hall, Suffolk, Sept. 1412 — Sept. 1413* (Chancery Misc. 4/8B, p. 3)

AKETONE [Acton].
Meals: breakfast 8, dinner 20, supper 20, Sum 48.
Thurs. 29 Sept., the feast of St. Michael, the Lady took her meals there with her household; in addition, Agnes Sampson, a certain groom [of] Robert Louell for the whole day, two friars of Norwich, Colbrook, and one of the household of John Cok at one repast.
PANTRY — 40 white loaves and 6 black loaves; wine from what remained; also from stock. KITCHEN — one quarter of bacon, one joint of mutton, one lamb, and 32 pigeons.
PURCHASES — in companage, 2d.
PROVENDER — hay from stock for 7 horses of the Lady and of the company; fodder for the same one bushel of oats.   Sum of the purchases 2d.

Meals: Breakfast 8, dinner 22, supper 10, Sum 40.
Frid., the last of Sept., the Lady took her meals with the household; in addition, Marg [aret] Sampson with her daughter, son, and one of her household. Thomas Malcher at one repast, 9 of the household of Colbrook Manor and one of the household of Thomas Barbour for the whole day. PANTRY — 46 white loaves and 6 black loaves; wine from what remained; ale from stock.
KITCHEN - haif a salt fish and one stockfish.
PURCHASES - in a hundred white herrings, 18d.
PROVENDER - hay from stock for 9 horses of the Lady and company; fodder one bushel one peck of oats.   Sum of the purchases, 18d.

published by the Suffolk Institute of Archaeology and Natural History, (1931)

Country houses

Source 4·4 *Extracts from the account of William Burgh, Steward of the Household of Lady Alice de Bryene from the Vigil of St. Michael 6 Henry V to the Vigil of the same feast 7 Henry V* (i.e. 28 Sept. 1418 — 28 Sept. 1419)

EXPENSES
Provision of divers victuals for the household, wheat [and] wine
In one pipe of red wine bought at London by the Lady, with the expenses for the same and carriage to Colchester, 67s. 2d. Item in 2 pipes and one hogshead of red wine bought of John Joye of Ipswich by the Lady, £8. 13s. 4d. Item in one hogshead of white wine bought of the same, 40s. In 12 qrs. wheat bought by the Lady of the rector of Stanstede, £4. 8s., price 7s. 4d. the qr.
[All expended] by the Lady.   Sum, £20. 15s. 6d.

Purchase of fish
In 5 cades of red herrings, 30s., price 6s. a cade.
In one barrel of white herrings from Skone, 18s.
Item in 3 barrels of white herrings, 36s. price 12s. a barrel.
In 18 "Chelyngges" bought by the said Steward with 8d. for expenses, 20s. 10d. of which 4 price 12d. the piece and 14 price 14½d. the piece, less 1d. on the whole. In 42 "lynges" bought by the Lady, 42s., price 12d. the piece, besides one "lynge" thrown in. In a hundred stockfish bought at Steresbregge by the Lady, 32s. price the piece 3d., ½ a farthing, and a ¼ farthing plus 1½d. on the whole. In half a barrel of salmon and quarter of barrel of salmon bought at Lavenham by the said Steward, 20s. Item in quarter of a barrel of sturgeon bought by the same Steward at Lavenham, 14s. In half a barrel of salt eels bought by the same Steward, 14s.
                    Sum, £13. 11s. 10d.
Whereof [expended by] the Lady, 119s., by the Steward £7. 12s. 10d.

Purchase of salt
In 3 bush. white salt bought by the Lady at Steresbregge, 16½d., price 5½d. the bushel.
In 4 stone of salt bought for the dovecote in the manor, 12d.
[Expended] by the Lady.   Sum, 2s. 4½d.

Purchase of spices
In 3 lb. pepper bought at London, 6s. 3d. price 2s. 1d. the lb. In ½ lb. saffron, 7s. 6d. In 2 lb. ginger, 3s. 10d., price 23d. the lb.
In 2 lb. cinnamon, 3s. 2d., price 19d. the lb.
In one lb. cloves bought at Steresbregge, 3s.
In one lb. mace, 2s. 6d. In 2 lb. soda-ash 20d.
In 40 lb. almonds, 8s. 4d., price 2½d. the lb.
In 4 lb. rice, 4d. In 2 bush. one pk. seed-mustard 2s. 3d., price 12d. a bush. In one frail and 4 lb. figs, 4s. 8d. In 6 lb. dates, 20d. of which 2 lb. price 8d. and 4 lb. price 12d. In one frail and 2 lb. raisins 4s. 3d. In 8 lb. raisins of Corinth 2s., price 3d. the lb. In one lb. white sugar bought by the said Steward, 18d.
                    Sum, 54s. 10d.

Whereof [expended] by the Lady, 53s. 4d. by the Steward, 18d.

Purchase of wax

In 40 lb. wax bought by the Lady, 15s., price 4½d. the lb. In 13 lb. wick 2s. 2d. In stipend of John Blast for making the said wax into torches, "tortys", "prykettes" and candles, 2s.
Sum, 19s. 2d.

Whereof [expended] by the Lady, 15s., by the Steward, 4s. 2d.

Purchase of Paris candles and clarified tallow

In 52 lb. candles, 5s. 10d., price 1¼ and ½ farthing the lb., less 1½d. on the whole. In 180 lb. clarified tallow 14s. 3d., price 1d. the lb. on an average, less 9d. on the whole. In 4 lb. cotton, 2s. 5½d. price 7½d. the lb. less ½d. on the whole. Item in 8 lb. cotton, bought by the Lady, 4s. 4d. price 6½d. the lb. In the wage of John Bocher with his servant for 5 days for making 525 lb. of Paris candles this year by agreement in the gross, 3s. 8d. besides [their] board in the household. Sum, 30s. 6½d.

Whereof [expended] by the Lady, 4s. 4d. by the Steward, 26s. 2½d.

Petty necessaries

... [many items the most interesting of which is] Item paid for the expenses of John Archentein being at Sudbury for 5 days about the feasts of Corpus Christi, St. John Baptist, and St. Peter, for the safe keeping of the herbage of the Lady's meadow there, so that it should not be taken away by the neighbours for strewing their houses therewith, or otherwise destroyed, 7d.

Wages of the household servants

In the wages of the Lady's maid and of the chamberlain, squires, chaplains, grooms, clerks of the chapel and boys, which the parcels more fully appear in the Lady's paper, £44 by the year

[Expended] by the Lady   Sum, £44.

Payments for livery of divers ministers of the Lady

For clothing of divers ministers of the Lady as well for the household servants as for divers others of the Lady's counsel and bailiffs, farmers and other officers retained in the Lady's service against the feast of the Nativity of Our Lord, £23. 17s. 1½d. Item for 20 furs of the said livery for gentlemen, 26s. 6d. price each fur on an average, 15¾d. and ½ a farthing, plus ½d. on the whole. Item paid for summer liveries for the said household servants this year, £10. 16d.   Sum, £35. 4s. 11½d.

Kitchen necessaries

In 7 "Naperounes" bought for the officers of the kitchen, 2s. 4d. In 6 yards of linen cloth for cleaning the windows and vessels of the kitchen, 20d. In one "streynour", 2d. In mending one tripod and one iron "cobet" in which the spit turns in roasting food, 11d. In 4 earthen pans bought to catch the dripping 6d. In sharpening one kitchen knife this year, 2d. In one pestle for crushing cooked food, 2d. In one new "Dressyngknyf", 20d. In 2 iron pans bought at Steresbregge, for taking the clarified fat 3s. 4d. In one basket bought for the kitchen, 7d.   Sum, 11s. 6d.

published by the Suffolk Institute of Archaeology and Natural History, (1931)

Country houses

Source 5·4 *Extracts from William Harrison's "The Description of England" — in the time of Elizabeth I, Bk. II ch. XII: "Of the Manner of Building and Furniture of Our Houses"*

In this extract Harrison describes the changes taking place in homes and furnishings of all people from Noblemen downwards.

Every country house is inwardly divided into sundry rooms above and beneath. The clay wherewith our houses are impaneled is either white, red, or blue; they are compelled to burn a certain kind of red stone as in Wales, and elsewhere other stones and shells of oysters and like fish found upon the seacoast. Within their doors also such as are of ability do oft make their floors of fine alabaster burned, which they call plaster of Paris.

In plastering likewise of our fairest houses over our heads, we use to lay first a layer or two of white mortar tempered with hair upon laths, which are nailed one by another and finally cover all with the aforesaid plaster. The walls of our houses on the inner sides in like sort be either hanged with tapestry, arras work, or painted cloths, wherein either divers histories, or herbs, beasts, knots, and suchlike are stained, or else they are paneled with oak of our own or wainscot brought hither out of the East [Baltic] countries, whereby the rooms are not a little commended, made warm, and much more close than otherwise they would be. As for stoves, we have not hitherto used them greatly, yet do they now begin to be made in divers houses of the gentry and wealthy citizens, who build them not to work and feed in as in Germany and elsewhere, but now and then to sweat in, as occasion and need shall require it.

This also hath been common in England, that many of our greatest houses have outwardly been very simple and plain to sight, which inwardly have been able to receive a duke with his whole train and lodge them at their ease. Of old time our country houses instead of glass did use much lattice, and that made either of wicker or fine rifts strips of oak in checkerwise. But as horn in windows is now quite laid down in every place, so our lattices are also grown into less use because glass is come to be so plentiful and within a very little so good cheap, if not better than the other.

Heretofore also the houses of our princes and noblemen were often glazed with beryl (an example whereof is yet to be seen in Sudley Castle) and in divers other places with fine crystal. But now these are not in use, so that only the clearest glass is most esteemed, for we have diverse sorts, some brought out of Burgundy, some out of Normandy, much out of Flanders, beside that which is made in England, which would be so good as the best if we were diligent and careful to bestow more cost upon it. Moreover the mansion houses of our country towns and villages (which in champaign ground stand all together by streets and joining one to another but in woodland soils dispersed here and there, each one upon the several grounds of their owners) are builded in such sort generally as that they have neither, dairy, stable, nor brewhouse annexed unto them under the same roof (as in many places beyond the sea and some of the north parts of our country) but all separate from the first and one of them from another. And yet for all this they are not so far distant in sunder but that the goodman lying in his bed may lightly hear what is done in each of them with ease and call quickly unto his household if any danger should seize him.

The ancient manors and house of our gentlemen are yet, and for the most part, of strong timber, in framing whereof our carpenters have been and are worthily preferred before those of like science among all other nations. Howbeit, such as be lately builded are commonly either of brick, or hard stone or both, their rooms large and comely, and houses of office further distant from their lodgings. Those of the nobility are likewise wrought with brick and hard stone, but so magnificent and stately as the basest house of a baron doth often match in our days with some honors of princes in old time. So that if ever curious building did flourish in England, it is in these our years, wherein our workmen excel and are in manner comparable in skill with old Vitruvius, Leon Battista, and Serlio.

The furniture of our houses also exceedeth and is grown in manner even to passing delicacy; and herein I do not speak of the nobility and gentry only but likewise of the lowest sort in most places of our South Country. Certes in noblemen's houses it is not rare to see abundance of arras, rich hangings of tapestry, silver vessel, and so much other plate as may furnish sundry cupboards, to the sum oftentimes of £1,000 or £2,000 at the least, whereby the value of this and the rest of their stuff doth grow to be almost inestimable. Likewise in the houses of knights, gentlemen, merchantmen, and some other wealthy citizens, it is not uncommon to behold generally their great provision of tapestry, Turkey work, pewter, brass, fine linen, and thereto costly cupboards of plate, worth £500 or £600 or £1,000. But as herein all these sorts do far exceed their elders and predecessors, and in neatness and curiosity ... so in time past the costly furniture stayed there, whereas now it is descended yet lower, even unto the inferior artificers and many farmers.

There are old men yet dwelling in the village where I remain which have noted three things to be marvelously altered in England within their sound remembrance. One is the multitude of chimneys lately erected, whereas in their young days there were not above two or three in most uplandish towns of the realm (the religious houses and manor places of their lords always excepted), but each one made his fire against a reredos [back of an open hearth] in the hall, where he dined and dressed his meat.

The second is the great (although not general) amendment of lodging, for our fathers, yea, and we ourselves also, have lien full oft upon straw pallets, on rough mats covered only with a sheet, under coverlets made of dagswain, and a good round log under their heads instead of a bolster or pillow. If it were so that our fathers or the goodman of the house had within seven years after his marriage purchased a mattress of flock-bed, and thereto a sack of chaff to rest his head upon, he thought himself to as well lodged as the lord of the town that lay seldom in a bed of down or whole feathers. As for servants, if they had any sheet above them it was well, for seldom had they any under their bodies to keep them from the pricking straws that ran oft through the canvas of the pallet and rased their hardened hides.

The third thing they tell of is the exchange of vessel, as of wooden platters into pewter, and wooden spoons into silver or tin. For so common were all sorts of wooden stuff in old time that a man should hardly find four pieces of pewter (of which one was a salt) in a good farmer's house. Such also was their poverty that if some one odd farmer or husbandman had been at the alehouse, a thing greatly used in those days, amongst six or seven of his neighbors, and there in a bravery to show what store he had did cast down his purse and therein a noble or 6s. in silver, unto them, it was very likely that all the rest could not lay down so much against it; whereas in my time, although £4 of old rent be improved to £40, £50, or £100, yet will the farmer, think his gains very small toward the end of his term if he have not six or seven years' rent lying by him, therewith to purchase a new lease, beside a fair garnish of pewter on his cupboard, with so much more in odd vessel going about the house, three or four feather beds, so many coverlets and carpets of tapestry, a silver salt, a bowl for wine (if not an whole nest) and a dozen of spoons to furnish up the suit [set].

William Harrison, *The Description of England*, George Edelen (Ed.), (Folger Shakespeare Library by Cornell University Press, New York 1968), pp. 196-203

Source 6·4 *Arthur Young's description of gardens and park at Wentworth Castle*

The Earl of Strafford's seat at Wentworth Castle, near Barnsley, is very well worth seeing. The new front to the lawn is one of the most beautiful in the world ...

But Wentworth Castle is more famous for the beauties of the ornamented environs, than for those of the house .... The water and the woods adjoining, are sketched with great taste. The first extends through the park in a meanding course, and ... having everywhere the effect of a real and very beautiful river; the groves of oaks fill up the bends of the stream. The water, in many places, is seen from the house between the trees of several scattered clumps most picturesquely; in others, it is quite lost behind the hills, and breaks every where upon the view ...

The shrubbery that adjoins the house is disposed with the utmost taste. The waving slopes dotted with firs, pine etc. are pretty, and the temple is fixed on so beautiful a spot as to command a sweet landscape of the park.

Winding up the hill among the plantations and woods, which are laid out in an agreeable manner, we came to the bowling green, which is thickly encompassed with evergreens; with a very light and pretty Chinese temple on one side of it; and from thence cross a dark walk catching a most beautiful view of a bank of a distant wood. The next object is a statue of Ceres in a retired spot ... The lawn which leads up to the castle is elegant, there is clump of firs on one side of it, through which the distant prospect is caught;

and the above mentioned statue of Ceres, in the hollow of a dark grove, one among the few instances of statues being employed in gardens with real taste. From the platform of grass within the castle walls (in the centre of which is a statue of the late earl who built it) over the battlements, you behold a surprising prospect on whichever side you look . . .

Within the menagerie, at the bottom of the park, is a most pleasing shrubbery extremely sequestered, cool, shady, and agreeably contrasted to that by the house from which so much distant prospect is beheld: the latter is what may be called fine; but the former is agreeable. We proceeded through the menagerie (which is pretty well stocked with pheasants, etc) to the bottom of the shrubbery, where is an alcove in a sequestered situation . . . The shrubbery, or rather plantation, is spread over two fine slopes, the valley between which is a long winding hollow dale, exquisitely beautiful; the banks are thickly covered with great numbers of very fine oaks . . . at the upper end is a Gothic temple, over a little grot, which forms an arch, and together have a most pleasing effect; on a near view, this temple is found a light and airy building. Behind it is a water sweetly situated, surrounded by hanging wood in a beautiful manner, an island in it prettily planted; and the bank on the left side rising from the water, and scattered with fine oaks. From the seat of the river God . . . the view into the park is pretty, congenial with the spot, and the temple caught in proper style.

Before I leave this very agreeable place, let me remark to you, that in no great house which I have seen have I met with more agreeable treatment, nor will you perhaps esteem it wrong to hint, that Lady Strafford retired from her apartment for us to view it; I mention this as an instance of general and undistinguishing politeness, a striking contrast to that unpopular and affected dignity in which some great people think proper to cloud their houses — such as the necessity of gaining tickets — of being acquainted with the family — of giving notice before-hand of your intentions; all which is terribly inconvenient to a traveller.

Arthur Young, *A six months' tour through the North of England interspersed with descriptions of the seats of the nobility and gentry, (1771)*, VOL. I, pp. 127-138

Source 7·4 *A description of the duties of male servants of the Newdigate family, who were Warwickshire landowners*

April 15 1836
Regulations to be observed in the Family & the particular duties of the House Servants each separately though it is hoped that every member of the Family will at all times be ready & willing to promote the welfare & comfort of the whole, & that they will be ready & willing to assist each other.

No servants are allowed to go out without leave first obtained. For fear of accidents by fire or otherwise Mr. Newdigate wishes it to be understood that when a bell rings more than once it *must* be answered, & that it is the duty of every Servant both male & female hearing a bell ring more than once, to ascertain that it be answered immediately. Also that it is the duty of every Servant finding the great Doors left open to shut them.

Butler Is answerable that all Men Servants perform their duties with alacrity, care & diligence. He is to see that the Great Doors at the Entrance are kept shut, & that the Wicket is off the latch before dusk. That all the Doors & Windows are fast & the fires safe at night — That all is quiet below stairs & that the Men Servants are in bed before him every night. He has the care of Mr. Newdigate's clothes & waits on him. He keeps the cellar Slate & the inventories.

He has the care of the Cellars, Plate & Glass & is answerable that the plate & glass are kept particularly clean.
He lays the Cloth & takes up the Parlour Breakfast & waits — He must hold himself in readiness to answer the House & Door Bells without delay. He attends the fires on the ground floor till 2 o'clock P.M. when the Footman is out on duty — He sees that the Coal Box in the School Room is filled in the morning to last the day. He attends to the Cisterns & Fountain when the water comes on, & observes that the supply comes in regularly & that none of the ball cocks are fast. He also attends to the Hot Water Pipes & keeps them supplied with water (about once per Week) when required etc. He observes that the circulation of Hot Water is regular throughout in about $\frac{1}{2}$ an hour after the fire is made.

> Both Servants take up & attend Luncheon & at the Parlour dinner. They both take away & clean up the glass etc. — They both attend with Tea & Coffee. The Coachman or Groom both *when required* will assist at the Parlour dinner that the other Servants need not be obliged to leave the Room. Mr. Newdigate earnestly hopes that all the Servants will pay particular attention to their language & manners it being quite impossible that a Servant can be agreeable [sic] without a civil & obliging manner particularly where Ladies are concerned.
>
> *Footman* Trims the Lamps, rubs the Dining Room & Drawing Room Tables, Cleans the Glass, Plate & Silver hafted Knives. He prepares for the Children Dinner & Luncheon at which both Servants attend. He answers the bells & attends to the fires on the Ground Floor after 2 o'clock — He attends the carriage & lays the Cloth for the Parlour Dinner, assists in Waiting & cleaning up after. He brushes & cleans the young gentlemen's clothes & takes them up. He assists to clean the Windows of the ground floor & is expected to be civil & to make himself generally useful. On no account is he to be absent without leave previously obtained.
>
> *Boy* Makes & attends to the fire in the furnace of the Pipes — Cleans the Young Gentlemen's Shoes, the Servants' Hall passages & half the Yard. He riddles Cinders & takes them for Laundry & Pipes — He must carry coals for the Nursery fires. He goes on errands & must make himself generally useful. He must always be civil & on no account to go out without leave previously obtained.

preserved at the Warwickshire County Record Office and quoted in Pamela Horn, *The Rise and Fall of the Victorian Servant*, (Gill & Macmillian, 1975), appendix B2

Course work for G.C.E. and C.S.E. assessment

Some history teachers may wish to devise Mode 3 C.S.E. and G.C.E. 'O' level syllabuses which include work on *History Around Us: Country houses*. The following items of course work could be completed by pupils and submitted in a folder as part of their final assessment.

1. Descriptions of houses visited supported by relevant maps, plans, sketches, photographs and any records or surveys.

2. Descriptions of other houses studied in the classroom including maps, plans, and sketches.

3. Work setting a house in its historical context and relating it to other houses:
e.g. an illustrated account explaining why a family chose to build and furnish a house in a certain style at a particular time, including a map showing the distribution of similar houses.
e.g. an illustrated account explaining why a country house fell into disuse or decay, including a map showing the distribution of similar houses.
e.g. an illustrated account describing and explaining the development of country houses between 1580 and 1850.

4. An imaginative reconstruction of:
either: A specific incident in the history of a house,
e.g. the fire which gutted Bramham House, West Yorkshire.
or: Life in a country house at a particular period,
e.g. the life of a servant 'below stairs' in a Victorian country house,
e.g. the life of a country gentleman in an eighteenth century house.
or: A study of the connections between a historical personality or family and a house,
e.g. Bess of Hardwick; the Parkers of Saltram; the Bedfords of Woburn.

Resources

Some of the books on this list are out of print. You should be able to obtain copies from your local library or from the Schools Library Loan Service.
Resources are listed by order of importance, within each section.

Teachers' books

Islay Doncaster, *Finding the History Around Us*, (Basil Blackwell, 1956) Ch. 3
W. G. Hoskins, *The Making of the English Landscape*, (Penguin, 1970) Ch. 5
W. G. Hoskins, *English Landscapes*, (BBC, 1973) Ch. 6
Alec Clifton-Taylor, *et. al. The Spirit of the Age*, (BBC, 1975)
T. W. West, *A History of Architecture in England*, (University of London Press, 1969)

Reference books for teachers and pupils

Olive Cook, *The English Country House*, (Thames & Hudson, 1974)
Doreen Yarwood, *The English Home*, (Batsford, 1956)
I. Brown, R. Dutton & A. F. Kersting, *Stately Home in Colour*, (Batsford, 1961)
Ralph Dutton, *The English Country House*, (Batsford, 1962)
Roy Strong, *et. al.* (Eds.), *The Destruction of the Country House*, 1875-1975, (Thames & Hudson, 1974)
Michael & Anna Meredith, *Museums and Historic Houses*, (Wayland, 1973)

Guide books for specific houses

Most country houses have their own guide books, but the following are of particular interest for schools in the appropriate areas:
The Story of a Great House, Syon House — Adam style, late eighteenth century, (Syon House Estate, 1968) available from Mr. P. Weathers, Curator, Syon House, Brentford, London.
Hardwick Hall — Elizabethan, available from Hardwick Hall, Doe Lea, Nr. Chesterfield, Derbyshire, S44 5QJ.
Speke Hall — circa 1490-1613, detailed information available from The Curator, Speke Hall, The Walk, Liverpool, LS4 1SD.
Ham House, Surrey — circa 1673, (HMSO)
Osterley Park, Middlesex — Adam Style, late eighteenth century, (HMSO)
Burton Agnes, Old Manor House, Humberside — Elizabethan, (HMSO)

Books for pupils

These deal with the visible evidence for houses and their furniture.
Doreen Yarwood, *English Houses*, (Batsford, 1966)
Treasure in the Home, (Dunlop Ltd.) free from the Education Section, Dunlop Ltd., 25 St. James Street, London, S.W.1.
E. O'Donnell, *The Modern Centuries*, 1600-1940, 'Look at the Past Series', (Ginn, 1964) set of six books dealing with houses, dress, furniture, glass pottery, porcelain and silver

Books for pupils and archive units

These contain primary source material about country houses and families associated with them.
Alison Plowden *Mistress of Hardwick*, (BBC, 1972)
Anthony Fletcher, *Elizabethan Village*, 'Then and There Series', (Longman, 1972) the first part of the book deals with Princes' Manor, Harwell and the Loder family.
Geffrye Museum, *Study Folder No. 1, Sixteenth Century, Study Folder No. 2, Seventeenth Century, Study Folder No. 3 Eighteenth Century, Study Folder No. 4, Nineteenth Century*, these contain photographs and other information about domestic interiors and are available from the Geffrye Museum, Kingsland Road, London E2 8EA.
Michael Cook & Joan E. Blyth (Eds.), *A Tudor House: Speke Hall and the Norris Family* 1500-1700, 'Liverpool History Teaching Unit No. 1' (Liverpool Education Committee, 1970, distributed by Parry Books Ltd., 49 Hardman St. Liverpool, L1 9AU.)
Gladys Scott Thompson, *Life in a Noble Household:* 1641-1700, (Cape, 1965)
Evelyn Curtis, *Life in the Palace Beautiful: The Account Books of Houghton House* 1675-89, 'Elstow Moot Hall Leaflets', (Bedfordshire County Record Office, County Hall, Bedford.)
Joyce Godber, *Wrest Park and the Duke of Kent*, (Henry Grey 1671-1740), 'Elstow Moot Hall Leaflets', (Bedfordshire County Record Office)
Ronald Fletcher, *Parkers at Saltram*, 1769-89, (BBC, 1970)
John Burnett, *The Useful Toil*, Autobiographies of Working People from the 1820s to the 1920s, (Allen Lane, 1974)
Pamela Horn, *The Rise and Fall of the Victorian Servant*, (Gill & Macmillan, 1975)
Mary Mauchline, *Harewood House*, (David and Charles, 1974)
David Cecil, *The Cecils of Hatfield House*, (Constable, 1973)

Reference books for pupils

These give background information about life in country houses at different periods.
Elizabeth Burton, *The Elizabethans at Home*, (Arrow Books, 1973)
Elizabeth Burton, *The Jacobeans at Home*, (Secker & Warburg, 1962)
Elizabeth Burton, *The Georgians at Home*, (Arrow Books, 1973)
Elizabeth Burton, *The Early Victorians at Home*, (Arrow Books, 1974)
Joan Clifford, *Capability Brown*, 'Lifelines Series', (Shire Publications, 1974)
Kay N. Sanecki, *Humphry Repton*, 'Lifelines Series', (Shire Publications, 1974)
W. K. Ritchie, *The Eighteenth Century Grand Tour*, 'Then and There Series', (Longman, 1972)

Slides

Many country houses have slides for sale, but they can also be obtained from:
The Department of the Environment for
Audley End, Essex
Chiswick House, London
Hampton Court, Middlesex
Kew Palace,
Osborne House, Isle of Wight
The Slide Centre Ltd, for
Styles of English Architecture
Development of the Domestic House
Life in Tudor England, 'S68 Castles, Palaces & Houses'
Life in Elizabethan England, 'S163 The Middle Classes, Nobility and Gentry'
Life in Stuart England, 'S170 The Middle Classes, Nobility and Gentry'
Life in Georgian England, 'S468 The English People: Upper Class Life'
Life in Regency England, 'S473 The Middle and Upper Class Life'
Life in Victorian England, 'S476 The Gentry'

Filmstrips

Some of these are out of print but may be available from Teachers' Centres or through the E.F.V.A.
Longleat, black and white, British Transport, 1960
Country Houses near London, black and white, British Transport, 1953
Oxfordshire Estate Maps, Bodleian Library, 1969
English Topography, showing eighteenth century mansions from the Gough MS drawings, Bodleian Library
Life in Tudor Times, colour, Longman/Common Ground
Life in Elizabethan Times, colour, Longman/Common Ground
Life in Early Stuart Times, colour, Longman/Common Ground
Life in Restoration Times, colour, Longman/Common Ground
Life in Early Georgian Times, colour, Longman/Common Ground

Filmstrips with tapes

Eighteenth Century Houses and Homes, The Slide Centre Ltd
Nineteenth Century Houses and Homes, The Slide Centre Ltd

Films

Tudor Houses, 8 mm cassette film, colour, Gateway, 1964

5 CHURCH BUILDINGS AND FURNISHINGS

Some objectives and outcomes

We hope that by the time pupils finish their study of churches they will:

1. have sufficient background knowledge to recognise when a church was built, extended and altered by looking at its architectural style and plan.

2. have had practice at recognising, recording, and interpreting the visible evidence about:
the site of a church and its position in the parish
the date when the church was built
the date of any extensions and alterations
the interior plan of the church building, e.g. the nave, aisles, chancel, vestry, tower, etc.
its fittings, furnishings and decorations, e.g. rood loft, chancel screen, stained glass, brasses, piscina, etc.
the graveyard and its monuments
the vicarage, rectory, church house and tithe barn.

3. have had practice at combining the study of visible remains and background documentary evidence to reconstruct a picture of:
a. a church building and its development, including the influence of local and national history on this process
b. the life and work of the parish priest or a monk
c. the part played by the church — or monasteries, in the religious and secular lives of the community in the past.

4. have the knowledge, skills and enthusiasm to explore churches and other aspects of their historical environment beyond school.

An approach

Teachers will wish to organise the course to suit the abilities of their pupils and to take account of the number and type of church buildings in the locality of the school. We hope that the following approaches will prove useful.

APPROACH 1

This could involve:
a. a detailed study of a parish church, concentrating first on the local church and using the visible evidence to explain:
the church building, its history and development
the parish priest — his status and livelihood
the role of the church and priest in the life of the local community in the past
b. a brief look at one or two different types of parish church which pupils see around them,
e.g. a cathedral church, a modern city church, one of Wren's London churches.

APPROACH 2

This could involve a study of two, three or four different types of church building,
e.g. a parish church, a Cathedral, an Abbey, a Non-Conformist chapel, a tithe barn.
In each case pupils could learn how to use the visible evidence to explain:
the history and development of the buildings
the life and work of the priest, minister or monks who used the building
its role in the life of the local community.

Studying church buildings: some questions and activities

The number, length and frequency of visits will vary from school to school, as will the form and amount of help teachers give to pupils studying churches in the classroom or by fieldwork. We hope that the following suggestions prove useful.

Church buildings and furnishings

Saxon church tower; Earls Barton, Northamptonshire

Norman-style church; Iffley, Oxfordshire

Church buildings and furnishings

Mediaeval tithe barn; Bradford-on-Avon, Wiltshire

The interior of the tithe barn, Bradford-on-Avon, Wiltshire

A wool church; Lavenham, Suffolk

Box pews and three decker pulpit; St. Mary's Church, Whitby, North Yorkshire

Methodist chapel; Yarm, Cleveland

85

Church buildings and furnishings

Parish church and priory ruins, Lindisfarne Priory; Holy Island, Northumberland

Transept and part of East range, Furness Abbey; Barrow-in-Furness, Lancashire

Cleeve Abbey; Old Cleeve, Somerset

Church buildings and furnishings

Fountains Abbey, North Yorkshire; in the foreground the lay brothers infirmary, middle distance the cellarium and cloister, background the church and Huby's tower

1. THE PARISH CHURCH

Because the parish church is often a palimpsest of interwoven clues and changes, it may be best to divide the study into four or five sections each having its own introductory lessons, visits and follow-up work.

a. Why study churches?

Teachers could give their pupils a brief introduction to the historical background about churches: the first introduction of Christianity, St. Augustine, the development of the church and its buildings during the Middle Ages, the importance of the church in the life of the community.

b. The origins and developments of the church buildings

Introductory lessons

These could be based on slides, a filmstrip, plans and drawings and give pupils the necessary background information to study the development of their own church using the visible evidence. The significance of the following clues should be explained:

The site of the church
This may be very ancient — built on a prehistoric religious site such as a pagan grove surrounded by yew trees or a burial mound. An ancient preaching cross (not to be confused with a market cross) may survive in the churchyard to show where the early churchmen held services before the church was built.

The dedication of the church
This may give clues about the date or reason for the foundation of the church.

List of incumbents
This is usually inside the church door and gives the names and dates of parish priests in the past.

The architectural style of the church
Since we know approximately when certain styles of windows, doors, pillars and arches were developed we can tell when parts of the church were first constructed and later extended and altered.

The plan of the church
The development of different parts of the church building could be explained. The simplicity or complexity of the plan reflects the age of the building and the wealth and size of the parish or advowson. The significance of the following could be discussed:
The chancel and sanctuary:
the priest's part of the church, built and maintained by him as a covering for the altar — the first part of a church to be built.

Figure 1·5 *Diagrams showing the development of typical church plans between the twelfth and fifteenth centuries* (dotted lines indicate the previous stages of development)

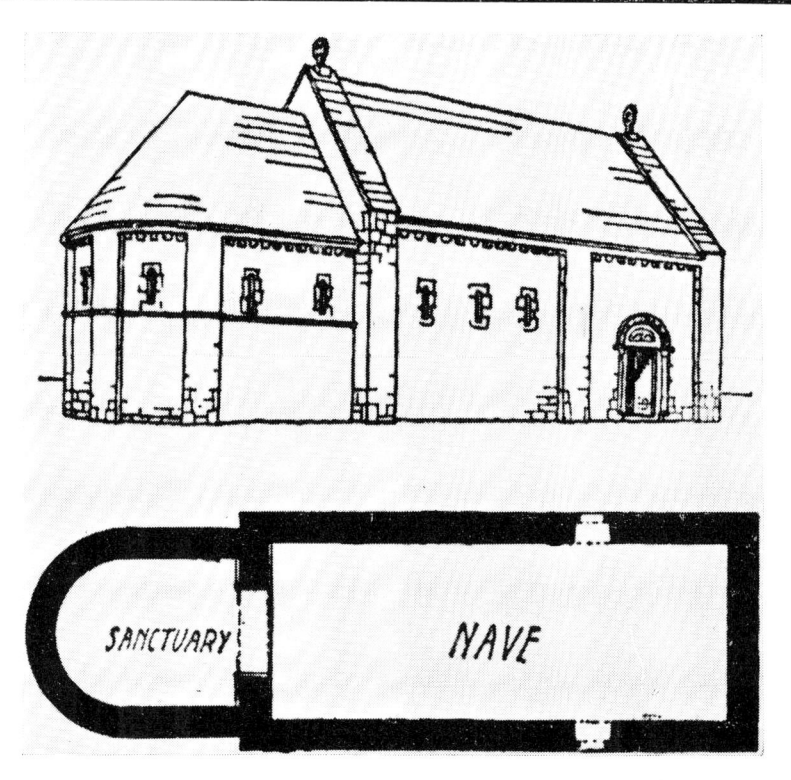

Twelfth century

Church buildings and furnishings

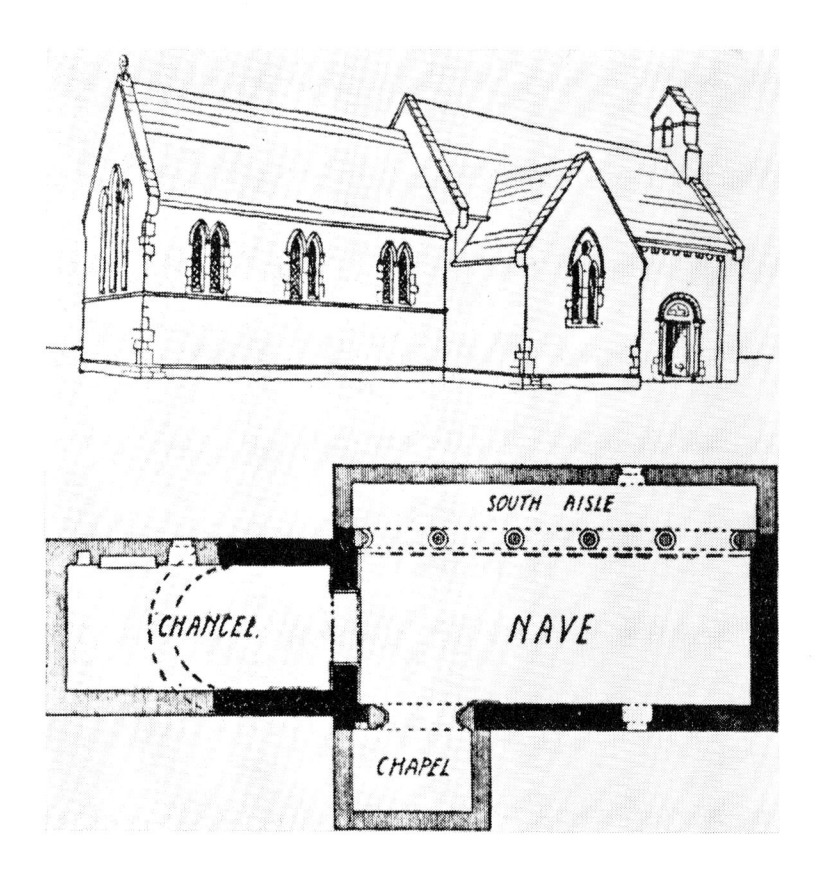

Thirteenth century

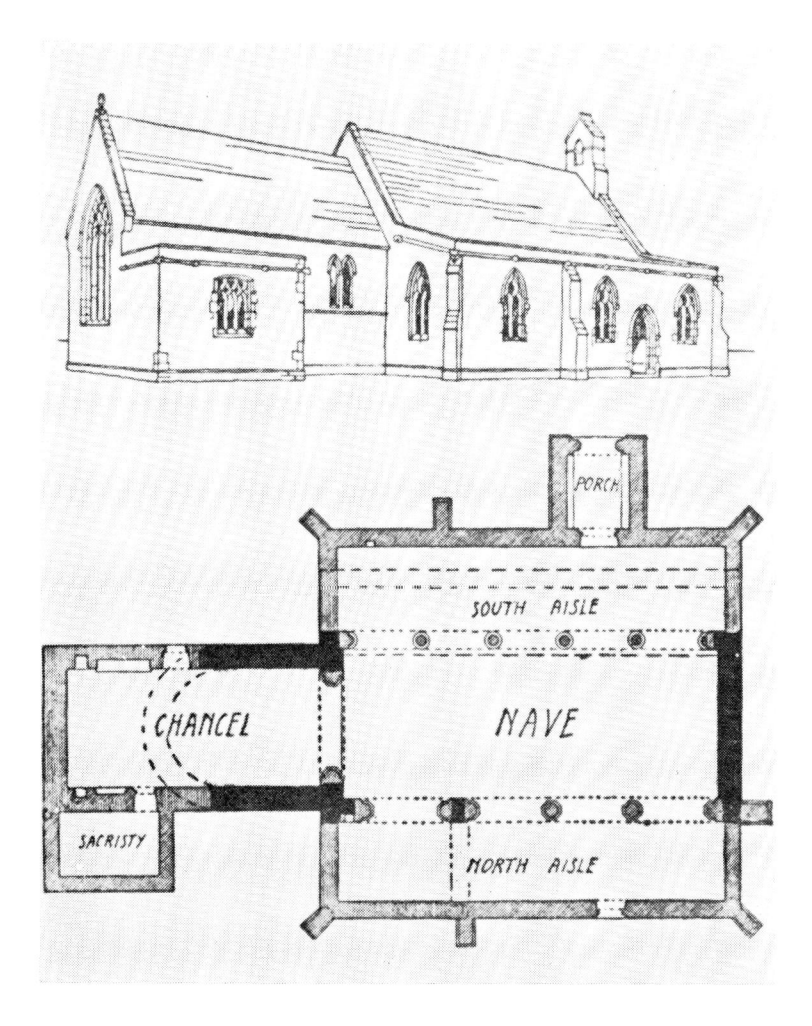

Fourteenth century

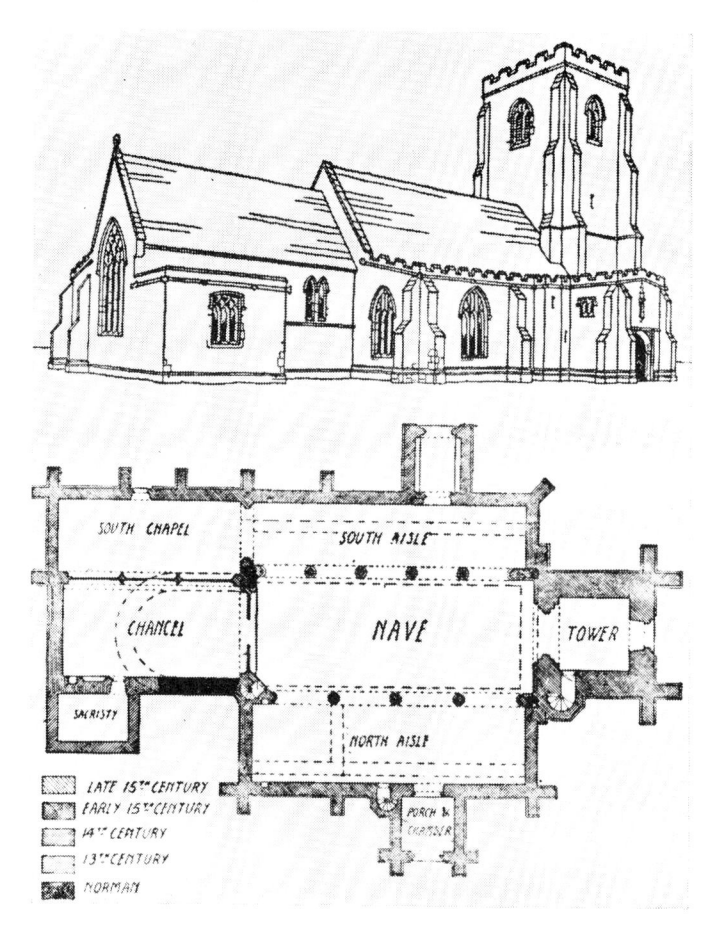

Church buildings and furnishings

Early fifteenth century

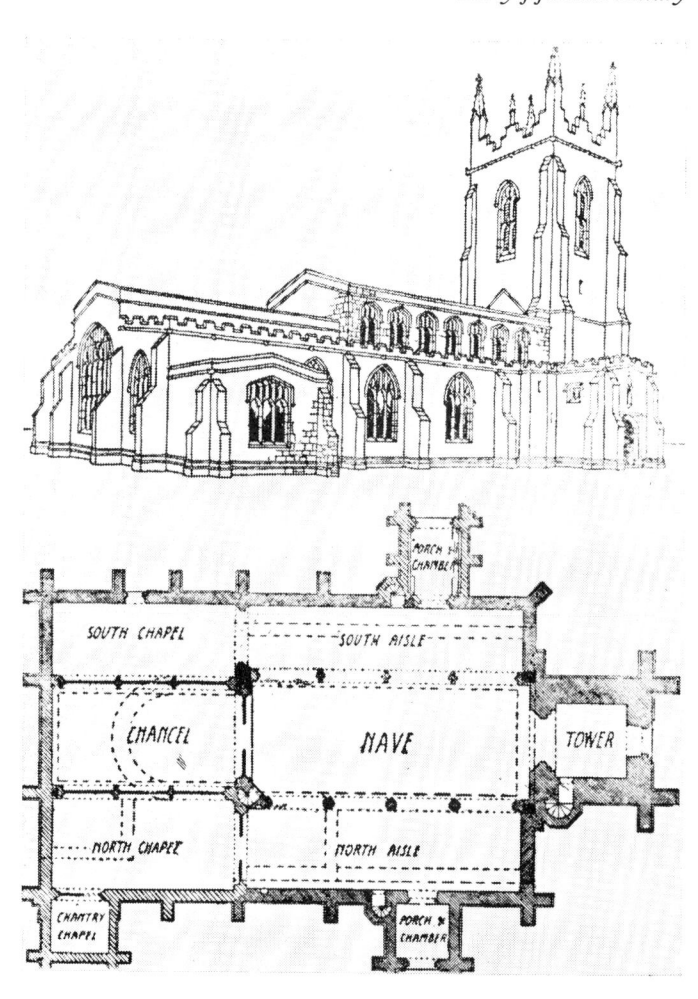

Late fifteenth century

reproduced from J. Charles Cox, *Parish Churches of England,* (Batsford, 1935) figs. 1-5

Church buildings and furnishings

The Nave:
the people's part of the church built later and maintained by them for shelter during services.
The tower or spire:
usually built later by the people as a place of refuge or a sign of the village's wealth and prestige.
Aisles:
added later by various people for numerous reasons,
e.g. by guilds as meeting places, by rich parishioners as places for altars, or for Lady chapels in honour of a family member, by the parishioners of an expanding community.
Porch:
first added between twelfth and fourteenth centuries to protect the church door or as a place for religious and secular business which could not be carried out in church such as the 'churching' of women after childbirth, or the signing of legal contracts.
Chantry chapels:
built by rich families or guilds as a place where hired priests could say masses and prayers for the souls of the dead.
Teachers may want their pupils to prepare 'clue sheets' with drawings showing the styles of church architecture at different periods and annotated sketches showing the development of the church plan see—*fig*. 1.5, before they visit the church.

A visit to the parish church

Pupils could record all the relevant information about the site, plan and architecture of the church — see *fig*. 2·5.

Follow-up work

The teacher and the class could catalogue and interpret all the clues about the development of the church building. They could then discuss the following questions:
Why was the church built on this site?
When was a church first built here?
Why was the church altered or extended during a particular period, i.e. did the community or one of its families prosper? Did its population grow? Was there rivalry between this and another parish?
The teacher may then consider the question:
How was the fabric of the church and its fittings maintained, and by whom?
Pupils could study extracts from the churchwardens' accounts for certain periods — see the section on background source material for examples. They could look at the first edition 25 inch Ordnance Survey plan of the church and its surroundings — see p. 185, for signs of a 'church house', built by some parishes for the brewing of church ale. Churchwardens would beg malt from the parish farmers, brew a vast quantity of strong ale then call upon people to come and drink it — at a price! Many became ale houses after church ales were abolished.

c. Church buildings and furnishings, their links with national events

Introductory lessons

These could:
a. explain the different furnishings and fittings which churches possessed at different periods, their purposes and function.
b. outline of national religious developments and events which brought changes to them.

A visit to the parish church

Pupils could record on their own plan of the church the location of all its fittings and furnishings, e.g. font, rood loft, chancel screen, stained glass, piscina, aumbry, sedilia, pews, pulpit, bells, and note their style, shape and state of preservation.

Follow-up work

The class could discuss their findings with the teacher and draw conclusions about the effect of national events on their church. The churchwardens' accounts for periods of change, especially the Reformation and the Victorian era, provide information about alterations made to the church fabric and fittings as a result of national developments.

d. The priest and his living

Introductory lessons

These could introduce and explain the visible evidence about the priest, his status and way of life in the past, e.g.
the church sign board
This states whether the priest is a vicar, rector or perpetual curate, so we know what his status and his income were in the past
the tithe barn and glebelands
This tells us about his income in the past — the remains of these may only be recalled in street and field names
the list of incumbents
This may show us that the priest was the younger son of a wealthy local family

Church buildings and furnishings

Figure 2·5 *An example of a survey sheet to record information about the site, plan and architectural style of a church*

Church	Date of visit
Site of Church	*Plan of Church*

External features of the church

Tower ....

Steeple ....

Porch ....

Gargoyles ....

Sundial ....

Building materials: walls/tower ....

                                    roof ....

Other interesting features ....

Internal features of the church

Feature	Architectural style	Roof
Nave		
Chancel		
Transepts		
Aisles		
Chapels		

Comments and conclusions

Church buildings and furnishings

plaques and memorials
The ones in the church may commemorate notable priests and their work
the vicarage or rectory
The size and style of the house and grounds gives us more information about the status of the priest and his life style during a particular period in the past.

A visit and/or map work

Some pupils may revisit the church to look at the sign board, the list of incumbents, plaques, memorials, and vicarage. Others may use the first edition 25 inch Ordnance Survey plan of the church and its surrounding area, the local 'church history', and the 1836 tithe map. These may give information about the location of the tithe barn and glebe lands and the size of the vicarage or rectory and its grounds.

Follow up work

Pupils could combine the information from the visit and/or map work to answer three questions: What was the status of the priest in the past and how did he get his living?
At what period in history did the priest appear to be most wealthy or influential? Can you explain the reasons for this?
Did the church have a notable or infamous priest at any time in its history? If so, give details.
If this section of the course stimulates interest teachers may want some pupils to study extracts from glebe terriers, to find out more information about the income and life style of the priest — see the section on background source material for examples.

e. The church and the community
Introductory lessons

These could introduce pupils to the kinds of visible evidence which help us to build up a picture of the role played by the church in the life of the community in the past.
The class could draw up lists of various types of evidence, e.g.
The religious life of the community: birth, life, death
baptism — font, parish register of births
marriage — parish registers
worship — robes, vestments, church plate, prayer books and hymnals, organ, orchestra gallery
religious instruction — pulpit, bible and lectern, wall paintings, stained glass windows
confession — confessional box
burial — brasses, tombs and monuments in the church, graveyard and gravestones, lych gate
care of souls — chapels
The secular life of the community
refuge in danger — tower
meetings and social gatherings — the nave, aisles, the church hall, the church house
markets and fairs — churchyard and market cross
the display of family and parish pride — towers, spires, chantries and other additions to the fabric of the church
striking of bargains and signing of contracts — the porch
education — church school, aisle used for Sunday school
poor relief and law and order — the vestry, almshouses
recording of events and personalities in the parish's history — the parish chest and its records, plaques, memorials and brasses.

A visit and follow up work

Pupils could answer the following questions by studying the visible remains and background information:

What do we know about the part played by the priest and the church in the life of the parish in the past from the evidence in and around the church?
Some pupils may revisit the church to locate and draw features such as the lych gate, market cross or tower, and to record information from brasses, memorials and plaques over the church school and hall.
This visible evidence may be explained or supported by background information from documentary records such as: visitation returns, lists of fairs, school log books.
See the section on background source material for examples.

From the visible evidence in and around the church what do we know about personalities and events in the history of the parish?
Some pupils may revisit the church to look at tombs and memorials in the church itself and gravestones in the churchyard—see *fig. 3·5*. These may give information about:
costume at certain periods
names of local families
the impact of the First World War on the parish
life expectancy at different times
any disaster which may have affected the community
the extent to which people travelled and died in other places.
This evidence may be combined with background information from parish records such as: accounts of the overseers of the poor, parish registers. See

Figure 3.5 *An example of a survey sheet to record information from gravestones and memorials in the churchyard*

Date of death	Surname	Christian names	Age at death	Other information e.g. place of origin, reason for death

the section on background source material for examples.

Concluding lessons

The teacher and class may discuss the changing role of the priest and the church today and the way this is reflected in the buildings and their use, e.g. the return to the mediaeval idea of the church building as a centre for the secular life of the community, or the growth of a new style church in office blocks and urban centres.

2. CATHEDRALS AND CHAPELS

The approaches, questions and activities suggested for a study of the parish church may be used in a modified form for cathedrals or chapels.
Teachers who intend to study chapels may find useful information in K. Lindley, *Chapels and Meeting Houses*.

3. ABBEYS

The study of an abbey may present more difficulties than the study of parish church because of its size and its ruined state. As the location of many abbeys is remote, it is unlikely that many schools will make more than one visit.
Pupils must be well prepared if they are to make the best use of their fieldwork. We hope the following suggestions prove useful.

Introductory lessons

These could introduce pupils to the historical background essential for studying the visible remains of abbeys, e.g.
the historical background and events leading to the founding of monasteries in Britain
an explanation of the monastic ideal
an examination of a typical monastic plan and the kind of monastic buildings associated with different orders
a discussion of the location and siting of various monasteries using maps
an explanation of the reasons for and effects of the dissolution of the monasteries.
Using maps and plans pupils could answer the following questions:
Why were abbeys sited in these places?
From the maps and plans what can we tell about:
a. worship and religious life in monasteries?
b. the daily work and livelihood of the monks?

A visit to an abbey

Pupils could record information about:

The site of the abbey
Where is it located and why was that particular site chosen?
When was it built and by whom?

The monastic buildings
Pupils could explore the abbey, finding and recording the different buildings and their features, e.g.
The church:
Where were the altars, saints' shrines, night stairs, effigies and grave slabs, dividing screens?
What is the plan of the church?
The cloister:
Where are the chapter house, reredorters, sacristy, warming room, parlour, lavers, book cupboard?
Outer buildings:
Where are the kitchens, bakehouse, brewhouse, abbot's house, infirmary, guest house, barns, dove-cote, fish pond, water mill, outer gate?
Water supply and drainage:
How did the abbey get its water for drinking and flushing the drains?
What architectural style are the buildings? What is the state of repair of the buildings?

Other buildings
Is there a nearby hall or manor house which may have been built using stone and lead from the monastery?

Follow-up work

Pupils could produce some of the following items of work:

a. An annotated sketch map showing the site of the abbey based on the 2½ inch Ordnance Survey map, explaining why it was located on this site.

b. An annotated plan of the abbey and an account describing the religious life of the monks and their way of producing food and wealth.
Teachers may want pupils to use documentary evidence such as:
the 2½ inch Ordnance Survey map, which may show signs of the abbey's sheep runs, or drove roads
accounts of the ritual and way of life in a monastery, e.g.
The Rites of Durham: a description of the ancient monuments, rites and customs in the monastical church of Durham before the suppression written in 1593 and reproduced in *The Publications of the Surtees Society*, VOL. 107, (1903)
inventories of the abbey's possessions, e.g.
the inventory of the furnishings of the abbot's lodgings at Peterborough made in 1460 reproduced in A. R. Myers (Ed.), *English Historical Documents*, VOL. IV, (Eyre and Spottiswoode, 1909) p. 1146.

c. A brief illustrated account explaining the fate of the abbey at its dissolution: this may involve a study of a local family who bought the abbey and took the stone and lead for their own house.
The suppression papers relating to the abbey may have been published by the local record society. These will give the names of the monks and nuns who still remained in the abbey when it was dissolved.
H. F. M. Prescott, *Man on a Donkey*, (Penguin Classics, 1969) is an imaginative reconstruction of the story behind the dissolution of Marrick Priory near Richmond in North Yorkshire. Extracts from it are most useful.

d. An annotated map showing the location of other abbeys which are:
either: within a day's travelling distance of home
or: in an area which pupils may visit while on holiday.

Some background source material

Types of background primary source material

Primary source material may be easier to find for some church buildings than for others. A number of documentary sources for the study of abbeys have been mentioned and some examples are included below.

A selection of the many types of documentary sources which can help pupils to understand the visible remains associated with parish churches is listed below:

1. Parish records

These may be available in manuscript form in the church or diocesan registry. Teachers may find printed extracts either in a local history book or amongst the volumes of the local record society in reference libraries. Parish registers, especially the list of burials, can give information about parishioners who came to worship in the church, e.g. their trades, occupations and their life expectancy.

Churchwardens' accounts record changes in the fabric of the church; glebe terriers list the lands and dues of the priest; the accounts of the overseers of the poor show how the parish officials who met in the church vestry, dealt with the poor.

2. Visitation returns

These were sent at intervals to every parish priest by the Archbishop to find out about the size of the congregation, their 'religious health' and the work of the priest in the parish. From these we can discover the number of Anglicans and Dissenters in a parish at any one time. They also give information about the educational and charitable work of the church such as the setting up of a church school or almshouses. Many visitation returns have been reproduced in print by local record societies and are available in reference libraries.

3. Owen's *Book of Fairs*

These lists tell us when fairs and markets were held and who first granted their charter. Some of these may have been held in the churchyard on the eve of a Saint's Day. Owen's *List of Fairs for Yorkshire*, 6th edn., (1770) has been reproduced in print by the Thoresby Society of Leeds, Vol 39, (1940). Lists for other counties may be found amongst the volumes of other local record societies.

4. Maps

These can be used to discover the location and extent of church land and buildings, e.g. tithe barn, church house, vicarage, glebe lands, etc. The most useful maps are the first edition 25 inch Ordnance Survey plan, 1860s onwards according to area, and the tithe map of the parish. Xerox copies of relevant sections of the 25 inch plan can usually be obtained from the local reference library or record office. Tithe maps and awards were produced for each parish at the time of the 1836 Tithe Commutation Act. They show all the properties in the parish whose owners were liable to pay tithes to the priest. Copies may be found in the local record office or diocesan registry.

5. Contemporary novels and diaries

These provide information about the work of the parson and the role of the church in the local community in the past. Some of the most interesting are:

Thomas Hardy, *Under the Greenwood Tree*, New Wessex edition (Macmillan, 1974). This tells the story of the Mellstock parish choir. Chapter Four describes the custom of carol singing. It incorporates much interesting discussion about the string instruments once played in church orchestra galleries, and the introduction of 'barrel organs and the things next door to 'em that you blow wi' your foot'.

George Eliot, *Scenes from Clerical Life* (Penguin, 1973). Chapter One has an interesting description of the changes made to one parish church in the early nineteenth century and the reasons for them.

Rev. James Woodforde, *Diary of a Country Parson*, John Beresford (Ed.), (4 Vols. O.U.P. 1949). This describes the day to day concerns of a parson in the late eighteenth century.

Source 1.5 *Extracts from Churchwardens' accounts, All Saints, Barwick-in-Elmet, West Yorkshire*

The following general entries are interesting. Amongst other things they show us the fabric of the church passing from the greater mediaeval beauty to the miserable condition it reached in the earlier half of the nineteenth century.

Year	Entry	Amount
1734	Received by old glass	2:6
	The glazier's bill	4:0:0
	Paid for stone getting from Huddlestone	11:0
	Paid the stone cutters bill for making two new windows in the church	2:16:0
	Wood for the Church stile and making	12:6
1735	Paid a quarter's learning for the Singers to sing	1:1:0
1740	Repairing horse block	1:4
1741	For a Book of Homilies	5:0
1743	New surplice 12 yards of Holland at 4s. 6d. per yard	2:14:0
	New surplice making	7:6
1746	Paid for a Book of Duty's	2:6
	For church whitening, varnishing and other work	4:4:9
1747	Paid for a book against swearing	8
1748	Paid for a new window in the bell chamber	17:6

Church buildings and furnishings

1752	To John Whitehead for making hearse	3:10:0
	To Stephen Burley for the iron work	1:12:0
1755	Going round the parish 2 days in search of strollers	4:0
1757	Whitewashing and reparing Church	2:10:3
1765	William Lumb for the Dial.	1:10:0
	William Dawson for cutting the road three times to the Church in the great snow	1:0
1768	Cleaning snow from ye bells etc.	9
	William Dawson for cutting road twice to Church	1:0
1769	Absolution for Elizabeth Watson	6
	Paid towards the base viol	2:12:6
	The names of the subscribers towards the new clock in Barwick Church	
	The Revd. Dr. Sumner	4:4:0
	Sir Thomas Gascoigne Bart.	3:3:0
	The Revd. James Brooke	2:2:0
	Robert Denison Esq.	1:1:0
	Thomas Shepley Esq.	1:1:0
	Mr. Eamonson of Lazincroft	1:1:0
	Mr. Poskitt	1:1:0
	Mr. Rooke	10:6
	Mr. Broadbent	10:6
	Mr. Robert Dawson	7:6
	Lord Bingley	2:2:0
	Sir William Milner Bart.	1:1:0
	William Ellis Esq.	1:1:0
	John Taite	2:6
	Samuel Varley	2:6
	Robert Smith Sen.	2:6
	Thomas Whitehead	2:6
	William Knapton	2:6
	Jacob Pease	2:6
	Richd. Lumb	2:6
	John Taite, Junr.	2:6
	Miles Jackson Milner	2:6
		£20:8:0

F. S. Colman, *History of Barwick-in-Elmet*, (Thoresby Society VOL. 17, 1908), pp. 269-70

St. Mary's, Devizes

The following items indicate the effect of the rapid changes of church policy and ritual in the sixteenth century on the church fabric.

1550	4 Edw. VI. Pd for their labor at the plucking down of the Alters, and for meat and drinke	xiv^d
	Pd for their labor at the taking downe of the side Altar	xii^d
1553	1 Mary. Pd to Bartlett for setting up the great Altar	viii^d
	Pd to James Benett the mason for his work about the Alter	vi^d

1554	2 Mary. Pd for holye oyle	iv^d.
	To Wm. Jefferies for ii tapers of a pound and a half and more	xviii^d.
	For the new making of the same tapers against Easter	xi^d.
	There is to be accounted for of old ix days work for George Tylar and his man, at vii^d. the day, for putting and making up of the organ loft	v^s.iii^d.
1555	3 Mary. Pd for defacing the Scriptures on the walls	ii^s.iv^d.
	Pd for making of the altar and for defacing the x commandments and putting . . . in the Rodloft	vi^s.
	Pd for making Mary and Joseph [? John]	v^s.iv^d.
1557	5 Mary. Pd for makyn of ii alters	iii^s.iii^d.
	Pd for stones for the same alters	ii^s.viii^d.
	For tymber to make the pyctor that standeth by the Rode named Mary and John	ii.^{s}
	For mendyng of a crewet	i^d.
	For mendyng of ii Albes	ii^d.
	For frankinscens	i^d.
1561	4 Elizabeth. For taking down of the Roodloft	vi^s.

J. Charles Cox, *Churchwardens' Accounts from the fourteenth to the seventeenth century*, (Methuen, 1913), p. 185

Bassingbourne, Cambridge.

There are frequent entries to the church ales in these accounts. In 1497-8 ten ales were held which realised £14. 7s. 3½d. towards the cost and carriage of a new treble bell from London.

Rec' att the Fryste may ale and all charges borne	xviii^s.ii^d.
Rec' att an Ale next after the seid may ale	vii^s.xi^d.ob.
Rec' att one other Ale in the Feste off the transfiguration off our lorde ihesu criste	x^s.ii^d.ob.
Rec' att an ale the next sondaye after the Assumption off our blyssid ladye	vi^s.ii^d.
Rec' att an Ale the next Sunday after Mich'daye	vii^s.viii^d.
Rec' att an ale that day xivth next after	v^s.ii^d.
Rec' atte one othir ale on the next Sunday aftyr and Feste of seynt Kataryn the virgin and martyr	vi^s.viii^d.
Rec' att an ale on Rogacion sondaye	vi^s.x^d.
Rec' att the laste maye ale with the towns and heynes obitt, as with bred and ale	xxxvi^s.viii^d.
Rec' att an ale on Mydleton sonday	vi^s.vi^d.ob.
In losse off evyll money taken at the may ale	viii^s.

J. Charles Cox, *Churchwardens' Accounts from the fourteenth to seventeenth century*, (Methuen, 1913), pp. 289-90

Church buildings and furnishings

Sources 2·5 *Extracts from glebe terriers for the church and rectory of Barwick-in-Elmet, West Yorkshire*

Extracts from the Glebe Terrier for 1693

A Perfect Terrier and Survey of the Houses and Outhouses, Gardens, Orchards, Meadows, and the Land or Gleab belonging to ye Parsonage of Barwicke in Elmett. Given in by the Minister, Churchwardens and other Parishioners for the year of our Lord God 1693 vizt:

Imprimis. The Parsonage House with a Garden, an Orchard, a foldstead, the Garner, a Dove Coate, a Hay Barn, a Stable, The Tyth Barn, with 2 dwelling houses thereunto belonging.
Item one little Toft or Croft at the Backe of the Tyth Barn.
Item in the Oxe Close, fourteen Beaste Gates and a half,
Item in the Meadow in Barwicke Moor eleven Acres.
Item in Meadow in the Ings, about Seaven Acres.
Item one Close called by the name of Syde Peice.
Item one Close called by the name of Hud Ing.
Item one Close called by the name of Dog Pitt Close.
Item one Close called by the name of Pye Garth.
Item one Close called by the name of Skye Close.
Item one Close called by the name of Coppley Close.
Item one Messuage house, a Barn and foldstead, a Garden, and two Acres of Arable land, one acre lying in the High field, the other one in the little field in the possession of James Orton.
Item one messuage house, a Barn, a foldstead, a garth. Three acres and three Rood of Arable land, two whereof lying in ye high field, one in Barwick More being Meadow and three rood of arable land in the Carr field in ye possession of Mary Taylor.
Item one Messuage house with a Barn and a foldstead in ye possession of John Barker.
Item one Messuage converted into a Barn by the Tennant, a foldstead, a Garth, 5 acres and a half of Land, whereof two acres lying in the little field, one acre of meadow lying in Barwick Moor, three rood in the high field and three rood in the Carr field, half an acre in the New Mill Beck field, half an acre in the Low field.
Item let to severall Tennants in the High field about twenty-five acres of arable land
Item in the Richmond field about fourteen acres and a half of arable land.
Item in ye Low field about Six acres and a half of arable land.
Item Concealed Gleab within Barnbow in the hands of Thomas Gascoigne esqr. of Barnbow, paying yearly for itt the sume of Two pounds ten shillings

                Sam: Dudson, Minister
                Joe: Taylor,
                P (?) Daniell
                Wm. Vevers
                ... Wright
                Thos. Norfolke

F. S. Colman, *A History of Barwick-in-Elmet*, (Thoresby Society VOL. 17, 1908), pp. 93-4

Church buildings and furnishings

Extracts from the Glebe Terrier for 1764

All the Glebe belonging to the Rectory of Barwick contains
    One Hundred and Thirty five Acres two Roods fifteen Perches,
All the Coal in the Glebe belongs to the Rector,
Tythes of Wool and Lamb is all due throughout the Whole Parish
    and Payable in kind, but the Rector Usually agrees to take one
    Penny for every fleece of Wool, and Threepence for every Lamb.
Barwick Township: All the Lands in the Township of Barwick pay all
    Tythes in kind to the Rector, except the Demesne Land of which
the Rector hath but only one third.

The Ancient Demesne in Barwick pay one third of the Tythe to ye Rector.
The known Customs of the Parish for Easter Reckonings, Surplice
    fees and other Ecclesiastical Dues are as follows (viz) to the Rector:

A Marriage by Licence	10s. 0d.
Banns and Publication	3s. 6d.
Churching a Woman	8d.
Registring Child's Name	4d.
Funeral Sermon	10s. 0d.
Funeral in the Body of the Church	6s. 8d.
In the Quire	13s. 4d.
In the Churchyard	1s. 0d.
Every Communicant	2d.
Every House Holder, a Hen or sixpence at Christmas	6d.

Bees per Swarm 1d.	House Dues 2d.	3d.
Plow 1d Foal 1d.	Cow 1d. Calf ½d.	3½d.

Source 3·5 *Extracts from the accounts of the overseers of the poor at Barwick-in-Elmet*

		£ s. d.
1734	Cloth for badges	7
	Pd Samuel Waite for setting them on	6
	Attending badging of the poor	6
1735	For the cure of Ester Thorn's legg	2: 2: 0
1736	To a person for seeking Ann Walker	2: 6
	ditto charges at the same time	1: 6
	For myself and horse 2: 6. Charges 1s. 6d.	4: 0
	Given to Ann Walker	2: 0
	To a person for assisting us in finding her	6
1738	Going to see Ann Walker	1: 6
	Given to a person for informing me	
	where she was	8
	For fetching her home	1: 6
1741	For myself and horse and charges	
	seeking Ann Walker	5: 0
1740	Going to Leeds, about the cure of heresy	1: 9
	To Mr. Davenport for the cure of heresy	12: 7

Church buildings and furnishings

1751	Going to Leeds to get licence for Jane Hopwood and charges	4: 6
	Paid for licence	1: 7: 6
	Wedding Dues	15: 0
	For meat and drink	15: 6
	To the ringers	1: 0
	A horse for John Hacksup	1: 0
	Attending the wedding	1: 6
	A pair of new shoes for Jane Hopwood	3: 0
	Gave John Hacksup for Jane's portion	2: 6
	Paid Thomas Hacksup for bringing about the wedding	10: 6
	To William Thompson for carrying her goods	6: 0
	Myself going with them and charges	2: 6
1754	Given to Edith Slaytor when sick	3: 0
	Going to Idle doctor for her	2: 0
	Paid for physick for her	3: 6
	A dozen of ale to take her medicines in	1: 0

F. S. Colman, *History of Barwick-in-Elmet*, (Thoresby Society, VOL. 17, 1908), p. 271

Source 4.5 *Extracts from parish burial registers of Aberford, in West Yorkshire*

Burials from Lady day 1803 to Lady day 1804 — Age

April	6	Joseph Mills, a youth at Ephraim Sanderson's school	12
	27	Joseph, son of Joseph Smith, carrier & Mary, his wife	4 months
May	1	James Clapham, warrener	60
	8	William Jackson, servant	51
	24	John, son of William Loryman, Labr & Hannah, his wife	9
	29	William Bullock, gentleman	63
June	28	Mary, wife of Joseph Wilkinson, cooper.	64
	28	Frances, dr of Joseph Pain, Labr & Mary, his wife	Infant
July	1	Alice, wife of Richard Sparling, labr.	63
August	2	Bartimeus, son of John Issott, bar-keeper & Mary, his wife. Headley Barr	4 months
	9	Ann, wife of Thomas Pattison, labr.	60
	16	Frances Pickering	74
	24	Emilia, dr of Darcy Lever, Esquire & Elizabeth, his wife	1
Octr.	30	Ann, dr of George Cowing, labr & Mary, his wife	1
	31	John, son of John Hollings, servant & Martha, his wife	Infant
Decr.	9	Francis Malthouse, labr. Burton Salmon	86
	20	James Heptonstall, farmer, Smaws Hall	47
	22	Thomas Layster, mason	52
Jan	3	1804. Francis, son of John Thompson, labr & Sarah, his wife	Infant
	10	Hannah McWilliam, widow, Hasslewood	68
	15	Robert Frew, barber	46
Febr	1	Charles Wright, butler	29
	12	Sarah, wife of Robert Howeroft, cordwainer	84

		13	George, son of Richard Bately, cordwainer & Elizabeth, his wife	1
March		9	Sarah Street, spinster	46
		9	John, son of Francis Shann, labr & Ann, his wife	4

Burials from Lady day 1804 to Lady day 1805

March		30	John, son of James Watson, collier & Sarah, his wife	9 months
		31	Ann, wife of Mark Hick, blacksmith	41
May		3	Hannah Milner, widow	72
		12	Samuel Carter, steward	69
July		5	Mark Hick, Blacksmith	38
		10	Henry Watkinson, labr.	76
August		13	Frances, wife of George Webster, servant	22
Octr		24	Frances, dr of George Webster, servant.	3 months
Novr		15	Jane Maltus, widow	78
Decr		2	Rev. William Hodgson, schoolmaster starved with cold	45
		28	Ellin, dr of Edward Nettleton, publican at Barkstone Ash	22

Aberford Parish Registers, (Thoresby Society VOL. XXVI, Leeds 1937)

Source 5·5 *Extracts from "The Rites of Durham: a description of the ancient monuments, rites and customs within the monastical church of Durham before the suppression" — written in 1593*

THE CLOISTER   The Northe Alley
In the north syde of ye cloister from ye Corn over against
ye Church Dour to ye corner over againste the Dorter dour was
all fynely glased from ye hight to ye sole within a litle of ye
grownd into ye cloyster garth, & in euy wyndowe iiij° pewes or
carrells where euy one of the old monks had his Carrell seuall by
him selfe, that when they had dyned they dyd resorte to that place
of cloister, and there studyed vpo there books, euy one in his
carrell all ye after none vnto evensong tyme, this was there
exercise euy daie: all there pewes or Carrells was all fynely wainscotted
and in euy Carrell was a deske to lye there bookes on; and ye
[71] carrells was no greater then from one stanchell of the
wyndowe to another. And over against the carrells against the
church wall did stande great almeries or Cupbords of
waynscott all full of bookes (wth great store of antient Manuscripts)
to help them in ther studdy, wherein dyd lye as well the old
auncyent written Docters of the Church as other . . . authors . . .
so that euy one dyd studye what Doctor pleased them best, havinge
the librarie at all tymes to goe studie in besydes there Carrells.

The Publications of the Surtees Society, (VOL. 107, 1902-3) p. 83

Source 6·5 *Extracts from the Rule of St. Benedict*

Chapter 22   *How the Monks are to Sleep*
If it be possible let them all sleep in a common dormitory, but if their great number will not allow this they may sleep in tens or twenties, with seniors to have charge of them. Let a candle be constantly burning in the room until morning, and let the monks sleep clothed and girt with girdles or cords. In this way the monks shall always be ready to rise quickly when the signal is given and hasten each one to come before his brother to the Divine office.

Chapter 33   *Ought monks to have anything of their own?*
None, without the leave of the abbot, shall presume to give, or receive, or keep as his own anything whatever, neither books, nor tablets, nor pens, nothing at all.

Chapter 48   *Daily Manual Labour*
Idleness is the enemy of the soul. Because this is so the brethren ought to be occupied at specific times in manual labour, and at other fixed hours in holy reading. We therefore think that both these may be arranged for as follows:
From Easter until the 1st October . . . let the brethren labour till about the fourth hour. From the fourth hour until about the sixth, let them enjoy themselves in reading. On rising from the table after the sixth hour let them rest on their beds, in strict silence. If any of them wishes to read to himself during this period, he shall read so as not to disturb the others. Let Nones be said somewhat . . . about the middle of the eighth hour, and afterwards all shall work at what they have to do until evening.

Chapter 53   *The Reception of Guests*
Let the abbot pour water on the hands of the guests, and let him and the whole community wash their feet . . . Let special care be taken of poor people and pilgrims. Let the charge of the guest place be assigned to a brother whose soul the fear of God possesses . . . No one, unless ordered may associate with or speak to the guests.

Chapter 55   *Of the clothes and shoes of the Brethren*
Let clothing suitable to the locality and the temperature be given to the brethren . . . In ordinary places it will be enough for each monk to have a cowl and tunic, in winter the cowl being of thicker stuff, in summer of finer or old cloth. He should have also . . . shoes and stockings for the feet.

Monks must not grumble at the colour or coarseness of these things; they shall be such as can be procured in the district where they live, or such as can be bought at the cheapest price.

A mattress, blanket, coverlet and pillow are to suffice for bedding. The beds shall be frequently searched by the abbot to guard against the vice of hoarding. And if anyone be found in possession of something not allowed by the abbot let him be subjected to the severest punishment.

Cardinal Gasquet (trans.), *The Rule of St. Benedict*, (Chatto & Windus, 1936)

Church buildings and furnishings

Source 7.5 *Extracts from Chaucer's descriptions of a monk and a parson from the Prologue to "The Canterbury Tales"*

The Monk
A Monk there was, one of the finest sort
Who rode the country; hunting was his sport.
A manly man, to be an Abbot able;
Many a dainty horse he had in stable.

His bridle, when he rode, a man might hear
Jingling in a whistling wind as clear,
Aye, and as loud as does the chapel bell
Where my lord Monk was Prior of the cell.
The Rule of good St. Benet or St. Maur
As old and strict he tended to ignore;
He let go by the things of yesterday
And took the modern world's more spacious way.
He did not rate that text at a plucked hen
Which says that hunters are not holy men . . .

Was he to study till his head went round
Poring over books in cloisters? Must he toil
As Austin bade and till the very soil?
Was he to leave the world upon the shelf?
Let Austin have his labour to himself.

This Monk was therefore a good man to horse;
Greyhounds he had, as swift as birds, to course.
Hunting a hare or riding at a fence
Was all his fun, he spared for no expense.
I saw his sleeves were garnished at the hand
With fine grey fur, the finest in the land,
And on his hood, to fasten it at his chin

He had a wrought-gold cunningly fashioned pin;
Into a lover's knot it seemed to pass,
His head was bald and shone like looking-glass;
So did his face, as if it had been greased . . .
Supple his boots, his horse in fine condition.
He was a prelate fit for exhibition,
He was not pale like a tormented soul.
He liked a fat swan best, and roasted whole.
His palfrey was as brown as is a berry.

The Parson
A holy-minded man of good renown,
There was, and poor, the Parson to a town,
Yet he was rich in holy thought and work.
He also was a learned man, a clerk,
Who truly knew Christ's gospel and would preach it
Devoutly to parishioners, and teach it.
Benign and wonderfully diligent,
And patient when adversity was sent
(For so he proved in great adversity)
He much disliked extorting tithe or fee,
Nay rather he preferred beyond a doubt
Giving to poor parishioners round about
From his own goods and Easter offerings.
He found sufficiency in little things,
Wide was his parish, with houses far asunder,
Yet he neglected not in rain or thunder,
In sickness or in grief, to pay a call
On the remotest, whether great or small,
Upon his feet, and in his hand a stave.

Nevill Coghill (trans.), *The Canterbury Tales*, (Penguin Classics, 1960) pp. 23-5, 32

Course work for G.C.E. and C.S.E. assessment

Some history teachers may wish to devise Mode 3 C.S.E. and G.C.E. 'O' level syllabuses which include work on *History Around Us: Church buildings and furnishings*. The following items of course work could be completed by pupils and submitted in a folder as part of their final assessment.

1. Descriptions of churches, abbeys, chapels, or cathedrals studied by fieldwork, supported by maps, plans, sketches or photographs.

2. Description of any church buildings studied in the classroom supported by maps, plans and sketches.

3. Work setting a site in its historical context:
e.g. an illustrated account explaining the architectural development of a church building and the effects of national events on it and upon its furnishings.
e.g. an illustrated account explaining the fate of a monastery after its dissolution.

4. An imaginative reconstruction of:
either: a specific incident in the history of a church or abbey,
e.g. the rebuilding or alteration of the church fabric in Reformation or Victorian times.
or: the role of a church and its priest in the life of the community at a particular time in the past.
or: life in an abbey during a particular period.
or: a study of the connection between a historical personality and a church,
e.g. Becket and Canterbury Cathedral,

e.g. A local wool merchant, or family, and the church.

Resources

Some of the books on this list are out of print. You should be able to obtain copies from your local library or from the Schools Library Loan Service.

Resources are listed by order of importance, within each section.

Teachers' books

Victor Bonham Carter, *Exploring Parish Churches*, (Routledge & Kegan Paul, 1961)
Kenneth Lindley, *Exploring Graves and Graveyards*, 'Local Search Series', (Routledge & Kegan Paul, 1972)
Kenneth Lindley, *Chapels and Meeting Houses*, (John Baker, 1969)
Joscelyne Finberg, *Exploring Villages*, (Routledge & Kegan Paul, 1958), see chapter on the parish church
T. D. Atkinson, *Local Styles in English Architecture*, (Batsford, 1947)
Thelma N. Nye, *An Introduction to Parish Church Architecture A.D. 600–1965*, (Batsford, 1965)
J. Charles Cox, *The Parish Churches of England*, (Batsford, 1935)
M. D. Anderson, *Looking for History in British Churches*, (John Murray, 1951)
Leonora & Walter Ison, *English Church Architecture through the Ages*, (Baker, 1973)
Alec Clifton-Taylor, *Cathedrals of England*, 'World of Art Series' (Thames & Hudson, 1967)
Arnold Fellows, *England and Wales: A Traveller's Companion*, (O.U.P. 1964), see chapter on the parish church
Helen & Richard Leacroft, *Cathedrals and Churches: Their Building and Use*, (Lutterworth, 1972)

Reference books for pupils

John Page, *Maklin's Monumental Brasses*, (Philips, 1972)
Henry Stanley Bennett, *Life on the English Manor 1150–1400*, 'Studies in Mediaeval Life and Thought', (O.U.P. 1956), see the imaginative reconstruction of a service in a mediaeval church
Pitkin Pictorials (Publishers), *Pictorial Guide to Cathedral Architecture*, (1973)
Pitkin Pictorials (Publishers), *Cathedrals at Work*
Pitkin Pictorials (Publishers), *Dissolution of the Monasteries*

L. F. Salzman, *Buildings in England down to 1540: A Documentary History*, (O.U.P., 1952)
Publications of the Surtees Society, *Rites of Durham; a description of all the ancient monuments, rites and customs within the monastical church of Durham before the Suppression*, VOL. 107, 1902–3, (written 1593)

Guide books

These can be obtained for many different abbeys, cathedrals and churches all over England, from HMSO and Pitkin Pictorials.

Books for pupils, dealing with visible evidence

Henry Pluckrose, *Churches*, 'On Location Series', (Mills & Boon, 1973)
Henry Pluckrose, *Monasteries*, 'On Location Series', (Mills & Boon, 1975)
Patrick Thornhill, *The Parish Church*, 'Get to Know Series', (Methuen, 1973)
Kenneth Lindley, *Discovering Graves and Graveyards*, 'Local Search Series', (Routledge & Kegan Paul, 1972)
John Harries, *Discovering Churches*, 'Discovering Books Series', (Shire Publications, 1972)
David Pepin, *Discovering Cathedrals*, 'Discovering Books Series', (Shire Publications, 1974)
Jane Sayers, *Life in the Medieval Monastery*, 'Focus on History Series', (Longman, 1969)

Books for pupils providing background information

Marjorie Reeves, *The Medieval Monastery*, 'Then and There Series', (Longman, 1958)
Gladys Scott Thomson, *Medieval Pilgrimage*, 'Then and There Series', (Longman, 1962)
A. J. Fletcher, *The Elizabethan Village*, 'Then and There Series', (Longman, 1967), see chapters on 'Going to Church' and 'The Churchwardens and their duties'
David Birt & Jon Nichol, *The Monastery*, 'Longman History Units: The Middle Ages', (Longman, 1975)

Maps and charts

Ordnance Survey, *Map of Monastic Britain*
Ordnance Survey, *Symonson's Map of Kent*, 1596, this shows churches as they actually appeared
Educational Productions, *Living History Wall Charts, No. 2 Churches*

Slides

These can be obtained for most of the important

churches, abbeys and cathedrals from the following organisations:

Department of the Environment, interiors and exteriors of cathedrals and abbeys

Woodmansterne Limited, interiors of cathedrals, abbeys and priories, stained glass windows

Slide Centre Ltd, *Cathedrals and Major Churches*

1000 *years of English Architecture*

Development of Stained Glass in England

Norfolk Churches and Stained Glass

Churches and Religions

Filmstrips

Some of these are out of print but may be available through Teachers' Centres or the E.F.V.A.

The Monastery, colour, Longman/Common Ground

The Cistercian Abbey: Rievaulx, colour, Educational Productions

Looking at Brasses, black and white, Educational Productions

The Parish Church, black and white, Hulton, 1950

The Parish Church, black and white, Educational Productions, 1956

Films

The Mediaeval Monastery, 16 mm, black and white, 17 mins. 1948 — distributed by Rank

Witness in Brass, 16 mm, black and white, 10 mins. Essex Education Committee, 1957

6 TOWN DEVELOPMENT AND DOMESTIC ARCHITECTURE

Some objectives and outcomes

We hope that by the time pupils finish their study of town development they will:

1. have sufficient background knowledge to:
a. suggest when some of the buildings in their area were constructed by looking at their architectural style and building materials
b. understand the significance of certain street names and street plans.

2. have had practice at:
a. recognising, and interpreting the visible evidence about the town's origins and development especially its domestic architecture
b. relating features such as market places, railways, roads, canals, harbour, mines, street names, street plans, factories, etc., to the development of the town as a whole
c. using the visible evidence gathered both by map work and field work to discover:
the original centre of a town, its function and the reasons for its foundation
the different stages in the town's growth and development.

3. have had practice at combining visible evidence and background information to help them:
a. discover some of the reasons why different areas of the town developed in certain ways at particular times
b. reconstruct *either* the life style and work of the inhabitants in different types of houses or in one street at a particular time
or the role played by a person or family in the development of the town
or a specific incident which affected the development of a town.

4. have the knowledge, skills and enthusiasm to:
a. trace the origins and development of other towns using visible evidence
b. continue exploring other aspects of their historical environment beyond school.

An approach

Teachers will wish to organise the course to suit the abilities of their pupils and to take account of the size of their town and the range and type of visible evidence relating to its origin and development.
We hope that the approach outlined below will prove useful.

STAGE ONE

A study of the origins and siting of the town

Teachers may introduce this section by discussing some of the important factors which have influenced the siting of towns and the evidence which is necessary for such a study. Geography colleagues may provide $2\frac{1}{2}$ inch Ordnance Survey maps showing the sites of different types of towns — a gap town, market town, castle town, etc. The maps and plans in M.D. Lobel, *Historic Towns* may be also useful here. For full details see Resources section at the end of the chapter.

Pupils would begin the study of their own town by looking at:
the $2\frac{1}{2}$ inch Ordnance Survey map of the town and its surrounding area

Town development and domestic architecture

a street plan
extracts from a place name dictionary which explain the name of the town and its streets (see reference books in the Resources section).

Teachers could describe and explain the types of visible evidence which can help pupils discover:
a. the original extent of the early town
b. when it was founded and the reasons for its foundation
c. why the particular site was chosen.

Pupils would look at:
ancient buildings and monuments,
e.g. castles, bridges, market crosses, Roman roads, Roman forts
the name of the town
street names in the centre of the town
the street plan of the centre of the town
geographical factors such as rivers, routeways, climate, water supply, highland, marsh, etc.
The significance of the evidence could be established by asking the following questions:

Do the street names provide us with any evidence about the origins and early development of the town?

Has the street plan been influenced by the entrances to a castle, fort or abbey?

Was the presence of a castle, fort or abbey the original reason for founding the town?

Has the street plan been determined by a market place or route over a bridge? Were these important factors in the origins or growth of the town? — see *fig.* 1·6

Do the street names tell us anything about the development of the town during the period of the Middle Ages?

Do any visible remains survive from the early years of the town, if so, what? If not, why not?

When pupils have completed their study of the visible evidence they could compare their findings with the earliest known maps of the town and extracts from local history books which incorporate evidence from primary sources.

Figure 1·6 *Part of the street plan of Pontefract, a small Yorkshire market town*

Note the influence of the castle gates and the market place on the street plan and street names.

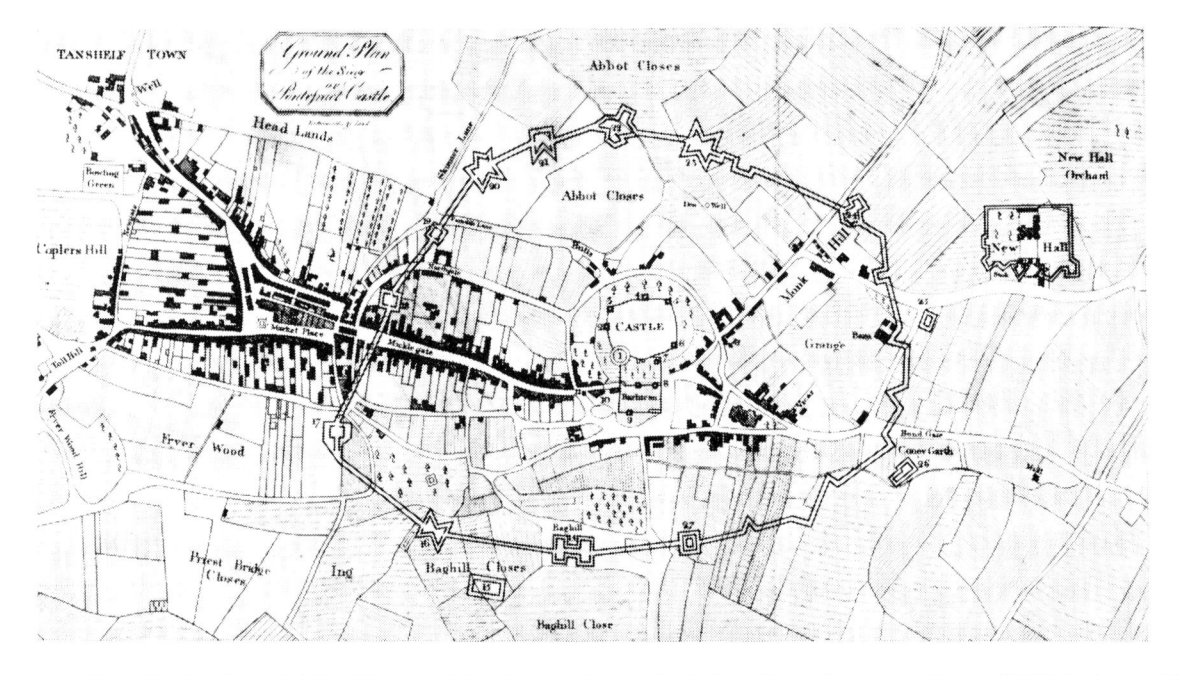

from B. Boothroyd, *The History of the Ancient Borough of Pontefract*, (private edition, 1807) facing p. 316

STAGE TWO

A study of the town's growth and development through time

1. Background lessons

a. The town in the Middle Ages

If little visible evidence survives to show the stages of the town's development in the Middle Ages, teachers may wish pupils to work out the extent of the town by 1500—or later if evidence of rapid growth begins between 1600 and 1800, using early maps and street names.

Then on an outline map of the modern town, based perhaps on the 6 inch Ordnance Survey map, pupils would mark the limits of the town in 1500. This would show them the extent of its growth over the last 400 years.

b. The town 1500–1970

The teacher could show pupils how it is possible to trace the stages in the growth of a town over the last 300 to 400 years. This will vary from town to town — for industrial towns it may be only 100 to 200 years. The architectural style and the type of building materials seen in houses in different areas of the town can provide evidence for the various stages of growth. See the Resources section for suitable teaching aids.

Pupils could be shown how to recognise different kinds of houses, and interpret the visible evidence which would help them to reconstruct the way of life, class and occupation of the people who lived in them. Pupils would then prepare clue sheets of annotated diagrams showing different types of houses — see *fig.* 2·6. Many teachers may prefer to prepare these themselves before a visit, to save time.

Jacobean half timbered house; The Old House, Hereford

18th century coaching inn; Yarm, Cleveland

Regency terrace; Royal Crescent, Bath, Avon

Town development and domestic architecture

A Victorian Villa

Victorian terraced workers' cottages; Eastwood, Nottinghamshire

Back to back housing; North-West Leeds, West Yorkshire

Town development and domestic architecture

1930s semi-detached houses 'Art Deco' style

1930s semi-detached houses 'Mock Tudor' style

1970s tower block

Town development and domestic architecture

Figure 2·6 *Two examples of clue sheets dating and describing houses in the Glossop region*

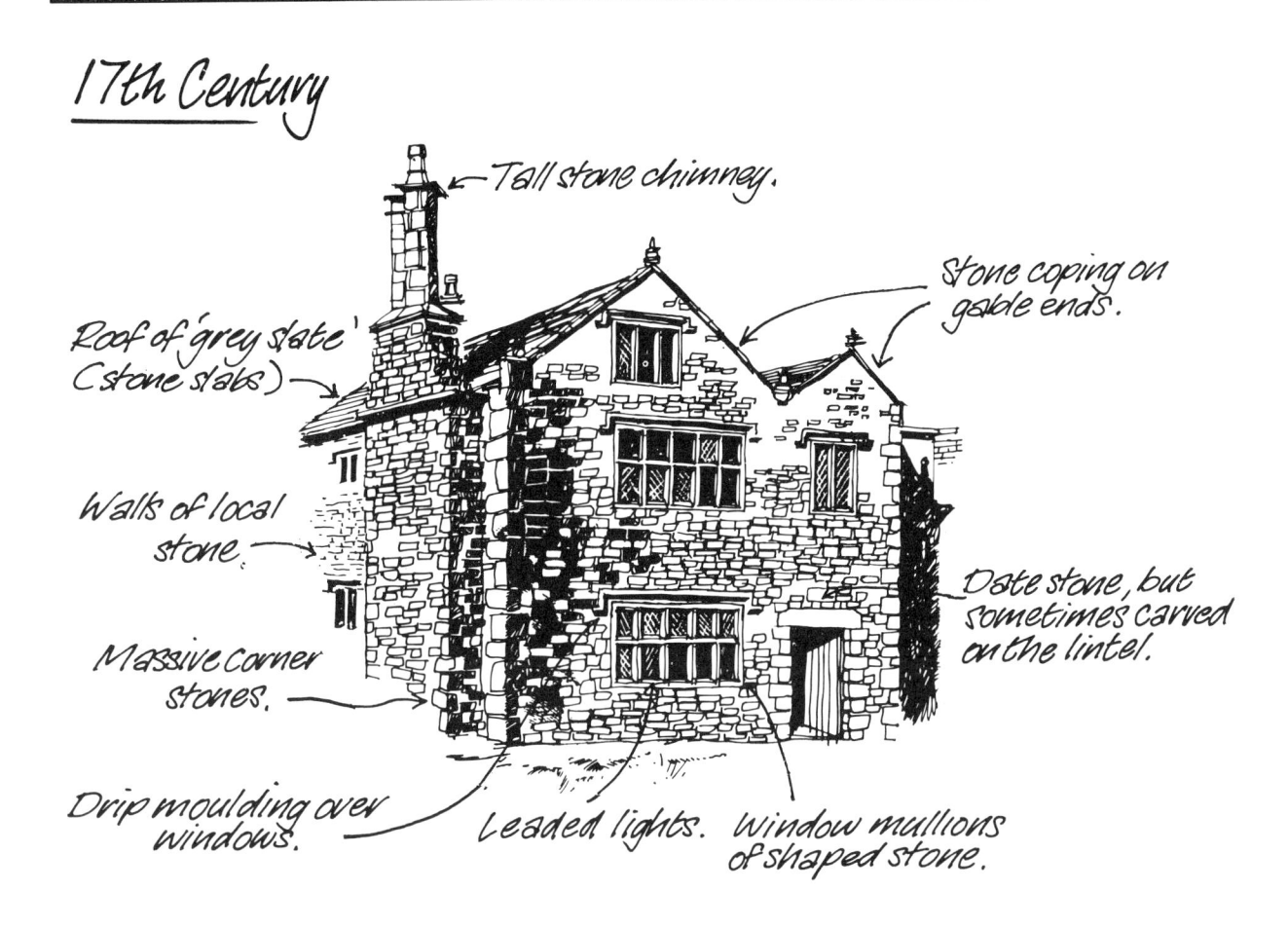

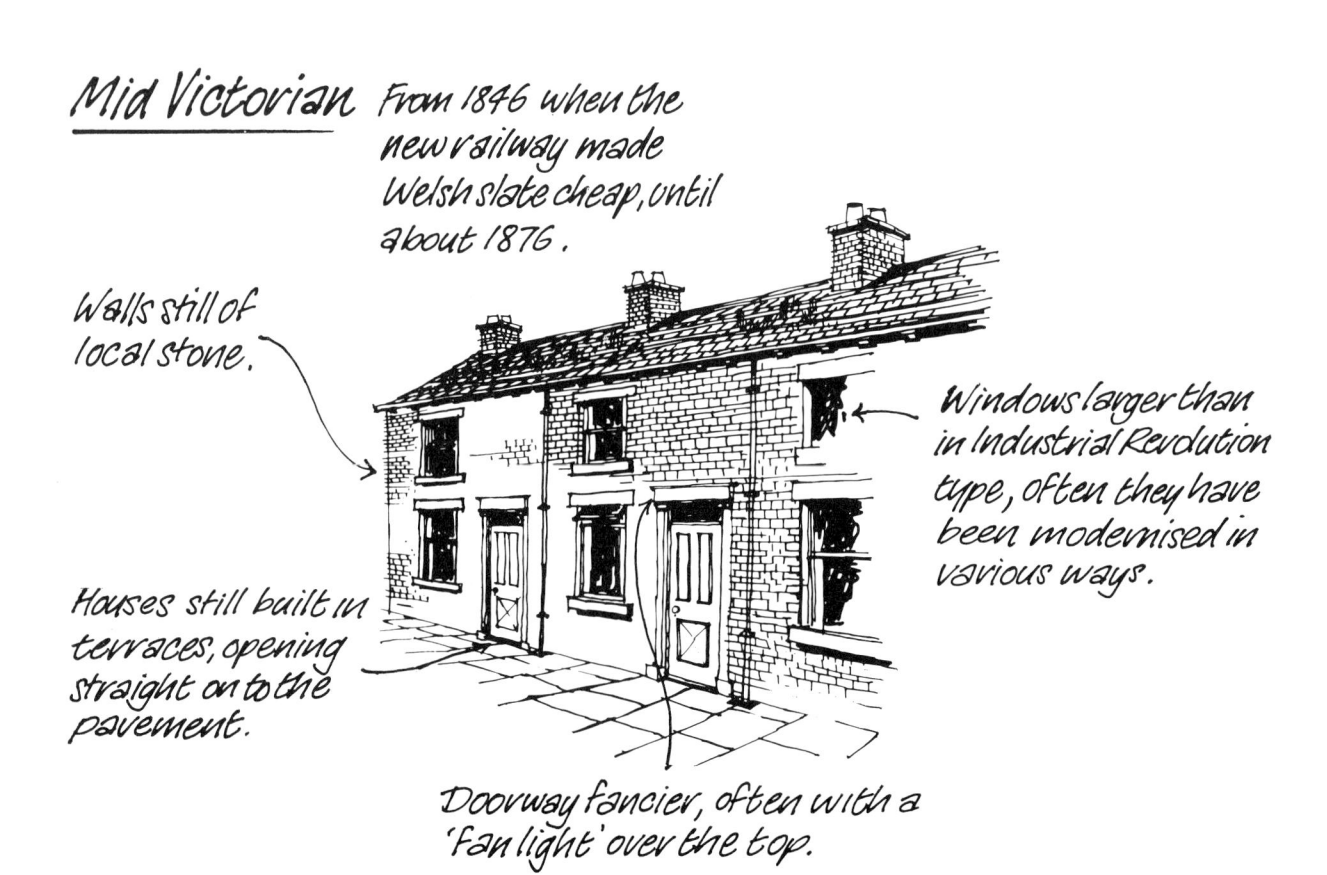

17th Century

- Tall stone chimney.
- Stone coping on gable ends.
- Roof of 'grey slate' (stone slabs)
- Walls of local stone.
- Date stone, but sometimes carved on the lintel.
- Massive corner stones.
- Drip moulding over windows.
- Leaded lights.
- Window mullions of shaped stone.

Mid Victorian

From 1846 when the new railway made Welsh slate cheap, until about 1876.

- Walls still of local stone.
- Windows larger than in Industrial Revolution type, often they have been modernised in various ways.
- Houses still built in terraces, opening straight on to the pavement.
- Doorway fancier, often with a 'fan light' over the top.

from drawings by Mr. J. Scott, Glossop School

Town development and domestic architecture

Figure 3·6 *Town plan of Portishead in Somerset showing the different zones of the town corresponding to the stages in its growth*

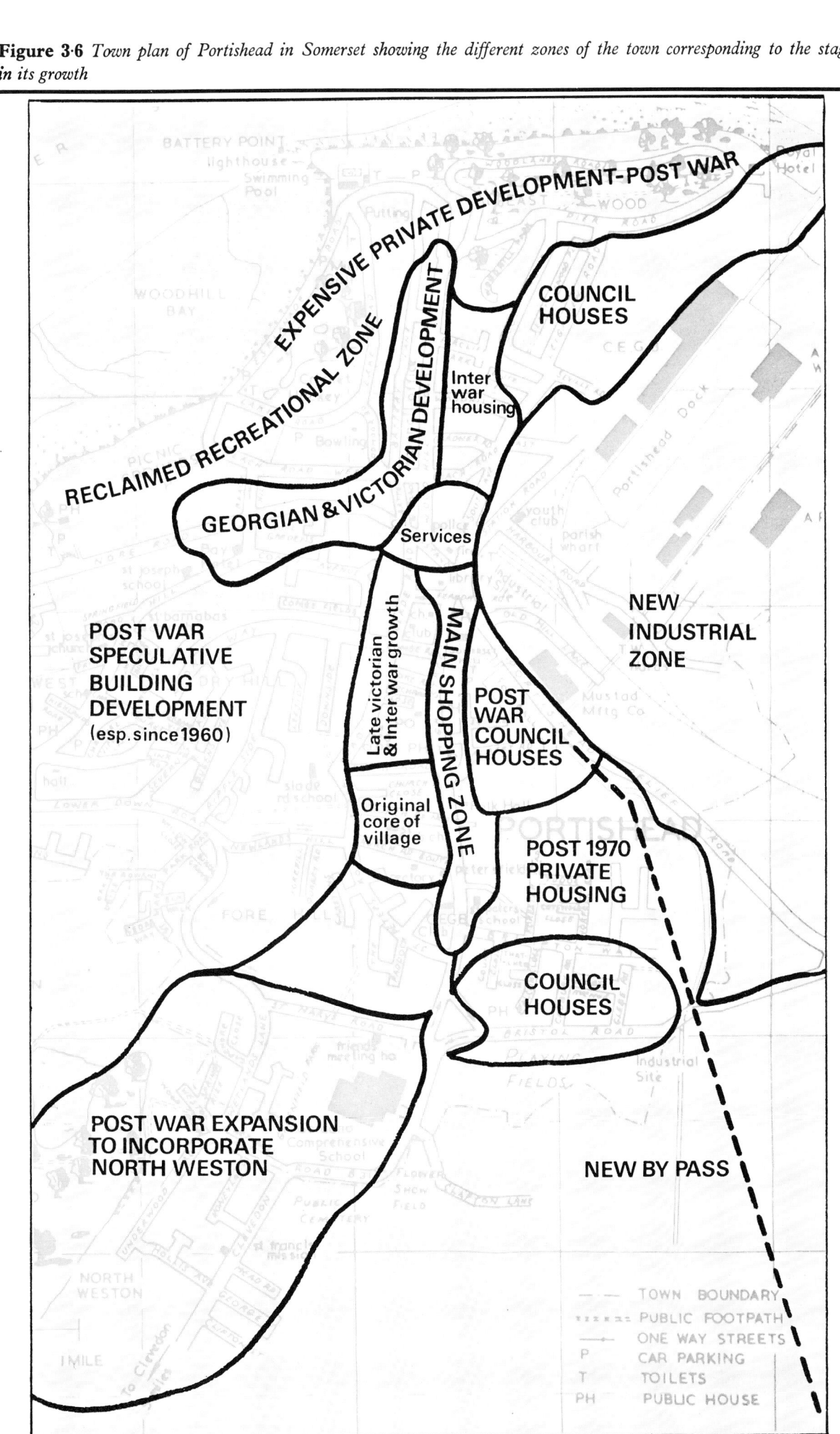

from a map overlay drawn by Mr. I. Plimmer, Gordano School

2. Fieldwork and mapwork

Using an outline map showing the present extent of the town — based perhaps on a street plan or the 6 inch Ordnance Survey map, (or 25 inch Ordnance Survey plan according to the size of the town) the teacher could divide the town into a number of zones — see *fig. 3.6*. These would correspond with the different stages in the growth of the town, e.g.

an area of nineteenth century workers' houses clustered round a factory

an area of inter-war semi-detached houses built in the suburbs for commuters

an area of Georgian town houses.

Pupils, either individually, or in groups or pairs would be assigned to different zones of the town for fieldwork. Within their zone they would carry out a number of surveys to classify the buildings, especially houses, according to:

building style
building material
type: terraced, semi-detached, detached
function: residential, commercial, etc.

Pupils would photograph or draw typical houses and note the location of other features such as canals, railways, factories, offices, shops, schools, churches, etc. This information would then be recorded on sketch maps based on a street plan of the area.

If the town being studied is too large to allow groups of pupils to study different areas, teachers may prefer the whole class to study one area in detail, assigning different streets to pairs of pupils.

3. Follow up work

Once the surveys have been completed pupils can begin to interpret the evidence they have collected and answer key questions:

When were most of the houses in this area built?
Is there any evidence that this area had previously been inhabited and that houses were rebuilt on original house sites?
What kind of people were the houses originally built for?

Information gathered by the various groups could be collected together and recorded on outline plans of the town. Different areas would be marked and shaded according to the period in which they developed. Important features such as railways, canals, factories, mines, etc. should also be marked. Finally, pupils would compare their findings with the evidence from any published maps or plans of the town drawn up at different times in the past.

If the town is small enough, a history trail could be arranged to show the whole class the various development zones.

STAGE THREE

A study of the factors which may have influenced town development

This study looks at different areas of the town during various periods of its history.

When pupils have found out the period their zone was first developed, they can investigate the area in greater detail. Using visible evidence from maps, photographs, further fieldwork and also background material — e.g. interviews with inhabitants, trade directories, census enumerators' returns, old guide books or gazetteers containing descriptions of the town, tithe maps, newspapers, etc., they could answer the following questions:

Who built and/or designed the houses?
e.g. the council, a jerry builder, Beau Nash, reputable local builders?
Where did the building materials come from?
Where did most of the inhabitants of the area work and what sort of jobs did they do?
(This may be obvious from the type of housing, e.g. workers' cottages near a factory or mine, otherwise pupils may have to consult trade directories and census enumerators' returns)
What other important buildings or features does the area have and when were they built?
e.g. mills, factories, mines, offices, schools, churches, etc.
Were these built before or after the houses?
Were these buildings or features connected in any way with the development of the area? If so, how?
What is the street plan of the area?
Was it planned by an architect before the houses were built?
Were the houses built along already existing streets?
Were the houses built on previously open country?
Who owned the land they were built on?
Does the street plan follow the pattern of any previous field boundaries or land holding?
— see *fig. 4.6*
(This may involve the study of enclosure or estate maps.)
Working from the information you have collected can you give the main reasons for the development of the area?

Town development and domestic architecture

Figure 4·6 *Housing development in Nottingham after the enclosure of the open fields in 1845*

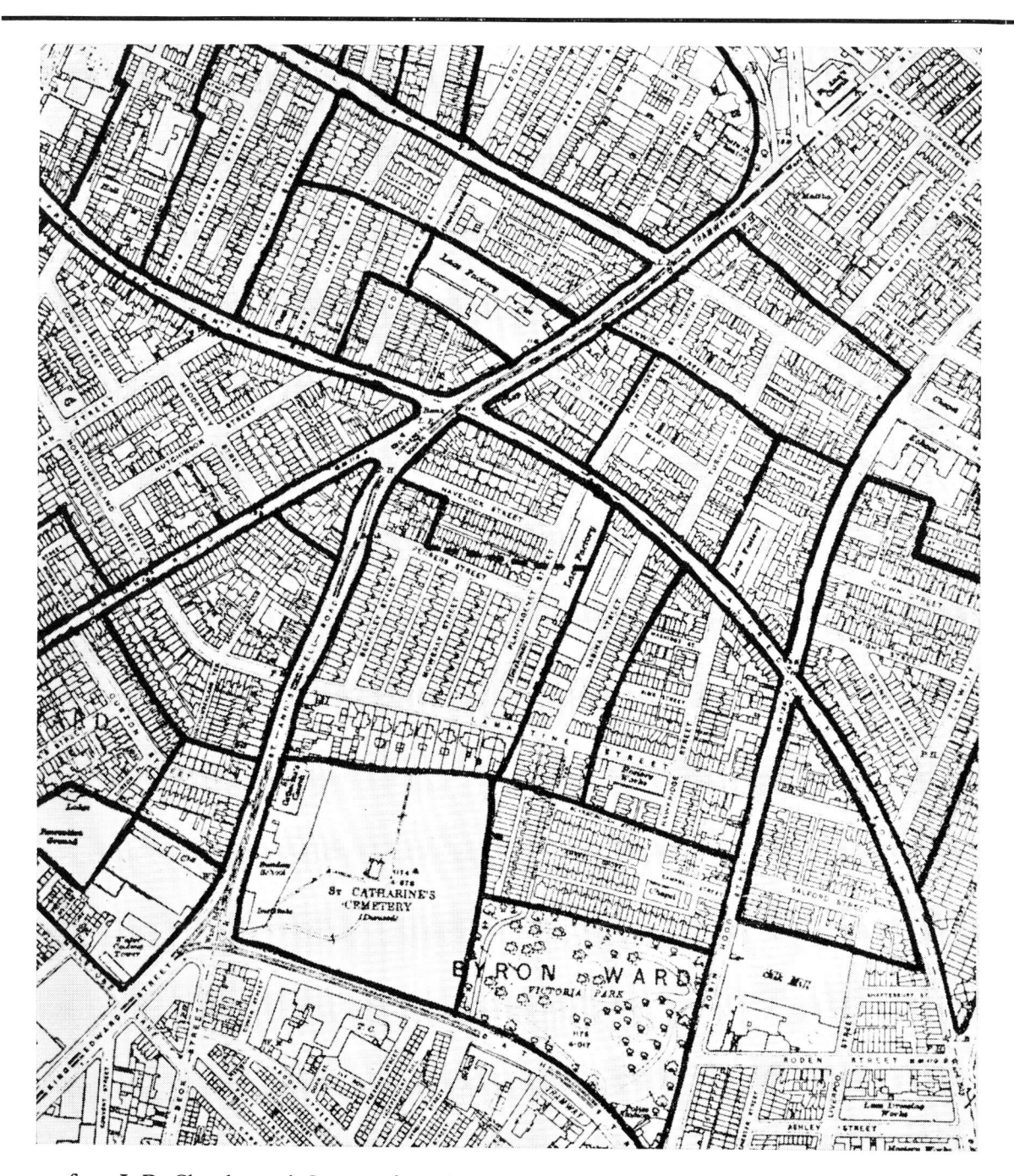

from J. D. Chambers, *A Century of Nottingham History* 1851–1951 (Nottingham University Press, 1952)

STAGE FOUR
A study of the homes and way of life of people in the area

When they know why their area developed, pupils could go on to find out more about the people who lived there. This would combine field work, map work and background information. Some alternative approaches are outlined below:

a. A study of life in one type of house or a comparison between two different types

Pupils could discover the plan of the house by looking at reference books, house plans submitted to the local authority or by visiting sympathetic house owners.

The location, size and condition of such features as the kitchen, living room, bedrooms, bathroom, toilet, fireplaces, etc. could be noted.

Pupils could research the following:

original furnishings and fittings — see Resources section for suitable reference books;

the daily routine of different members of the household, (using information from autobiographies of people who originally lived there, and interviews with elderly inhabitants)

the original condition of the houses and area

(using information from elderly local inhabitants if the period is within living memory, or government reports on working class housing).

b. A study of life in one street at a particular time

(information is most readily available for the nineteenth century)

Using a trade directory, the census enumerators' returns — if the period being studied is 1841 to 1871, or a tithe map of 1836, pupils may discover the names and occupations of inhabitants in one street at a particular time. They could then research and reconstruct the life style of the inhabitants of one house using the methods suggested above.

c. A study of a particular person or family who had an important influence on the development of the area

This could be a local factory or mill owner who built accommodation for his workers, e.g. Titus Salt of Saltaire. Family papers, newspaper articles or a local history book may have relevant information. These are usually available in reference libraries or record offices.

d. A study of an incident which affected the homes and lives of people living in the area

This could be a flood, fire, slum clearance or bombing in the war. Local history books, newspaper reports and even the memories of local inhabitants — if the incident is within living memory, can be useful sources of information.

STAGE FIVE
Concluding lessons

These would draw together all the information gathered by various groups of pupils in different areas of the town. This would give the whole class an overall picture of its development.

Members of each group could prepare illustrated talks to give to the rest of the class. One member of each group would explain when and why their area developed while others would describe a specific incident — life in one type of house, life in one street, the role of one person or family in the development of the neighbourhood and so on.

At the end of the exercise pupils could produce an illustrated account describing the different stages in the development of the town. They could also explain the reasons for its growth. A brief study of another town would provide a useful comparison.

Finally, teachers and pupils may wish to discuss possible trends for the future growth of the town.

Some background source material

It is impossible in this book to give a detailed list of all the different types of primary sources which provide background information for pupils. J. E. Exwood and R. E. Unwin, *Yorkshire Topography*, and John Haddon, *Discovering Towns*, are useful for teachers requiring greater detail. See Resources section for full details. We hope however that the following suggestions prove useful.

1. Maps and plans

Ordnance Survey maps
Both first editions, 1840s onwards depending on the scale and the area, and recent editions are useful. The 25 inch, 6 inch and $2\frac{1}{2}$ inch maps have their different uses, outlined in the Approach section of this chapter. Twenty towns were surveyed using a larger scale, e.g. 5 feet to one mile between 1845 and 1894. Examples of 6 inch and 25 inch maps can be seen in the section on Background source material in Chapter 9. Xerox copies of relevant sections of these maps can usually be obtained from the local reference library or record office.

Town plans
These were produced for most large towns on different scales by cartographers in the seventeenth, eighteenth and nineteenth centuries. Comparisons between them show us when and how the town developed. Copies are usually available in the local museum or reference library.

Tithe maps
These were made for each parish affected by the Tithe Commutation Act of 1836. They were part of a detailed survey showing all lands, houses, industrial or agricultural premises subject to tithes. They can be used to find the owners and the different functions of buildings in parishes during 1836. They may be in local record offices or in the diocesan registry.

2. Photographs and prints of town views and streets

These show us what different parts of the town looked like during various periods. They may be available from local reference libraries. Reecntly many booklets and pamphlets containing old photographs of towns have been published — for full details see the Resources section.

3. Gazetteers and trade directories

These were first published in the late eighteenth and early nineteenth centuries. They usually give a brief description of towns, mentioning changes and developments and include lists of tradesmen. They are normally available in public reference libraries.

4. Census returns

These are useful for pupils who wish to study the inhabitants of a particular street. The enumerators' note books, available only for 1841 to 1871, list the inhabitants of every household and often a precise address. The 1851 enumerators' note books have been placed on microfilm. Copies, together with a catalogue, can be found in most county or city reference libraries. Alternatively Xerox copies of schedules from the note books can be obtained from the Public Record Office.

5. Travellers' descriptions

These often provide a good picture of towns at different periods and include comments about their growth and reasons for their development. Useful extracts may be found in:
Daniel Defoe, *A Tour through the whole island of Great Britain*, (1722–6) P. Rogers (Ed.), (Penguin, 1971)
Celia Fiennes, *The Journeys of Celia Fiennes* (1685-1703) C. Morris (Ed.), (Cresset Press, 1949)
John Leland, *Itinerary* (1535-1543) L. Toulmin Smith (Ed.), (Centaur Press, 1971).
Leland and Fiennes can probably be found in the local reference library.

6. Parliamentary reports and private sociological reports

These may be useful for pupils who wish to find out about living conditions in Victorian working class areas, e.g.
The Report of the Select Committee on Artisans and Labourers Dwellings, 1881
Report of the Select Committee on Housing of the Working Classes, 1906
Reports of the Commissioners inquiring into the state of large towns and populous districts, 1844–5
H. Mayhew, *London Labour and the London Poor* (1851-62), 4 Vols. (Dover Publication, 1909)
C. Booth, *Life and Labour of the people of London* (1889-1903), 17 Vols. (Kelley, USA, 1970)
S. Rowntree, *Poverty, a study of town life*, (Macmillan, 1901)
F. Engels, *The Condition of the Working Class in England*, 1844, (Panther, 1969)
These are usually available in local reference libraries.

7. Local newspapers and nineteenth century magazines

e.g. *The Builder*
These may contain references to housing development schemes in the nineteenth and twentieth centuries.

8. Family papers and personal reminiscences

These may provide information about people who lived in an area or who were associated with it. They may be available in manuscript form in the local record office or reference library. Extracts may be printed in local histories. John Burnett, *The Useful Toil* contains interesting accounts by domestic servants and other workers in the nineteenth century.

9. Borough records

Minute books, order books and court records for the period after 1500 can provide information about new building schemes or demolition of old houses.

10. Housing plans

These were deposited with the local authorities under public health legislation and local Byelaws give plans, sections and elevations of different types of house.

11. Local town histories and biographies

They often contain interesting primary as well as secondary source material. They can usually be found in the local reference or lending library.

Some examples of primary source material

A selection of primary source material appears on the pages which follow.

Town development and domestic architecture

Source 1·6 *Hollar's map of Hull* 1640

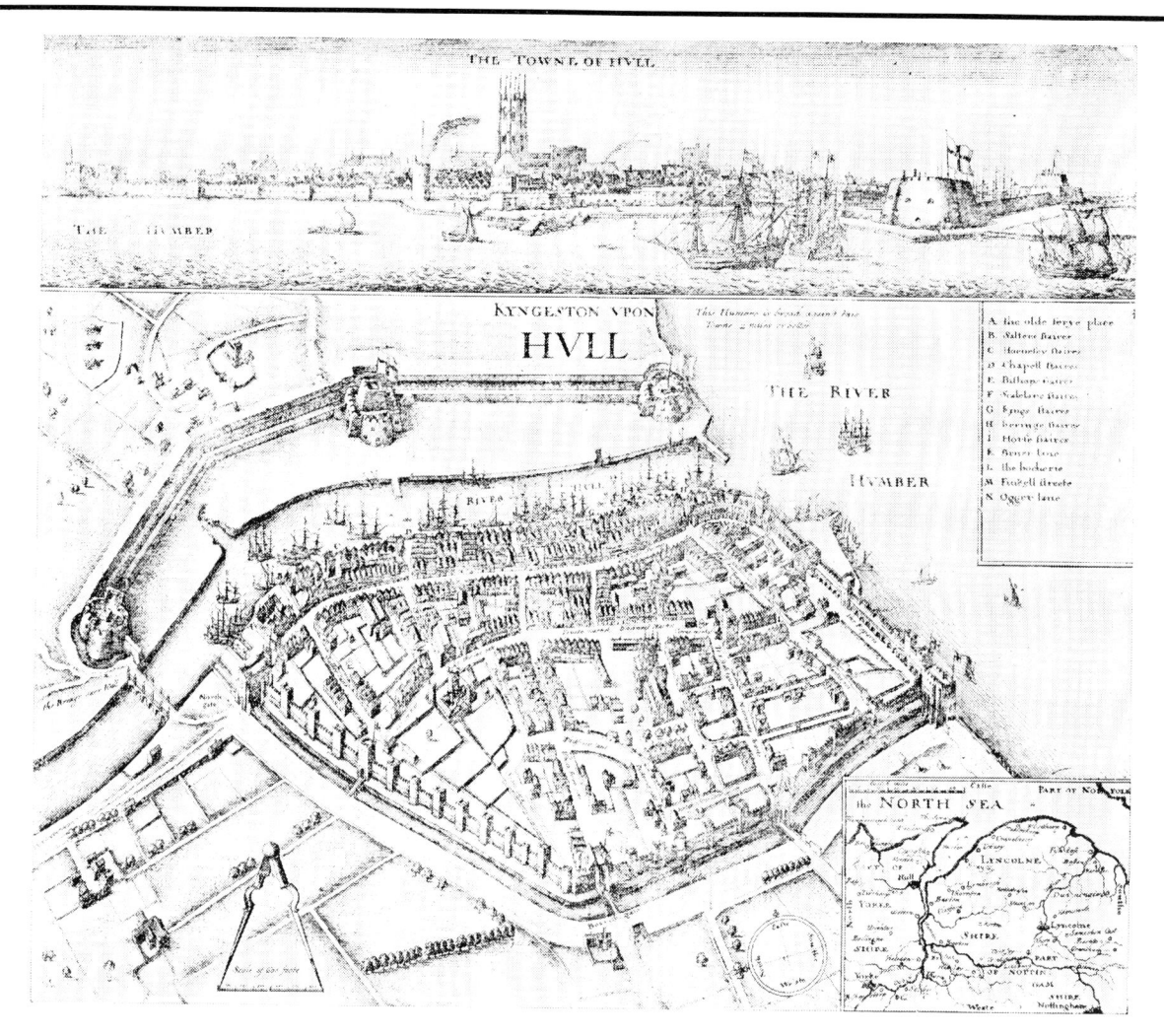

Source 2·6 *Goodwill and Lawson's "New Plan of Hull"* 1842

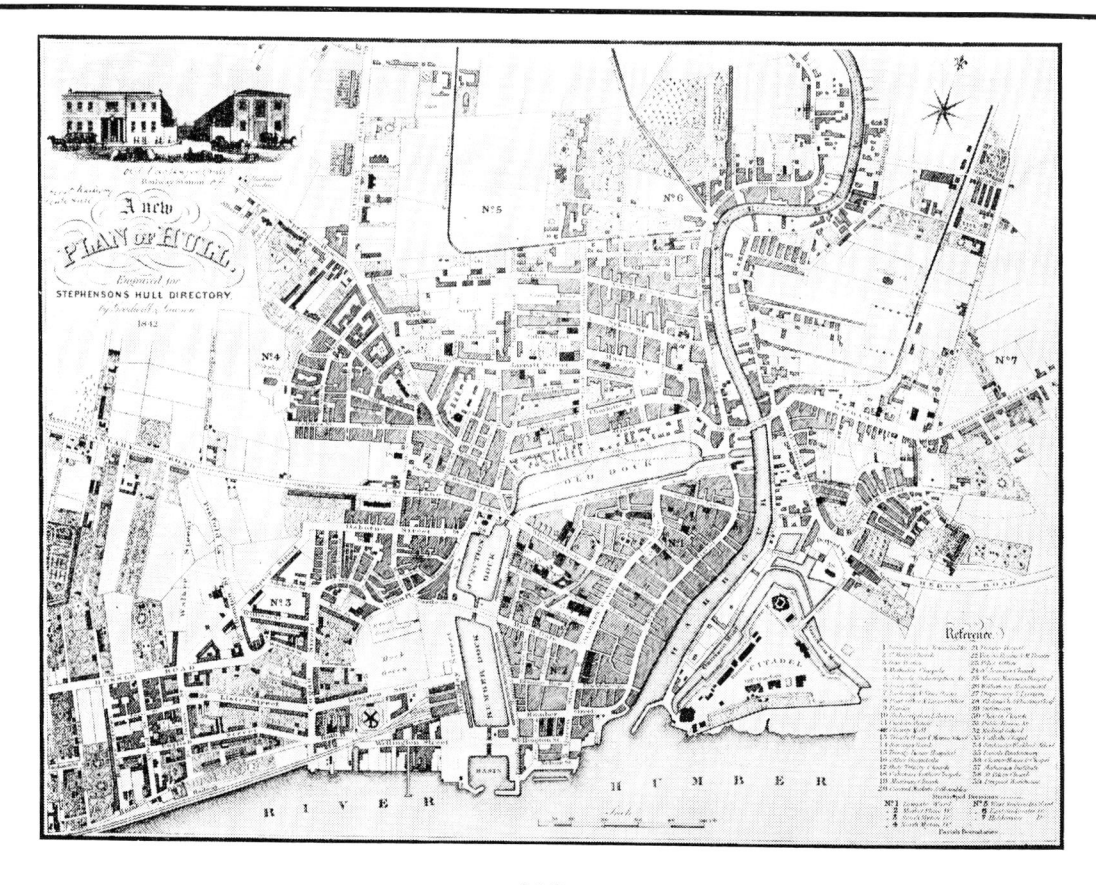

Town development and domestic architecture

Source 3·6 *A section of a large scale map of Leeds in the nineteenth century, 5 feet to 1 mile, 1850 edition*

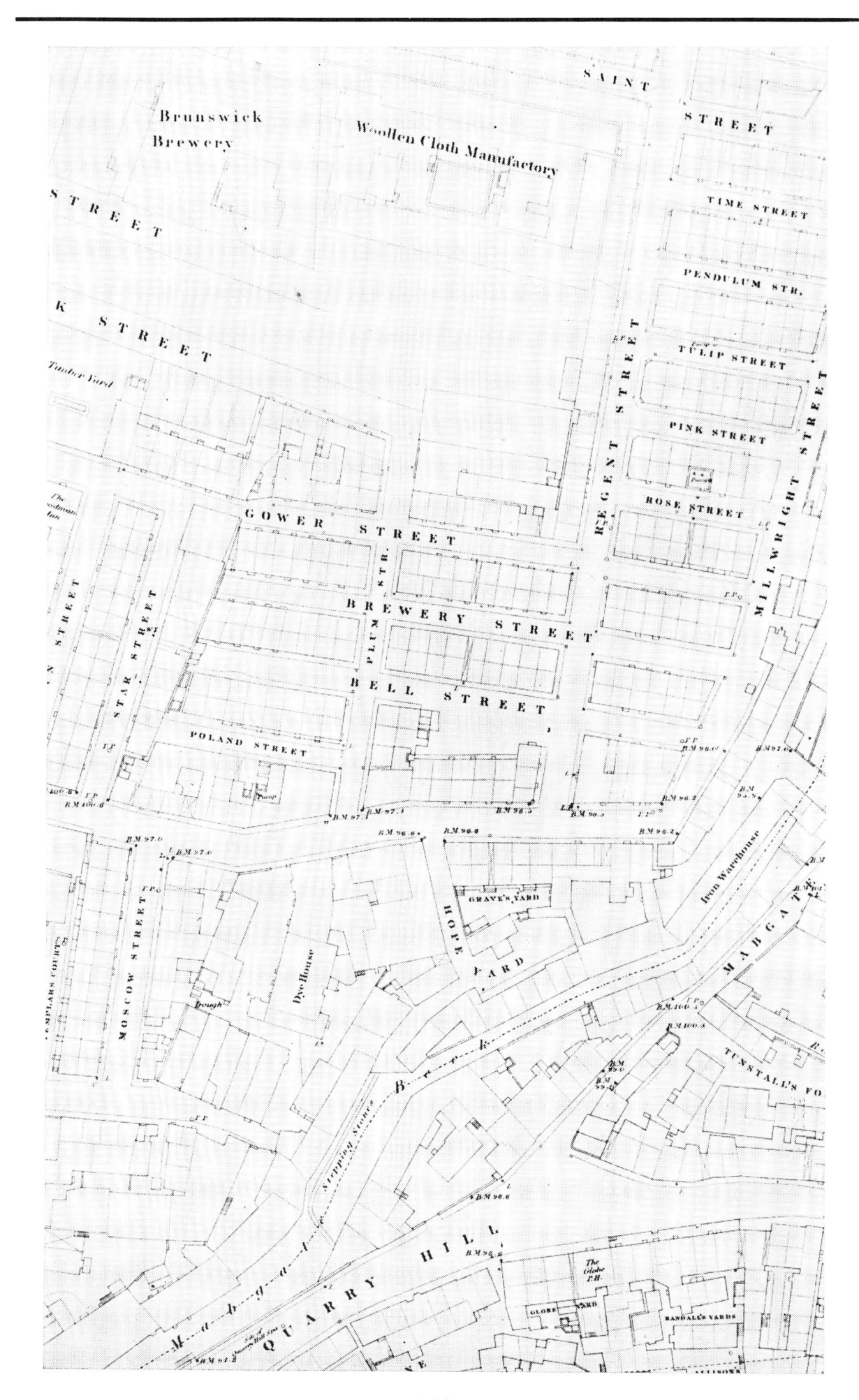

Town development and domestic architecture

Source 4·6 *Extract from Edward Baines, "History, Directory and Gazetteer of the County of York," (1822) Vol. 1, (David and Charles, 1969) showing part of the information relating to Pontefract*

PONTEFRACT. [*Towns.*] PONTEFRACT. **241**

William Tomlinson, Esq.
C. M. Torre, Esq.
Edward Trueman, Esq.
Robert Smith, Esq.
George Alderson, Esq.
Lord Viscount Pollington.
Robert P. Milnes, Esq.
Thomas Oxley, Esq.
Grosvenor Perfect, Esq.

The temple of Fame has not been crowded by the historian of Pontefract. 'Few men,' he says, 'who have ranked high in church or state, or who have been distinguished in the annals of literature, have either been born or resided in this town.' Amongst these few he mentions Bishop Bramhall, Primate of Ireland, who was a native of Pontefract, and rose by his talents and learning to his distinguished honour and high station in the church. The indefatigable antiquarian, Dr. Nathaniel Johnson, who made large collections for the history of Yorkshire resided here; and Lun, the facetious barber and keen satarist, who wrote the Poem of "The Newcastle Rider," and several other pieces not unworthy the pen of a Churchill, *shaved* both with lather and without, in this ancient borough for a number of years. Pontefract, standing off the great North road, has hitherto not been a place of much intercourse, but the communication recently opened by means of the new Barnsdale road is expected to enliven the town, and to confer substantial and permanent benefits upon its inhabitants. A hope is entertained, grounded upon the propriety and expediency of the measure, that the Glasgow mail from and to London, instead of taking the present route by Wetherby and Boroughbridge, will speedily pass through Pontefract, Leeds, Harewood, Harrogate and Ripon, and thus open a direct mail communication which cannot fail to promote the accommodation and advance the interests of a very populous and opulent line of country. The population of Pontefract, according to the returns of 1821, amounts to 4447.

POST MISTRESS—MARY HAYWARD, *Office, Finckle-Street.*

Places from whence Letter Bags are reced.	Miles from Pontefract.	Postage	Hours of Arrival.	Hours of Departure.
London	175	11d.	½ p 6 evening.	8 evening.
Wakefield	9	4	7 morning.	6 evening.
Barnsley	14	6	ditto.	ditto.
Leeds	13	4	½ p 9 morning.	½ bfr. 4 afternoon

DIRECTORY.

Academies, Boarding & Day Schools.
Dagley Miss, (ladies' bdg.) Beast fair
Edwards M.A. (ladies') Corn market
Martin C. A. (national) Micklegate
Tolston Nathan, (classical & commercial) Castle house

Agents, General and Particular.
Jackson Isabella, (East India Company) Ropergate
Moorhouse Michael, (London Genuine Tea Company) Salter row
Page Barbara, (East India Company's Tea) Corn market

Architects.
Hartley Bernard, Ropergate

Attornies.
Clough & Brook, Ropergate
Coleman James, Ropergate
Forrest William, Ropergate
Horner William, Market place
Mitton & Pearson, Ropergate
Smithson & Ramskell, Market place
Whitaker William, jun. Ropergate
Wood William, Corn market

Auctioneers.
Carr Thomas, Church lane
Dickinson James, Micklegate
Haigh George, Corn market
Wright Benjamin, Micklegate

Bacon and Ham Factors.
Dawson Ann, Market place
White Michael, Middle row

Bakers.
Bradbury John, Shoe market
Pease John, Middle row
Senior Joseph, Beast fair
Vaux Richard, Micklegate

Banks.
Leathams, Tew, Trueman, Tew, & Co. Market place, (on Jos. Denison and Co.)
Perfect & Co. Ropergate, (on Sir J. W. Lubbock, Bart. & Co.)

Basket and Skip Makers.
Bilbrough William, Beast fair
Fountain John, Tanshelf
Sadler Richard, Micklegate
Wrigglesworth Dobson, Ropergate

Y

Town development and domestic architecture

242 PONTEFRACT. [*Towns.*] PONTEFRACT.

Blacksmiths and Farriers.
Hunt Joseph, Back lane
Kay Michael, Salter row
Mathers Thomas, Tanshelf

Booksellers, Stationers & Binders.
Brown Sarah, (stationer) Market pl.
Fox John, (& printer) Market place
Hunt William, (& printer) Market pl.

Boot and Shoemakers.
Birkby Thomas, Northgate
Brown Ann, Shoe market
Brown George, Court house yard
Carter James, Salter row
Lacy Benjamin, Tanshelf
Lea Thomas, Market place
Makin Richard, Beast fair
Steel William, Beast fair
Stephenson William, Northgate
Thomlinson George, Beast fair

Braziers and Tinsmiths.
Drew William, Market place
England Joseph, near the Market pl.
Nunns Thomas, jun. Market place
Thompson Joseph, Beast fair
Wilson John, (tinman) Market place

Bricklayers.
Boys Samuel, Baxtergate
Moody F. & W. Market place
Moody John, Micklegate
Moxon Wm. (& maker) Baxtergate

Butchers.
Burton William, Micklegate
Greenwood Francis, Market place
Lodge William, Micklegate
Malcolm Mark, Beast fair
Tasker Thomas, Micklegate
White Michael, (pork) Middle row

Butter Factors.
Dawson Ann, Market place
Morley Joseph, (& bacon) Salter row

Cheesemongers.
Ashton John, Bridge
Dawson Ann, Market place
Nunns Thomas, Market place
Wilson Joseph, Beast fair

Chemists and Druggists.
Brice John, Market place
Parkinson William, Market place
Ramsden John, (druggist) Beast fair

Clock and Watch Makers.
Booth G. B. Wool market
Booth James, Market place
Farrer Benjamin, Beast fair
Farrer Joshua, Beast fair
Sheppard W. R. Micklegate

Confectioners.
Bradbury John, Shoe market
Moore Sarah, Market place
Senior Joseph, Beast fair

Coopers.
Bilbrouh William, Beast fair
Sadler Richard, Micklegate
Worfolk George, Market place

Corn and Flour Dealers.
Barratt Thomas, Ropergate
Baumforth Thomas, Beast fair
Colley Thomas, (flour) Micklegate
Eyre Thomas, Corn market
Gelder George, (flour) Market place
Gelder William, Micklegate
Moorhouse Michael, (flour) Salter row
Pinder Joseph, Ropergate
Walshaw Thomas, (flour) Salter row
Warwick Wm. (& malt) Micklegate
Watson Thomas, (corn & malt) Low Bailey gate

Corn Millers.
Nodder John, St. Thomas Hill
Nodder Thomas, near Bubwith house
Pease William, Boreas Union mill
Womack Richard, Corporation mill

Curriers and Leather Cutters.
Handley Joseph, Micklegate
Poppleton Richard, Gilleygate
Robson James, Market place
Winterburn Richard, Wool market

Fellmonger.
Purslove Thos. near the Old church

Fire and Life Insurance Offices.
County, F. G. Osburn, Ropergate
Phœnix, Wm. Whitaker, Ropergate
Sheffield, John Fox, Market place

Fishmonger.
Dawson Ann, Market place

Gardeners and Seedsmen.
Barratt Thomas, Ropergate
Hunter Timothy, (seedsman) Bridge
Knapton William, Baxter street
Oxley Thomas and Scholey, (nursery & seedsmen) Beast fair
Pollard Tempest, (seedsman) Micklegate
Swallow Christopher, Micklegate

Glass, China, & Earthenware Dealers.
Aukland Geo. (earthenware) Micklegate
Knowles Elizabeth, (earthenware) Shoe market

Glove and Breeches Makers.
Brook Matthew, Market place
Riley Wm. (breeches) Market place

Grocers and Tea Dealers.
Dawson Matthew, Market place
Dawson William, Market place
Firth Thomas, Market place
Gelder William, Micklegate
Hunter Timothy, Bridge
Johnson M. & E. Market place
Nunns Thomas, Market place

Source 5.6 *Extract from the 1851 census enumerator's returns for Somerset Place, Bath*

House No.	Name of Street etc.	Name & Surname	Relation	Condn.	Age	Rank, occupation etc.	Birthplace
5	Somerset Place	Amy M. Roberts	Head	U	48	Proprietor of Ladies Boarding School	Cork
		Mary A. Creyte	Visitor	U	30	Fundholder	Radcliffe, Yorks.
		Isabella Rickards	Visitor	U	20	Annuitant	Madras, B.S.
		Marianne Townsend	Pupil	U	19	Scholar (lady)	Clonalarty
		Kary Townsend	Pupil	U	17	Scholar (lady)	Clonalarty
		Kate Hicky	Pupil	U	17	Scholar (lady)	Cape of Good Hope
		Sophia Hickey	Pupil	U	16	Scholar (lady)	Cape of Good Hope
		Hardy Blanchard	Visitor	M	43	Perpetual Curate of Seacroft, Leeds	Northallerton, Yorks.
		Frances Blanchard	Visitor	M	42	Wife	Beverley, Yorks.
		Ellen Blanchard	Visitor	U	5		
		Robert Creyke	Visitor	U	3	Daughter	Seacroft
		Eliza Parker	Servant	U	28	Parlourmaid	Castle Cary, Som.
		Eliza Francis	Servant	M	28	Nurse	Gwinap, Cornwall
		Susan Watts	Servant	U	23	House servant, Cook	Barnstaple, Devon.
		Maria Rawlins	Servant	U	16	Housemaid	Bath, Som.
6	Somerset Place	Richard Hare	Head	M	57	Lieutenant, R.N.	London, Middlesex
		Mary C. Hare	Wife	M	40		Little Grimsby, Lincs.
		Mary H. Hare	Daughter	U	10		Ewnshill, Som.
		Elizabeth Hampton	Servant	U	21	Lady's maid	Weston, Som.
		Maria Ball	Servant	U	26	Cook	Bath, Som.
		Mary A. Gell	Servant	U	20	Parlourmaid	Woolwich, Kent.
		Eliza Allen	Servant	U	24	Housemaid	Shoreditch, Middx.

Town development and domestic architecture

Source 6·6 *An extract from the Daniel Defoe "Tour through the whole island of Great Britain" (1722-26)*

WAKEFIELD

The first town of note we came into was Wakefield, a large, handsome, rich clothing town, full of money and full of trade.

Wakefield is a clean, large, well built town, very populous and very rich. Here is a very large church, and well filled it is, for here are very few dissenters. The steeple is a very fine spire and by far the highest in this part of the country, except that at Sheffield. They tell us there are here more people also than in the city of York, and yet it is no corporation town; and the highest magistrate, as I understand was a constable.

Here also is a market every Friday for woollen cloaths after the manner of that at Leeds, tho not so great; yet as all the cloathing trade is encreasing in this country, so this market too flourishes with the rest; not but that sometimes as foreign markets receive interruption either by wars, by a glut of the goods, or by any other incident there are interruptions of the manufacture too, which when it happen, the clothiers are sure to complain of loss of trade, but when the demand comes again they are not equally forward with their acknowledgements and this I observed was the case everywhere else as well as here.

Source 7·6 *An extract from a description of Manchester and its inhabitants in 1832*

The township of Manchester chiefly consists of masses of houses, inhabited by the population engaged in the great manufactories of the cotton trade. Some of the central divisions are occupied by warehouses and shops, and a few streets by the dwellings of the more wealthy inhabitants; but the opulent merchants chiefly reside in the country, and even the superior servants of their establishments inhabit the suburban townships.

Manchester, properly so called, is chiefly inhabited by shopkeepers and the labouring classes. Those districts where the poor dwell are of very recent origin. The rapid growth of the cotton manufacture has attracted hither operatives from every part of the kingdom, and Ireland has poured forth the most destitute of her hordes to supply the constantly increasing demand for labour . . .

Having been subjected to the prolonged labour of an animal — his physical energy wasted — his mind in supine inaction — the artizan has neither moral dignity nor intellectual nor organic strength to resist the seductions of appetite. His wife and children, too frequently subjected to the same process, are unable to cheer his remaining moments of leisure. Domestic economy is neglected, domestic comforts are unknown. A meal of the coarsest food is prepared with heedless haste and devoured with equal precipitation. Home has no other relation to him than that of shelter — few pleasures are there — it chiefly presents to him a scene of physical exhaustion, from which he is glad to escape. Himself impotent of all the distinguishing aims of his species, he sinks into sensual sloth, or revels in more degrading licentiousness. His house is ill furnished, uncleanly, often ill ventilated, perhaps damp; his food, from want of forethought and domestic economy, is meagre and innutritious; he is debilitated and hypochondriacal, and falls the victim of dissipation . . .

James Phillips Kay, *The moral and physical condition of the working classes employed in the cotton manufacture in Manchester* (1832), pp. 6-11

Town development and domestic architecture

Source 8·6 *An extract from a description of Saltaire a model town built in the 1850s by Titus Salt for the workers at his mill*

But Mr. Salt's great conception did not end with the erection of the mill. It also embraced what was still more dear to him — the provision of comfortable dwellings, church, schools, — in fact, every institution which could improve the moral, mental, and religious condition of the workpeople. The number of "hands" employed at "the works" was, at that time, between 3,000 and 4,000, who had, for the most part, to be housed at Saltaire.

With a lithographed plan of the town before us, let us notice a few points about it which serve to illustrate some features of Mr. Salt's personal character. His loyalty is to be recognised, for the three chief thoroughfares of the town are Victoria Road, Albert Road, and Albert Terrace. His affection for his family comes out, for Caroline Street bears the Christian name of his wife, and other streets are named after his children, grandchildren, and other members of his family. Again, his esteem for his architects is expressed in the names Lockwood Street and Mawson Street. In all, there are twenty-two streets, besides places, terraces, and roads, which contain 850 houses, and forty-five almhouses making a total of 895 dwellings, covering an area of twenty-five acres.

Let us enter one of the dwellings, and examine its internal arrangements. From the sample the whole bulk may be judged. It is built to the same stone as the mill, and lined with brickwork. It contains parlour, kitchen, pantry, and three bedrooms. Some of the houses are designed for larger families, and others for boarding-houses. These dwellings are fitted up with all the modern appliances necessary to comfort and health; they are well ventilated, and have each a back garden, walled in, and flagged; the rents are moderate, and the houses are in much request. Part of Victoria Road is occupied by tradesmens shops, the post-office, the savings bank, and the office of *The Shipley and Saltaire Times*. The whole cost of dwellings, in 1864, amounted to £106,562, exclusive of the land.

With so much consideration for the welfare of the workpeople, it was not likely that the educational wants of the children would be forgotten. In laying out the town, a central and most convenient site was set apart on which elementary schools were to be built. From the first, provisional accommodation had been made elsewhere, but it was not till 1868 that the site was occupied. The report of the Government Inspector, after their erection, was "that the school buildings, for beauty, size, and equipment, had no rivals in the district". The cost of their erection was £7,000. They are situated on the west side of Victoria Road, and provide accommodation for 750 children. The style adopted is Italian, which is uniform with the other buildings of Saltaire.

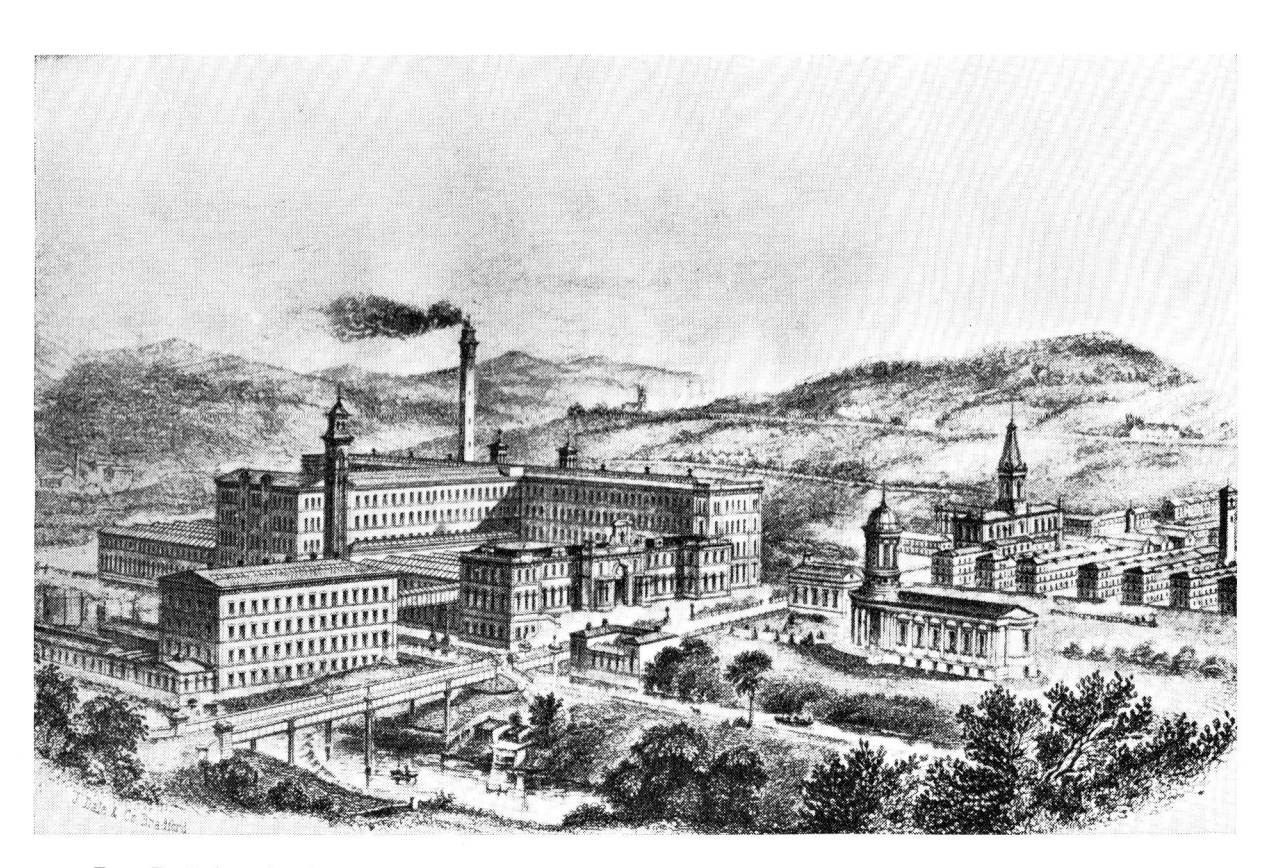

Rev. R. Balgarnie *Sir Titus Salt, Baronet: his life and its lessons*, (Hodder & Stoughton, 1877), pp. 135-137

Town development and domestic architecture

Source 9·6 *Extracts from the Richmond borough coucher — or minute, books in the eighteenth century*

2 March 1759	Committee set up to plan rebuilding of and alterations to the Town Hall
9 March 1759	Plans approved
20 March and 19 June	Further plans approved and money borrowed for same
18 October 1759	The Town Hall to be seated round and to be wainscotted and the Hall to be partitioned from the low counting room
25 April 1760	The Music Gallery to be finished in time for the Races Assembly
12 May 1761	Committee set up to supervise the building of tenements adjacent to the Toll Booth
4 March 1762	Corporation Committee appointed to view the present condition of the Shambles and to lay plans for their rebuilding
	Corporation offered land below Bell Banks and Newbiggin to Thomas Yorke Esq. to make part of his great garden for £279.5.0. Sale went through 6 April
20 July 1762	Plans approved
12 April 1763	Agreed to purchase some shops and chambers at the head of the Flesh Shambles for £184.10.0. Appointed Committee to plan building of new shambles
24 May 1763	Agreed that old shambles should be pulled down and new ones built
20 February 1764	Shambles to be built at the east end of the Common Hall
27 March 1766	Appointed Committee to let all the shops except the two uppermost ones in the new shambles
26 October 1787	Application from Samuel Butler to the Corporation to build a more commodious theatre in Richmond. Application granted 1 November

Course work for G.C.E. and C.S.E. assessment

Some history teachers may wish to devise Mode 3 C.S.E and G.C.E. 'O' level syllabuses which include work on *History Around Us: Town development and domestic architecture*. The following items of course work could be completed by pupils and submitted in a folder as part of their final assessment:

1. Descriptions of an area, street or town studied by fieldwork, with relevant maps, sketches, plans, diagrams and any records and surveys.

2. Descriptions of other areas, streets or towns studied in the classroom together with maps, plans, sketches, etc.

3. Work setting a town or area of a town in its historical context and relating it to other towns or areas:
e.g. an illustrated account describing and explaining the development of the town and comparing it with the development of another town.
e.g. an illustrated account comparing the development of two or three different areas of a town at a particular time and relating it to the domestic architecture.

4. A piece of work involving the imaginative reconstruction of:

either: a specific incident which affected the homes and lives of people in an area,
e.g. a flood, fire, slum clearance or air raid in the war.
or: the life and homes of people at a particular time,
e.g. life in one type of house, or a comparison between different types of houses and life styles, e.g. life in one street.
or: the part played by a person, or family in the development of an area,
e.g. Titus Salt, Robert Arkwright, Beau Nash.

Resources

Some of the books on this list are out of print. You should be able to obtain copies from your local library or from the Schools Library Loan Service.

Resources are listed by order of importance, within each section.

Teachers' books

John Haddon, *Discovering Towns*, 'Discovering Books Series', (Shire Publications, 1970)
Alan Rogers, *This was their World*, (BBC, 1972)
H. J. Dyos (Ed.), *Study of Urban History*, (Edward Arnold, 1971)
H. J. Dyos (Ed.), *Victorian Suburb: Study of the Growth of Camberwell*, (Leicester University Press, 1974)
G. A. Chinnery, *Studying Urban History in Schools*, 'Teaching of History Series', (Historical Association, 1971)
J. T. Smith & E. M. Yates, 'On the dating of English houses from external evidence', reprint from *Field Studies*, Vol. 2, No. 5, 1968 — available from E. W. Classey Ltd., 353 Hanworth Road, Hampton, Middlesex.
R. W. Brunskill, *An Illustrated Handbook of Vernacular Architecture*, (Faber, 1971)
J. Elizabeth Exwood & R. G. Unwin (Eds.), *Yorkshire Topography: A Guide to Historical Sources and their Uses*, (University of Leeds, Institute of Education, 1974)
Michael Aston & Trevor Rowley, *Landscape Archaeology: An Introduction to Fieldwork Techniques on Post-Roman Landscapes*, (David & Charles, 1974), see the chapter on towns
David Iredale, *Discovering This Old House*, 'Discovering Books Series', (Shire Publications, 1968)
W. G. Hoskins, *The Making of the English Landscape*, (Penguin, 1970), see the chapter on 'landscape of towns'
Asa Briggs, *Victorian Cities*, (Penguin, 1968)

Alec Clifton-Taylor, *The Pattern of English Building*, (Faber, 1972)
Maurice Willmore Barley, *The English Farmhouse and Cottage*, (Routledge & Kegan Paul, 1961)
Nikolaus Pevsner *et. al.*, (Ed.), *The Buildings of England Series* (Penguin), this series now has volumes for most counties, covering each town and describing and dating interesting houses
Ulster Architectural Heritage Society — lists and surveys all buildings of historic interest in Ulster
A. J. Rowan & C. E. B. Brett, *Queen's University Area of Belfast*, (U.A.H.S., 1969)
C. E. B. Brett & Lady D. H. Dunleath, *Lisburn*, (U.A.H.S. 1969)
W. D. Girvan *et. al.*, *Antrim and Ballymena*, (U.A.H.S. 1971)
W. D. Girvan & A. J. Rowan, *West Antrim*, (U.A.H.S. 1971)
C. E. B. Brett & R. J. McKinstry, *Joystreet and Hamilton Street area, Belfast*, (U.A.H.S. 1971)
R. Oram & P. J. Rankin, *Dungannon and Cookstown*, (U.A.H.S. 1971)
C. E. B. Brett, *Glens of Antrim*, (U.A.H.S. 1973)
C. E. B. Brett (Ed.), *Historic Buildings etc. in the Towns and Villages of East Down*, (U.A.H.S. 1973)
C. E. B. Brett, *Court Houses and Market Houses of the Province of Ulster*, (U.A.H.S. 1973)

Books for pupils dealing with the development of houses

Doreen Yarwood, *English Houses*, (Batsford, 1966)
Frank E. Huggett, *Housing the People*, 'Studies in Modern History Series', (Nelson, 1974)

Reference books for teachers and pupils dealing with town development

Eilert Ekwall, *The Concise Oxford Dictionary of English Place Names*, (O.U.P. 1960)
English Place Name Society, various volumes on twenty counties — write for further details.
Mary D. Lobel, *Historic Towns*, Vol. 1, (Lovell Johns, Cook Hammond & Kell Organ, 1969)
Edward Blishen & J. C. Armitage, *Town Story*, 'Book 1, Today — 1901', 'Book 2, 1851–1588', 'Book 3, 1399–300 A.D.' (Blond, 1964)
C. J. Lines & L. H. Bolwell, *History in Towns*, 'Discovering Your Environment Series', No. 8 (Ginn, 1970)
Geoffrey Martin, *The Town*, (Vista Books, 1961)

A. Ball & D. Merritt, *Yesterday in Bath: A Camera Record*, (Pitman, 1972)

B. Coe & M. Millward, *Victorian Townscape*, (Ward Lock, 1974)

Maurice Gorham, *Ireland from Old Photographs*, (Batsford, 1971)

George Chandler, *Victorian and Edwardian Liverpool and the North West from Old Photographs*, (Batsford, 1972)

Dorothy McCulla, *Victorian and Edwardian Birmingham from Old Photographs*, (Batsford, 1973)

Charles Sinclair Minto, *Victorian and Edwardian Scotland from Old Photographs*, (Batsford, 1970)

George Chandler, *Victorian and Edwardian Manchester and East Lancashire from Old Photographs*, (Batsford, 1974)

John Betjeman & David Vaisey, *Victorian and Edwardian Oxford from Old Photographs*, (Batsford, 1971)

S. Price, *Birmingham Old and New*, (Educational Productions, 1975)

R. Winstone, *Bristol Old and New*, (Educational Productions, 1975)

E. B. Newbold, *Coventry Old and New*, (Educational Productions, 1975)

F. Rodgers, *Derby Old and New*, (Educational Productions, 1975)

M. Gorham, *Dublin Old and New*, (Educational Productions, 1975)

C. Cruft, *Edinburgh Old and New*, (Educational Productions, 1975)

J. House, *Glasgow Old and New*, (Educational Productions, 1975)

T. Suthers, *Hull Old and New*, (Educational Productions, 1975)

C. Middleton, *Ipswich Old and New*, (Educational Productions, 1975)

W. Kidd, *Leicester Old and New*, (Educational Productions, 1975)

T. Lloyd-Jones, *Liverpool Old and New*, (Educational Productions, 1975)

F. Mullineux, *Manchester Old and New*, (Educational Productions, 1975)

M. Scaife, *Newcastle Old and New*, (Educational Productions, 1975)

G. M. Denison, *Nottingham Old and New*, (Educational Productions, 1975)

M. Shaw, *Norwich Old and New*, (Educational Productions, 1975)

D. Francis, *Portsmouth Old and New*, (Educational Productions, 1975)

J. E. Vickers, *Sheffield Old and New*, (Educational Productions, 1975)

G. Hampson, *Southampton Old and New*, Educational Productions, 1975)

N. L. Thomas & D. G. Bowden, *Swansea Old and New*, (Educational Productions, 1975)

E. P. Reprints, (Educational Productions) have a comprehensive library of reprints of town histories. They cover most areas of the country. Send for a current catalogue as the list is under constant revision — see address list in Chapter 1.

Reference books for teachers and pupils dealing with the development of houses

Doreen Yarwood, *The English Home*, (Batsford, 1956)

A. E. Priestley, *The English Home*, (Frederick Muller, 1971)

Maurice Willmore Barley, *House and Home*, (Vista books, 1963)

Vanessa Parker, *The English House in the Nineteenth Century*, (Historical Association, 1970)

R. J. Unstead, *Houses*, (A. & C. Black, 1972)

Walter Ison, *Georgian Buildings of Bath from 1700 to 1830*, (Kingsmead reprints, 1969)

Walter Ison, *Georgian Buildings of Bristol*, (Faber, 1952)

R. B. Wood-Jones, *Traditional Domestic Architecture in the Banbury Region*, (Manchester University Press, 1963)

Joseph Sprittles, *Links with Bygone Leeds*, (Thoresby Society, 1970)

Derek Linstrum, *Historic Architecture of Leeds*, (Oriel Press, 1969)

Geoffrey Booth, *Terrace to Tower Block*, (Wayland, 1974)

Reference books for pupils and teachers

These give background information, including primary source material about the homes and working lives of people in towns.

John Burnett, *The Useful Toil: Autobiographies of Working People from the 1820s to the 1920s*, (Allen Lane, 1974)

Margaret Powell, *Below Stairs*, (Pan, 1970)

Pamela Horn, *The Rise and Fall of the Victorian Servant*, (Gill & Macmillan, 1975)

Frank E. Huggett, *A Day in the Life of a Victorian Factory Worker*, (George Allen & Unwin, 1973)

Keith Dawson & Peter Wall, *Public Health and Housing*, 'Society and Industry in the Nineteenth Century', (O.U.P. 1970)

Marjorie Reeves, *The Medieval own*, 'Then and There Series', (Longman, 1954)

Marjorie Reeves & Paul Hodgson, *Elizabeth Citizen*, 'Then and There Series', (Longman, 1961)

Edith Joan Sheppard, *Bath in the Eighteenth Century*, 'Then and There Series', (Longman)

Town development and domestic architecture

Juliet Dymoke, *London in the Eighteenth Century*, 'Then and There Series', (Longman, 1958)
E. G. Power, *A Textile Community in the Industrial Revolution*, 'Then and There Series', (Longman, 1969)
John Addy, *A Coal and Iron Community in the Industrial Revolution*, 'Then and There Series', (Longman, 1970)
Tom Hastie, *Home Life*, 'Past into Present Series', (Batsford, 1967)
Molly Harrison, *People and Furniture*, (Ernest Benn, 1971)

Archive units

These contain maps and/or primary source material on town development and housing (listed in alphabetical order by town).

St. Albans, *Shire Archives Series, No. 1.*, (Shire Publications)
Birmingham, *Birmingham Prospects: South West Birmingham* 1731 by Buck, *East Prospect* 1732 by W. Westley, Maps 1778 (available from the City Museum)
Bristol, *Bristol Topography*, (Bristol Association for the Teaching of History), Archive Teaching Set No. 3
Cheadle, *Directories of Cheadle & District* (Staffordshire Education Department) Local History Source Book, L 10
Essex, *Essex Towns 1540-1640*, (Essex Record Office) Teaching Portfolio No. 2
Essex, *Town Life in Essex 1750-1950*, (Essex Record Office — in preparation)
Hull, *The Development of Kingston upon Hull*, shown through contemporary maps and views, (Local History Library, Hull City Library)
Leek, *Directories of Leek*, (Staffordshire Education Department) Local History Source Book L. 11
Leek, *Leek in Maps*, (Staffordshire Education Department) Local History Source Book L. 3
Morpeth, (Northumberland Record Office — in preparation)
Northamptonshire, *A Woman's Work: Housekeeping in Northamptonshire 1600-1900*, (Northampton Record Office) Archive Teaching Unit No. 3
Nottingham, *Public Health and Housing in Early Victorian Nottingham*, (Nottingham University Library) Archive Teaching Unit No. 3
Oxford, *Oxford the Town Beneath your Feet*, T. G. Hassall, (Oxfordshire Archive Unit, 1974)
Staffordshire, *The State of Large Towns in the Nineteenth Century — North Staffordshire*, (Staffordshire Education Department) Local History Source Book, G. 12 — in preparation)
The State of Large Towns in the Nineteenth Century — South Staffordshire, (Staffordshire Education Department), Local History Source Book G. 13 — in preparation

Slides

The Home and the Changing Role of Women 1870-1970, (Nicholas Hunter Filmstrips), 25 slides
Georgian Architecture of Bath, (The Slide Centre), eight sets
The Development of the Domestic House, (The Slide Centre), three sets
Living in Cities, (The Slide Centre), five sets, showing city life past and present

Filmstrips

Some of these are out of print but may be available from Teachers' Centres or through the E.F.V.A.

Market Town (Richmond, Yorkshire), black and white, British Council — distributed by Rank
How to Look at a Town, black and white, Common Ground, 1947
How to Look at a Seaport, black and white, Common Ground, 1968
Cathedral City (Salisbury), black and white, British Council, 1954 — distributed by Rank
The Town, 'Medieval Life Series', colour, Longman/Common Ground
Factories and their Towns, colour, Nicholas Hunter Filmstrips
Villages, Market Towns and Resorts, 'Introduction to the Industrial Revolution Series' No. 1, black and white, Common Ground
English Architecture, set of nine filmstrips, Visual Publications
Houses in Towns, colour, Hugh Baddeley Productions
Vernacular and Suburban Architecture, 'Arts and Humanities 'Environment' Series', BBC radiovision programme
Evolution of the English Home, 'Part Three: Middle Ages', 'Part Five: Jacobean to Queen Anne', 'Part Six: Georgian to Regency', 1714-1837', 'Part Seven: Victorian to George V, 1837-1939', black and white, Common Ground
The Development of the Dwelling House, colour, Hugh Baddeley Productions

Films

Cathedral City (Canterbury), 16 mm, black and white, 21 mins. G.B. Instructional, 1949 — distributed by Rank
Tudor Houses, 8 mm cassette film, colour, Gateway, 1964

7 INDUSTRIAL ARCHAEOLOGY

Some objectives and outcomes

We hope that by the time pupils finish their study of industrial archaeology they will:

1. have sufficient background information about the Industrial Revolution and the purpose and techniques of industrial archaeology to:
a. recognise different types of industrial sites and remains
b. set them in their wider historical context.

2. have had practice at recording and interpreting a number of different types of industrial sites and remains.

3. have had practice at combining visible evidence and background information, from both primary and secondary sources, to reconstruct the jobs and working conditions of people associated with different industrial sites.

4. have the knowledge, skills and enthusiasm to:
a. continue discovering and recording industrial remains beyond school
b. begin the exploration of other aspects of their historical environment beyond school.

The approach

Industrial archaeology is concerned with the visible remains of different industries, e.g. coal mining, textiles, pottery, iron and steel; transport systems, e.g. canals and railways; forms of power, e.g. wind, water, steam, electricity; as well as visible evidence relating to building, agriculture and rural crafts.

The following schemes outline two approaches to teaching an industrial archaeology course in schools. We hope they will prove useful. Both courses were designed for pupils aged 15-16, studying *History Around Us*, as part of G.C.E. and C.S.E. courses.

APPROACH 1
A study of a particular industrial community

Cromford, Derbyshire, 1770-1850. This includes the study of its associated forms of power and its transport system.

STAGE ONE
An introduction to industrial history and industrial archaeology

This is designed:
a. to introduce pupils to the aims of industrial archaeology and the techniques of studying and recording industrial remains
b. to set Cromford and its cotton mills in their historical context.

STAGE TWO
A study of the Cromford mills area

Two visits are made to the mill area to record and interpret the visible remains relating to the mill, its water power system and the workers' houses.
After the visits pupils attempt to set the visible remains in their industrial and historical context and to reconstruct the lives of people who worked in the mills.

Follow up work

a. a written account including sketches, plans, photographs and diagrams of the mill area and answers to the following questions:
What was produced at the mills?
Why are the mills situated here?
What different buildings were at the mill site?
How were they laid out and when were they built?
How were the mills constructed?
How was the spun cotton produced?
What machines were used and how did they work?
How was water power supplied?

Industrial archaeology

Why were the mills significant in the history of the industry?

What problems did the mills face?

b. a short biography of Sir Richard Arkwright: his background, invention, work at Cromford, achievements, etc.

c. an imaginative reconstruction: "Living and working in Cromford 1700-1850".

This work involves the study both of visible remains and evidence from written sources. For examples see the section on background source material in this chapter.

STAGE THREE
A study of the Cromford and High Peak Railway and the Cromford Canal

Background work on the railway and canal system precedes visits to two sites: the Middleton Top engine house and High Peak junction. During the visits pupils record details of the visible remains to show, for example, how the engine and incline workings functioned.

Middleton Top engine house on the Cromford and High Peak Railway

Follow up work
a. Site descriptions together with annotated diagrams and illustrations explaining the different features of the railway, their functions and construction

b. an imaginative reconstruction of:
either: the collapse of Jessop's aqueduct,
or: how a train ran away on an incline,
or: the work of the men involved with the railway

c. discussion of the interrelationship between the High Peak Railway and other canal, tramway and early railway sites in Derbyshire.

Pulley system outside the Middleton Top engine house Cromford and High Peak Railway

Engine shed and tensioning wheel pit at the bottom of the sheep pasture incline on the Cromford and High Peak Railway

STAGE FOUR
A comparative study of other industrial sites at Belper, Ironville, Ambergate

After visits to these sites follow work includes:
a. work on the industrial development of Sheffield, Chesterfield, South Lancashire and West Yorkshire to set these sites in their historical context

b. discussion and essay work attempting to link the sites by answering questions such as:
Are these places connected in any way with Cromford? If so how?
How are they different or similar?
Why did they develop later?
Why did Cromford's development and the development of its attendant communication system cease?

APPROACH 2
A study of a number of different aspects of industrial archaeology

This includes a study of the visible remains in the Dudley area of the West Midlands.

STAGE ONE
What is industrial archaeology and how do you become an industrial archaeologist?

Through a study of the visible remains of an iron furnace pupils are introduced to the aims, methods and techniques of industrial archaeology.

STAGE TWO
A study of the visible remains of an industry: the iron industry

Visits are made to a number of sites connected with the iron industry:
Coalbrookdale: Abraham Darby's furnace, furnace pool, great warehouse.
Blists Hill Open Air Museum: steam engines, iron making, early transport methods.
Avoncroft Museum of Building: nailers' and chain makers' shops.

STAGE THREE
A study of different forms of power

Two forms of power are studied: wind and water power. Pupils investigate the visible remains of windmills and water-mills in the locality and Danzey Green Windmill at the Avoncroft Museum of Building

STAGE FOUR
A study of different forms of transport

This involves the study of a number of railway lines — The Pensnett Railway, the Gibbon Works Railway, Oxley Junction and Kingswinford Junction branchline, and their interrelationship with:
a. the local clay, coal and stone industries,
b. the local canal and turnpike system.

Studying sites: some questions and activities

The amount of help given to pupils studying industrial remains in or outside the classroom will vary. Some teachers may prefer to introduce their pupils to fairly well preserved remains first and then move on to more difficult sites.

Industrial Museums

There are a number of industrial museums in different areas of the country, which would be ideal for first visits, e.g.
Abbeydale Industrial Hamlet, Sheffield — enquiries to: Sheffield City Museum, Weston Park, Sheffield, S10 2TP
Avoncroft Museum of Building, Bromsgrove, Hereford and Worcester
Blists Hill Open Air Museum — enquiries to: Ironbridge Gorge Museum Trust, Church Hill, Ironbridge, Telford, Salop, TF8 7RE
Bradford Industrial Museum, Moorside Mills, Eccleshall, Bradford, West Yorkshire
City of Salford Science Museum, Buile Hill, Hill Park, Salford 6 — this museum has a reconstruction of Buile Hill No. 1 pit
Coalbrookdale Museum and Furnace Site — enquiries to: Ironbridge Gorge Museum Trust, Church Hill, Ironbridge, Telford, Salop, TF8 7RE
Cusworth Hall Museum — The South Yorkshire Industrial Museum, Near Doncaster, South Yorkshire
Higher Mill Museum, Helmshore, Rossendale, Lancashire — Honorary Curator; D. Pilkington, 515 Elm Terrace, Helmshore
Llechwedd Slate Caverns, Blaenau Festiniog, Merionethshire
Museum of Science and Engineering, Exhibition Park, Great North Road, Newcastle upon Tyne
Nether Alderley Mill, Cheshire — enquiries to the Custodian, Mr. A. I. Oldham, 53 Stoneacre Road, Manchester, M22 6BN
North of England Open Air Museum, Beamish, Co. Durham
The Science Museum, Exhibition Road, South Kensington, London, SW7 2DD
Shepherd Wheel Water Powered Grinding Shop, Whiteley Wood, Sheffield
Ulster Folk and Transport Museum, Cultra Manor, Holywood, Co. Down
Weald and Downland Open Air Museum, Singleton, Chichester, Sussex
Welsh Folk Museum, St. Fagans, Cardiff, Glamorgan

Industrial archaeology

Slate splitting at Dinorwic Slate Quarry Museum, Llanberis, Gwynedd

Interior of a chain workshop, at Avoncroft Museum of Building, Bromsgrove, Hereford and Worcester

The first iron bridge in the world, built 1779; Ironbridge, Salop

Industrial archaeology

Danzey Green Windmill, at Avoncroft Museum of Building; Bromsgrove, Hereford and Worcester

Alderley Old Mill; Nether Alderley, Cheshire

Weaver's house, linen bleach green and watchman's hut; Ulster Folk and Transport Museum, Co. Down

Industrial archaeology

Pit head winding gear and rolling stock; Eppleton Colliery, Tyne and Wear

The fulling room at the Higher Mill Museum; Helmshore, Lancashire

All these museums either prefer or require advance notice of party bookings.

Industrial sites and remains

Suggestions for questions and activities for the study of three different types of industrial remains are outlined below:

1. Studying the coal mining industry: a disused coal mine

Background lessons

Using filmstrips, slides, maps, etc. the teacher could introduce pupils to background information about:

a. the coal mining industry in general

b. the particular disused coal mine
e.g. the names of the mine owners, the name and location of the mine, mining methods being used at the time, methods used to transport coal at the time, markets for the coal at the time.
This information is necessary for pupils to recognise and interpret the visible evidence.

A study of visible remains

Using slides, maps, photographs and diagrams, pupils could learn how to locate and recognise evidence of old mines on maps and on the ground. With an outline map of the area based on the 25 inch Ordnance Survey plan, pupils — individually, in pairs or groups, could make a series of

Figure 1.7 *Record Cards*
Card for a factory or mine

NATURE OF SITE (factory, mine etc.)			COUNTY	REF. NO.
Grid reference or location	Industry	Dating	Parish/Township	Date of Report
DESCRIPTION: dimensions; present condition; architectural features, etc. (Further remarks or photo/sketch may be recorded on the back)					
Machinery and fittings				
Danger of demolition or damage				
Printed, manuscript or photographic records				
Reporter's name and address: Institution or Society:				Return
C.B.A. Industrial Archaeology Report Card				

Industrial archaeology

General Card

NATURE OF SITE		COUNTY	NRIM Ref. No.
GRID REF. LOCATION		TOWN/ PARISH	DATE OF REPORT
DESCRIPTION			
ORES/SEAMS WORKED (with dates)			
ENGINES/MACHINERY/EQUIPMENT			
DOCUMENTARY/PHOTOGRAPHIC RECORDS			
OWNER OF SITE	REPORTER'S NAME AND ADDRESS		
INDUSTRIAL ARCHAEOLOGY REPORT CARD: MINES SECTION			
RETURN TO *Centre for the Study of the History of Technology, University of Bath, Claverton Down, Bath*			

visits to different sites connected with the disused mine, e.g.
the pit head, its engine house and spoil heaps
the trackway used to transport coal to the despatch depot
the coal depot, staithes, manager's house, workers' cottages
coal owner's house.

The location of various sites could be marked on the outline map. Each site could be surveyed and recorded in detail using photographs, sketches, notes, etc.

Some teachers may wish their pupils to complete record cards instead of assignment sheets — see *fig.* 1·7.

If the site has not been recorded pupils could send their record card to: The Director, Centre for the Study of the History of Technology, University of Bath, Claverton Down, Bath, Avon.

Follow up work

Pupils could reconstruct:
a. the day to day running and organisation of the mine, its trackway and coal depot, etc. at a certain period
b. the lives and work of the people associated with the mine at a certain period.
This work involves not only detailed investigation of the visible remains, but also the study of background information — secondary histories of the mining industry, maps and, wherever possible, primary sources relating to the particular mine. A visit to a museum which has items of mining equipment would be helpful. The Schools Museum Service may provide models of workings or items such as miners' lamps.

Some questions for investigation

How did the miners get down the mine?
How did they work the coal?
How was coal transported from the face to the surface?
How was the coal transported from the pit head to the depot?
What happened to the coal at the depot?
Which market was the coal from this mine destined for?
How did it reach its market?
What different jobs were involved in the daily working of the mine?
Where did the mine workers live and how did they get to work?
What were their living conditions like?
What were their working conditions like?
How much did they earn?
Who was the mine owner and where did he live?
Do we know of any notable incident in the history of the mine at this time?

Possible work and activities

These could include:

An annotated plan of the mine and its associated visible remains explaining the function of the different remains.

A sketch map of the area showing:
a. the markets for the coal,
b. the route and means of transport used to get the coal to its market.

An imaginative reconstruction of a mine workers' day, describing the different sites and remains associated with the mine and his work.

An illustrated account describing an incident in the mine's history, e.g. a strike or disaster.

2. Studying transport: a canal

Background lessons

Using filmstrips, slides, maps, etc. the teacher could introduce pupils to:
a. background information about canals in general: their location, the dates when they were built, methods of construction, reasons for their construction, goods transported, etc.
b. basic details about the canal to be studied: date of construction, engineer, route, etc.

A study of the visible remains

Using maps, slides, photographs, etc. pupils would learn how to locate and recognise evidence of a canal on a map and on the ground. With an outline map of the section of the canal to be studied, pupils could make a series of visits to locate, survey, and record the different features of the canal, e.g.

the general lie of the land around the canal which helps to explain its route
bridges: wooden or cast iron, cantilever, swing or lift
embankments and cuttings
aqueducts, tow-paths
buildings: wharfs and warehouses, lock keepers' cottages, boat building yards, toll houses, canal inns, tunnel keepers' houses
other features: tunnels, reservoirs, locks
transport: barges, nearby roads and railways.

Follow up work

Pupils could research aspects of the canal's history, e.g.
the construction of the canal
its daily traffic during the particular period being studied
the work of the men connected with the canal and its traffic
the reasons for the decline of the canal
the industries which the canal served.

This work involves the interpretation of visible remains and the use of background information from both primary and secondary sources.

Some questions for investigation

Why did the canal follow that particular route?
What problems did the engineer have to face when building the canal and how did he overcome them?
Why was the canal originally built?
What cargoes did the canal barges carry at this time?
Which industries and markets did it serve?
What evidence survives of these industries along the canal banks?
What different types of work were involved in operating the canal?
Why did the canal decline?

Possible activities

These could include:

An annotated map of the section of the canal studied, explaining the different features of the canal and their functions.

An annotated sketch map of the whole length of the canal showing the different industries and markets which it served and its relationship with the road and river system.

An imaginative reconstruction of a bargee's journey along a section of the canal at a particular time describing the loading and unloading of cargo and the various features of the canal.

An illustrated account describing the problems faced by the engineer when building the canal and his solutions to those problems.

3. Studying power: windmills and water-mills

The approach to this topic is similar to the one used for the mine and the canal. Teachers may wish pupils to attempt comparative studies of the two main types of windmill — the post-mill and the tower or smock-mill as well as the two main types of water-mill — overshot and undershot. They may wish pupils to use and complete the appropriate record card for the Society for the Preservation of Ancient Buildings — see *fig. 2·7*.

Questions and activities

Some of the questions and activities given below were used by pupils studying wind and water-mills in the Dudley area:
What is Molinology?

Figure 2·7 *Record Card*

NAME AND ADDRESS OF MILL			COUNTY	REF. NO.
Nat. Grid reference or location	Industry	Dating	Parish/ Township	Date of Report
DESCRIPTION		WHEEL OR SAILS		
CONDITION				
Danger of demolition or damage				
Printed, manuscript or photographic records				
Reported by		Owner of Mill		
Return card to		Tenant of Mill		
S.P.A.B. Wind & Water-mill Section Water-mill Record Card				

MACHINERY DETAILS	
DRIVE SYSTEM	MILL MACHINERY
AUXILIARY MACHINERY	REMARKS etc.

Industrial archaeology

What sort of work have mills been used for in the past?

Look at the sketch of the working parts of a post-mill. You will see that this has a more complicated arrangement of wheels than Danzey Green. Explain:

a. how it works?
b. why the system is different?
c. the advantages of this system over the one used at Danzey Green.

Explain the differences between smock and tower-mills.

What were the advantages of the tower-mill over the post-mill?

Draw a diagram of a tower-mill and explain how it works.

What mistakes might poor millwrights make in building a tower-mill?

Explain the purposes of mill races and mill ponds?

From the map showing Heath Mill, can you say whether this was a good site on which to build a mill or not?

Why were there so many mills on Smestow Brook?

Look at the diagrams of waterwheels:

a. state whether the direction of each wheel shown was clockwise or anti-clockwise
b. state why the three types of wheel are necessary in your own area.

Write an explanation of how the two gearing systems shown work.

Why did the ancient manor of Sedgley have so many mills?

Why have the mills fallen into disrepair?

Imagine you were present at the collapse of Ruiton old mill. Tell the tale using the historical facts you know, and using the technical terms you have learnt.

Imagine you are a farmer living at Cotwallend some time before 1800. Explain your job, the landscape, why you use the mill and which mill you go to.

Some background source material

Types of primary source material

Background material from both secondary accounts and primary sources is essential to the study of industrial remains. Its provides important information about:

a. the existence and location of long forgotten or hidden remains
b. the dimensions, structure and appearance of derelict or destroyed buildings and remains
c. the working and function of obsolete or damaged machines
d. the lives and work of people associated with industrial remains.

Teachers may not find it easy to collect primary source material relating to specific industrial sites in their locality. Fortunately, many extracts from documents and maps relating to different types of sites have been published in books or archive units.

Details of some of these can be found in the Resources section.

1. Maps

The first edition 25 inch Ordnance Survey plan or 6 inch Ordnance Survey map of the area often reveals industrial remains which may not be obvious at first sight, e.g. a disused colliery railway, an old water-mill converted into a garage. Xerox copies of relevant sections of these maps can usually be obtained from the local reference library or record office.

The business records of companies, and the estate papers of mine and factory owners often contain maps and plans of proposed projects such as a canal or mill — see No. 8 overleaf.

2. Prints and photographs

These can be invaluable sources of information about the structure and appearance of derelict buildings such as old mills.

These are often to be found in the photographic and print collections of local history libraries, in old local history books or in histories of specific industries.

3. Trade directories and gazetteers

These were produced from the 1780s onwards and usually include a history and general description of the district and its industry as well as a list of trades and professions.

These may reveal the existence of an industry which has since vanished and so start a search for its visible remains.

Directories for each area published in the nineteenth and twentieth centuries, e.g. Baines', White's, Kelly's, can usually be found in the local history or reference libraries.

4. Travellers' descriptions of the area

These can provide useful descriptions of industrial sites or processes when they were still being used. Extracts may be found in the following accounts:

Daniel Defoe, *A Tour through the Whole Island of Great Britain*, 1722-6, (Penguin, 1971)
Viscount Torrington, *Diaries* — written in 1780s, C. F. Andrews (Ed.), 'Illustrated Library Reprints', (Methuen, 1970)
J. Aikin, *A description of the country for thirty to forty miles around Manchester*, 1795, (David & Charles reprint, 1968)
Copies of these and other examples may be in the local reference library either as separate volumes or amongst the volumes of the local record society.

5. Newspaper articles

Old newspapers often provide valuable information about local industries, e.g. advertisements listing goods and prices, stories about specific incidents in the history of a mill, canal or mine. Copies of old newspapers may be found in reference libraries.

6. Posters

These give useful information about canals, turnpikes and railways. They may be found amongst the estate papers of local landowners or industrialists — many of these have been deposited with local record offices, or amongst the business records of firms — see No. 8 below. Many have been published in local archive units.

7. Reminiscences of workers in the industry

If the site being studied was still in use within living memory pupils may be able to interview elderly people who worked there. Otherwise pupils may be able to use written accounts of working people connected with a type of site. Sometimes manuscript copies of such accounts, including photographs, are in local reference libraries.
Some autobiographies of working people have been published, e.g. John Burnett, *The Useful Toil*, see Resources section for full details.

8. Business records and estate papers

Business records about local canals, rivers, railways, roads, mills, etc. have often survived. They may be in the form of plans, accounts, letters, patents, title deeds, private Acts of Parliament, leases, etc.
Some date from the time when buildings were first planned to the time when operations or production ceased.

These archives are in a number of places, e.g. North of England Institute of Mining and Mechanical Engineers' Library, Neville Hall, Westgate Road, Newcastle-upon-Tyne 1.
British Railways Board Historical Records Office, 66 Portchester Road, London W.2.
University Libraries, e.g. Bristol University Library for the Brunel papers, Leeds University Library for the Gott Papers.
Solicitors' offices.
Local record offices.
Many industrialists were also landowners — especially the coal owners. Their estate papers often contain plans and letters about their business undertakings.

9. Parliamentary papers

Sections of the famous nineteenth century government reports referring to working conditions in local factories and mines can be seen in the local reference library.
For a list of reports teachers could look at:
Percy & Grace Ford, *A Select List of British Parliamentary Papers*, 1833-99, (Irish University Press, 1970)
William Raymond Powell, *Local History from Blue Books*, (Historical Association, 1962).

10. Local histories, technical histories and reports

These often contain primary and secondary source material on industry, power and transport. Technical histories and reports were sometimes produced by engineers of railways, mines, mills and canals.
They describe the technical problems involved in constructing a canal, sinking a mine or producing cotton. Some of these reports are in the business records of industrial companies. Others have been published in book form and may be available in local reference libraries, e.g.
J. B. Priestley, *Historical Account of the Navigable Rivers, Canals and Railways in Great Britain* 1831, (David and Charles, 1969)
Simon Shaw, *History of the Staffordshire Potteries* (1829), (David and Charles, 1970) or County History Reprints, (Educational Productions, 1970).

Some examples of primary source material

A selection of material appears on the pages which follow.

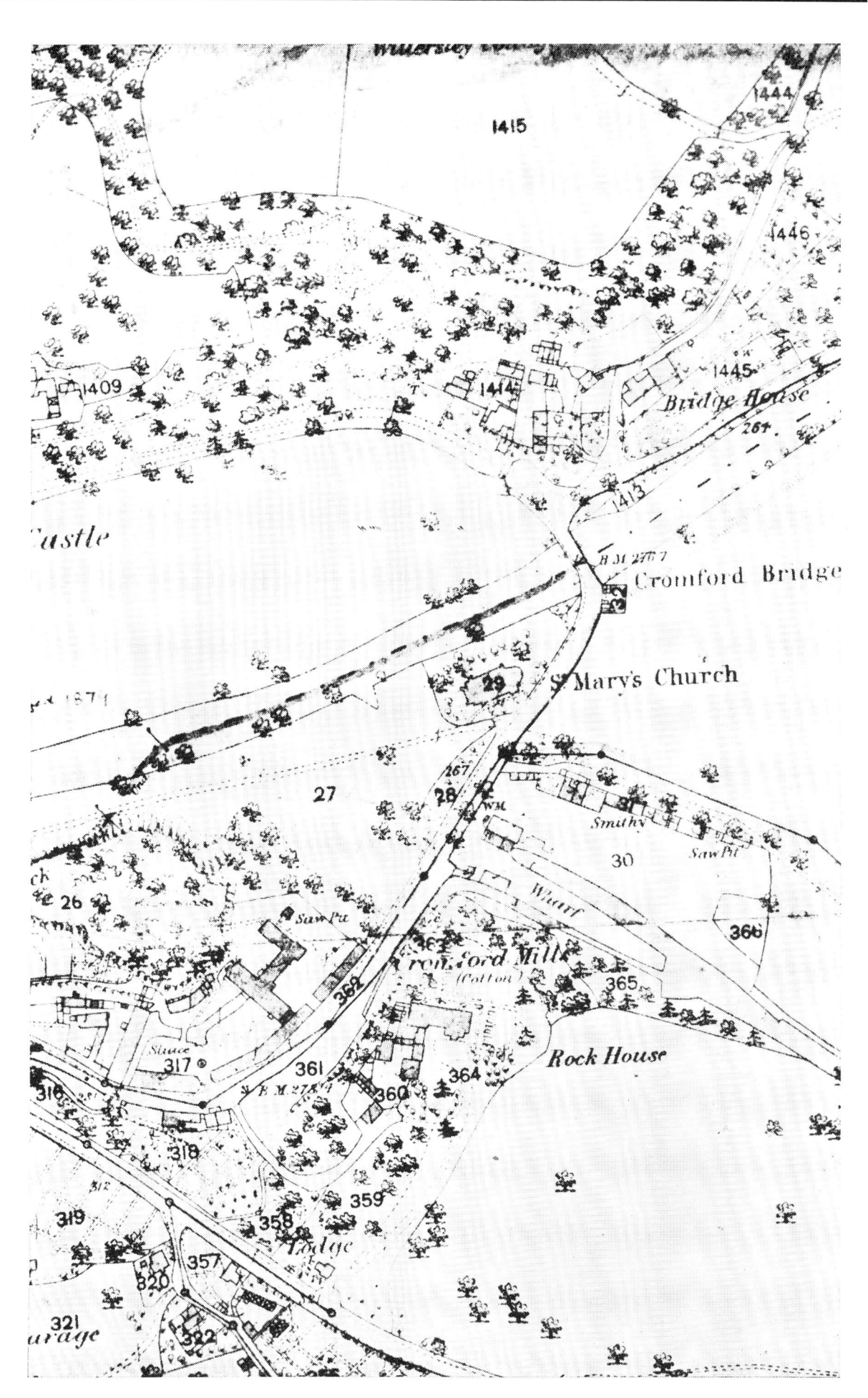

Industrial archaeology

Source 1·7 *A section of the 25 inch Ordnance Survey plan* (1880) *showing the Cromford Cotton Mills*

Industrial archaeology

Source 2·7 *Prints showing two processes involved in lead smelting in the sixteenth century*

Men tending furnaces

Breaking and washing ore
Robert T. Clough, *The Lead Smelting Mills of the Yorkshire Dales,* (private edition 1962)

Source 3·7 *An extract from F. White's "History and Gazetteer of Derbyshire 1850"*

> Cromford's colour works, lead mines, wharfs, canal and
> the railroads together with extensive smelting mills,
> hat manufactory and worsted mills at Lea not only give
> employment to the numerous and increasing population
> but renders the town of Cromford of commercial importance...
> Fairs were formerly held here, but are now discontinued...
> The large number of hands employed at the mills is not so
> large as previously in consequence of a considerable portion
> of the supply of water being diverted into another channel...

Industrial archaeology

Source 4·7 *Extracts from F. Aikin "A description of the country for thirty to forty miles around Manchester"* (1795) *pp. 533-5, relating to the pottery industry of Staffordshire*

To the preceding general account of the manufacture, we shall add a more particular description of the process used in manufacturing the earthen ware, which has been communicated to us by a person on the spot. A piece of the prepared mixture of clay and ground flint, dried and tempered to a proper consistence, is taken to be formed into any required shape and fashion, by a man who sits over a machine called a wheel, on the going round of which he continues forming the ware. This branch is called throwing and as water is required to prevent the clay sticking to the hand, it is necessary to place it for a short time in a warm situation. It then undergoes the operation of being turned, and made much smoother than it was before, by a person called a turner ... Dishes, plates, tureens, and many other articles are made from moulds of ground plaister, and when finished, the whole are placed carefully (being then in a much more brittle state than when fired) in saggars, which in shape and form pretty much resemble a lady's band-box without its cover, but much thicker, and are made from the marl or clay of this neighbourhood. The larger ovens or kilns are placed full of saggars so filled with ware, and after a fire which consumes from twelve to fifteen tons of coal, when the oven is become cool again, the saggars are taken out, and their contents removed, often exceeding in number 30,000 various pieces; but this depends upon the general sizes of the ware. In this state the ware is called biscuit, and the body of it has much the appearance of a new tobacco pipe, not having the least gloss upon it. It then is immersed or dipped into a fluid generally consisting of sixty pounds of white lead, ten pounds of ground flint, and twenty pounds of a stone from Cornwall burned and ground, all mixed together, and as much water put to it as reduces it to the thickness of cream, which it resembles. Each piece of ware being separately immersed or dipped into this fluid, so much of it adheres all over the piece, that when put into other saggars, and exposed to another operation of fire, performed in the glossing kiln or oven, the ware becomes finished by acquiring its glossy covering, which is given it by the vitrification of the above ingredients. Enamelled ware undergoes a third fire after its being painted, in order to bind the colour on.

A single piece of ware, such as a common enamelled teapot, a mug, jug, etc. passes through at least fourteen different hands before it is finished, viz:

    The slipmaker, who makes the clay;
    The temperer, or beater of the clay;
    The thrower, who forms the ware;

The ballmaker and carrier;
The attender upon the drying of it;
The turner who does away its roughness;
The spoutmaker;
The handler, who puts to the handle and spout;
The first, or biscuit fireman;
The person who immerses or dips it into the lead fluid;
The second, or gloss fireman;
The dresser, or sorter in the warehouse;
The enameller, or painter;
The muffle, or enamel fireman.

Several more are required to the completion of such piece of ware, but are in inferior capacities, such as turners of the wheel, turners of the lathe, etc., etc.

Source 5·7 *An extract from the "Derby Mercury" 15 November 1781 describing a mill fire in Nottingham*

... the fire raged with such fury, that in two hours after the spacious building was reduced to a mere shell. All the machines, wheels, spindles etc. employed for spinning and weaving and winding cotton were entirely consumed, and not a single article contained therein, the books excepted, could possibly be saved, not withstanding the exertions of many inhabitants, who used their utmost to preserve it and the adjacent house from inevitable destruction. From what cause the fire originated we are unable to tell.

Source 6·7 *An advertisement from the "Derby Mercury" relating to the Cromford Cotton Mills*

Cotton Mill, Cromford 10th Dec. 1771

WANTED immediately, two Journey men Clock-Makers, or others that understand Tooth and Pinion well; Also a Smith that can forge and file — Likewise two Wood Turners that have been accustomed to Wheel-making, Spole-turning, etc. Weavers residing at the Mill, may have good Work. There is Employment at the above Place, for Women, Children, etc. and good Wages.
N.B. A Quantity of Box Wood is wanted:
    Any Persons who the above may suit, will
    be treated with by Messrs. Arkwright and
    Co. at the Mill or Mr. Strutt, in Derby.

Industrial archaeology

Source 7·7 *Extract from the minutes of a board meeting at the Lagan Navigation Company (Northern Ireland Record Office document COM 1/1/1)*

At a Board held 16th November 1795.
Present Wm. Bristow. Ed Kingsmill, Stwt Banks, Waddel Cummingham, George Black
The following anonymous letter enclosed in a letter from Sir Chas Talbot being read and an answer to the same considered — viz.

Belfast, 15th September 1795

Sir
I wrote you on 22nd ulto to which I yet refer. Since that time I have visited the banks of the Canal. I am still the more convinced of the propriety of the recommended cutts to be carried thro, namely as they can be done for a few hundred pounds, I would proceed to give you the plan and exact expense according to my judgment were it not that you will see it necessary first to remove the following obstructions. I at present would stand alone in the business — the Commissioners seem to think that they should have been consulted before any improvement was recommended which I certainly would have done, had consultations or requisitions been admitted from any elsewhere. True it is that the Linen Drapers still continue to draw the water off the upper level improperly — some new sluices have lately been put into a penweir so low as leave only 11 inches of water on the level above — some of the gates being bad they have thrown in large quantities of earth behind the locks to prevent a loss of water — it is also believed that some have lowered the gegs from their original design, all that their mills may have a better supply of water in dry weather, *a time when Canals should not be robbed of their right* — These impositions and neglects have almost destroyed the great design you had in view and disappointed the merchants whose interes in this with Lord Donegall is mutual. What pity to see so much money as it were lost from use and the merited preference which this respectable town has obtained cut off from their friends in the counties of Derry and Tyrone — what goods are ordered from hence must go by land carriage. Bulky articles which would pay well to a Canal and advance the shipping interests here for the sake of conveyance, are taken from Newry, a place they otherwise would avoid — the merchants, the people who ply on Canal and the superintendent Mr. Graham have laid the above with many other grievances before the Commissioners — my report recommended to them by the Chamber of Commerce in the year '93 was treated in a manner which prevents my observations going before men whom I revere individually but not as Commissioners on the Lagan Navigation — Altho' you promised to remedy these inconveniences I do not expect you entirely to rely on what I suggest — have recourse to other men of judgment, who will speak and act *impartially*, with them I will act, and make every exertion in assisting you in the arduous task you have done so much to accomplish — Be assured that without your particular interference nothing can be done.

Industrial archaeology

Source 8·7 *Extracts from the minutes of a meeting about the buildings of the Pensnett Railway*

April 24, 1826. Proposed Railway to be made from Shut End to the Staffordshire and Worcestershire Canal to Greensforge in the parish of Kingswinford.

Terms and Conditions for the consideration of Messrs. John Bradley and Co. and subject to the approbation of Lord Dudley. Lord Dudley to make and maintain a railway from the Staffordshire and Worcestershire Canal near to Greensforge to certain lands belonging to John Cox near to the Church in Kingswinford for the conveyance of coal, limestone, ironstone and other materials.

The railway to be made in such direction as shall prove to be most practicable and convenient — to be formed and constructed in a suitable and approved manner and if required, adapted to the use of steam engines, to be employed in propelling the carriages to be used thereon.

Lord Dudley to keep and maintain such Railway in good repair and condition, also to make and maintain all necessary wharfs and loading places that may be required and upon any lands and premises belonging to him.

Messrs. John Bradley and Co. to be empowered to make use of such railway for the conveyance of coal, slack, coke, limestone, ironstone, iron and other materials at all times during the term of years from Lady Day last on the terms and conditions herein after mentioned viz:—

To pay to Lord Dudley a rate on tonnage of 4d. a ton per mile, and not less than 8d. a ton on the whole length for each and every ton of coal slack, coke, limestone, ironstone, iron and other materials that shall or may be taken and conveyed by them upon such railway . . .

from an unclassified manuscript in the Dudley Reference Library, reproduced in Angus Dunphy, *The Pensnett Railway*, (Dudley Teachers' Centre Resources Bank Item No. 3616)

Source 9·7 *Extract from the second report of the Children's Employment Commission 1843 describing the "Little Black Dens" of Sedgeley*

The nature of the occupation of the children and young persons in the parish of Sedgeley is almost entirely that of nail-making at the forge. Many of the forges (i.e. workshops) are at the back of the hovels in which the working classes reside . . . The best kind are little brick shops of about 15 feet long by 12 feet wide, in which seven or eight individuals constantly work together, with no ventilation except the door and two slits, or loop-holes, in the wall; but the great majority . . . are very much smaller, filthily dirty, and in looking in upon one of them when the fire is not lighted, it presents the appearance of a dilapidated coal-hole or little black den . . . In this dirty den there are commonly at work a man and his wife and daughter, with a boy and girl hired by the year. Sometimes there is an elder son with his sister, and two girls hired; sometimes the wife (the husband being a collier, too old to work, has taken to drinking, or is perhaps dead) carries on a forge with the aid of her children.

These little work-places have the forge placed in the centre generally, round which they each have barely standing room at an anvil; and in some instances there are two forges erected in one of these shops. There is scarcely ever room for anyone to pass round to his or her stand while others are at work, so that men and women, and boys and girls, are almost continually obliged to clamber over each other's bodies, or else step upon hot cinders to get over the forge, in order to reach the door.

The effluvia of these little work-dens, from the filthiness of the ground, from the half-ragged, half-naked unwashed persons at work, and from the hot smoke, ashes, water, and clouds of dust (besides the frequent smell of tobacco) are really dreadful . . .

Industrial archaeology

Source 10·7 *An extract from J. B. Priestley "Historical Accounts of the Navigable Rivers, Canals and Railways in Great Britain 1831", pp. 190-1*

The Cromford and High Peak Railway

It is in length thirty-three miles and seven furlongs, and it attains an elevation of 990 feet above the head level of the Cromford Canal, and 1271 feet above the level of the sea at low water, by means of six inclined planes ...

Mr. Josias Jessop was the engineer employed to lay out this railroad, and he estimated the cost (including £20,000 for stationary engines to work the inclined planes) at the sum of £155,079.16s.8d. The act for making it received the royal assent on the 2nd May 1825 ...

It was obtained by a company consisting of one hundred and sixteen persons, amongst who were the Dowager Viscountess Anson, the Honourable Edward Curzon, Sir Charles H. Colville, and Admiral Digby, who were incorporated by the name of "The Cromford and High Peak Railway Company," and empowered to raise, among themselves, the sum of £164,000, in sixteen hundred and forty shares, of £100 each, (which sum was subscribed before going to parliament,) and, if necessary, the further sum of £32,880, by mortgage of the undertaking.

TONNAGE RATES.

	d.
Dung, Compost, and Manure, Lime-stone, Free-stone, Paving-stone, and all other Stone, Mineral, and Metallic Ores, Pig Iron, Bricks, Tiles, Slate, Clay, and Sand	1 per Ton per Mile.
Coal, Coke, Lime, Bar and Plate Iron, and Iron Castings, Lead and other Metals, and Timber	1½ ditto
Corn, Malt, Flour, and Meal	2½ ditto
All other Goods, Wares, and Merchandize	3 ditto
All Articles (except Lime and Limestone) which do not pass the whole Length of Railway	6 per Ton, in addition
All Goods, Wares, and Merchandize, conveyed on any of the Inclined Planes	1½ per Ton, at each of them, in addition

Source 11·7 *Extract from a list of fines levied at Strutt's Mills at Belper*

Frequently looking thro' window.
Riotous behaviour in room.
Making noises in counting house.
Riding on each other's back.
Making disturbances on Gang way.
Dancing in Room
Going out of the room in which she works to abuse the hands in another room.
Neglecting his work to talk to people.
Making a noise when order'd not.
Quarreling.
Throwing bobbins at people.
Throwing a bobbin at F. Shipton.
Tellings lies.
Telling lies to Mr. Jedediah.
Striking T Ride on the nose.
Making T Ride's nose bleed on the hanks.
Throwing tea on Josh Bridworth.
Beating Wm. Smith Jr.
Striking T Hall with a brush.
Playing tricks with Wm Hall
Abusing G Haywood about her Daughters work.
Quarreling with the pickers & abusing Geo Haywood.
Quarreling in the room with Mr. Hodgkinson.
Using ill language.
Fighting.

R. S. Fitton & A. P. Wadsworth, *The Strutts and the Arkwrights* 1780-1830, (Manchester University Press, 1973) pp. 234-237

Course work for G.C.E. and C.S.E. assessment

Some history teachers may wish to devise Mode 3 C.S.E. and G.C.E. 'O' level syllabuses which include work on *History Around Us: Industrial archaeology*.

The following items of course work could be completed by pupils and submitted in a folder as part of their final assessment:

1. Descriptions of sites studied by fieldwork supported by relevant maps, plans, photographs, sketches, record cards, surveys.

2. Descriptions of sites studied by classroom. investigation, supported by sketches, maps and plans.

3. Work setting a site in its historical context and relating it to other sites:
e.g. an illustrated account explaining why a mill was built in a particular spot at a particular time, and comparing it with earlier and later mills.
e.g. an illustrated account explaining the route taken by a canal, its relationship with local industries, the communication system of the region — roads and other canals, and the reasons why it declined.

4. Work involving the imaginative reconstruction of:
either: life at a site at a particular time,
e.g. the work of miners in bell pits in the Forest of Dean during the nineteenth century,
e.g. working life in an iron foundry or cotton mill in the nineteeth century.
or: a specific incident in the history of a site,
e.g. a colliery accident,
e.g. the collapse of Ruiton old mill.
or: the connection between a historical personality or family and a site,
e.g. Abraham Darby and Coalbrookdale,
e.g. Richard Arkwright and Cromford,
e.g. The Earl of Dudley's mineral agent and the building of the Pensnett Railway,
e.g. The engineer of the Lagan Navigation.

Resources

Some of the books on this list are out of print. You should be able to obtain copies from your local library or from the Schools Library Loan Service.
Resources are listed by order of importance within each section.

David and Charles have a long list of books relating to regional and national industrial history and archaeology. Only a few have been listed below, interested teachers should send for a full catalogue.

Teachers' books

For books relating to industrial remains in your area, look in your local reference and lending libraries.
R. A. Buchanan, *Industrial Archaeology in Britain*, (Penguin, 1972)
Kenneth Hudson, *Industrial Archaeology*, (John Baker, 1966)
Kenneth Hudson, *Handbook for Industrial Archaeologists*, (John Baker, 1967)
Schools Council, Project Technology Handbooks, Book 10 *Industrial Archaeology for Schools*, (Heinemann Educational, 1973)
Schools Council, Project Technology Handbooks, Book 11 *Industrial Archaeology of Water-mills and Water power*, (Heinemann Educational, 1975)
Charles Hadfield, *British Canals: An Illustrated History*, (David & Charles, 1974)
Robert Sherlock, *Industrial Archaeology of Staffordshire*, (David & Charles, 1975)
R. A. Buchanan & Neil Cossons, *Industrial Archaeology of the Bristol Region*, (David & Charles, 1970)
A. C. Todd & P. Laws, *Industrial Archaeology of Cornwall*, (David & Charles, 1972)
Helen Harris, *Industrial Archaeology of Dartmoor*, (David & Charles, 1968)
Frank Nixon, *Industrial Archaeology of Derbyshire*, (David & Charles, 1969)
William Branch Johnson, *Industrial Archaeology of Hertfordshire*, (David & Charles, 1970)
Owen Ashmore, *Industrial Archaeology of Lancashire*, (David & Charles, 1969)
Frank Atkinson, *Industrial Archaeology of North East England*, Vols. 1 & 2, (David & Charles, 1974)
Helen Harris, *Industrial Archaeology of the Peak District*, (David & Charles, 1971)
John Butt, *Industrial Archaeology of Scotland*, (David & Charles, 1967)
Kenneth Hudson, *Industrial Archaeology of Southern England*, (David & Charles, 1968)
Frank Booker, *Industrial Archaeology of the Tamar Valley*, (David & Charles, 1971)
D. Morgan Rees, *Industrial Archaeology of Wales*, (David & Charles, 1975)
A.R. Griffin, *Coal Mining*, 'Industrial Archaeology Series', (Longman, 1971)
Anthony Bird, *Roads and Vehicles*, 'Industrial Archaeology Series', (Longman, 1969)
L. T. C. Rolt, *Navigable Waterways*, 'Industrial

Archaeology Series', (Longman, 1969)

W. English, *Textile Industry*, 'Industrial Archaeology Series', (Longman, 1969)

Geraint Jenkins, *The Craft Industries*, 'Industrial Archaeology Series', (Longman, 1972)

Reference books for teachers and pupils, dealing with visible remains

Brian Bracegirdle, *The Archaeology of the Industrial Revolution*, (Heinemann, 1973)

Geoffrey Booth, *Industrial Archaeology: The Midlands*, 'Regional Studies', (Wayland, 1974)

Brian Bracegirdle & Patricia Miles, *The Darbys and the Iron Bridge Gorge*, (David & Charles, 1974)

T. H. Hair, *Series of Views of the Collieries in the Counties of Northumberland and Durham*, 1884, (David & Charles, 1969)

D. Bremner, *Industries of Scotland* 1869, *Their Rise, Progress and Present Condition*, (David & Charles, 1969)

Barrie S. Trinder, *The Industrial Revolution in Shropshire*, (Phillimore, 1973)

John Reynolds, *Windmills and Watermills*, 'Excursions into Industrial Archaeology', (John Evelyn, 1970)

Frank Atkinson, *Industrial Archaeology: Top Ten Sites in North East England*, (Frank Graham, 1972)

A. F. Tait & Edwin Butterworth, *Views on the Manchester-Leeds Railway*, 1845, (Frank Graham reprints, 1972)

Peter Smith, *Waterways Heritage*, (Luton Museum & Art Gallery, 1972)

Ernest Straker, *Wealden Iron, A Monograph on the former Iron Works in the Counties of Sussex, Surrey and Kent*, (David & Charles, 1969)

Books for pupils, dealing with visible remains

Roy Christian, *Factories, Forges and Foundries, Industrial Buildings of Britain*, 'Local Search Series', (Routledge & Kegan Paul, 1974)

Rowland W. Purton, *Rivers and Canals*, 'Local Search Series', (Routledge & Kegan Paul, 1972)

Warren Farnworth, *Canals*, 'On Location Series', (Mills & Boon, 1974)

Warren Farnworth, *Railways*, 'On Location Series', (Mills & Boon, 1973)

Christine Vialls, *Cast Iron*, 'Industrial Archaeology Series', (A. & C. Black, 1974)

Christine Vialls, *Crossing the River*, 'Industrial Archaeology Series', (A. & C. Black, 1971)

Christine Vialls, *Windmills and Watermills*, 'Industrial Archaeology Series', (A. & C. Black, 1974)

Christine Vialls, *Roads*, 'Industrial Archaeology Series', (A. & C. Black, 1971)

C. J. Lines & L. H. Bolwell, *Crafts and Industries in the Past*, 'Discovering Your Environment Series', (Ginn, 1971)

John Norman Thatcher Vince, *Discovering Windmills*, 'Discovering Books Series', (Shire Publications, 1973)

F. G. Cockman, *Discovering Lost Railways*, 'Discovering Books Series', (Shire Publications, 1973)

G. J. Howister Short, *Discovering Wrought Iron*, 'Discovering Books Series', (Shire Publications, 1970)

Thomas John Taylor, *Archaeology of the Coal Trade*, (Frank Graham, 1971)

Robert Charles Bell & M. Gill, *Potteries on Tyneside*, (Frank Graham, 1973)

Reference books for pupils

These provide information and primary source material about the people connected with industrial remains.

E. Royston Pike, *Human Documents of the Industrial Revolution in Britain*, (Allen & Unwin, 1966)

Frank E. Huggett, *A Day in the Life of a Victorian Factory Worker*, (Allen & Unwin, 1972)

R. S. Fitton and A. P. Wadsworth, *The Strutts and the Arkwrights*, 1758–1830, (Manchester University Press, 1973)

John Burnett, *The Useful Toil: Autobiographies of Working People from the* 1820s *to the* 1920s, (Allen Lane, 1974)

M. O. Greenwood, *Roads and Canals in the Eighteenth Century*, 'Then and There Series', (Longman, 1953)

Karen McKechnie, *A Border Woollen Town in the Industrial Revolution*, 'Then and There Series', (Longman, 1968)

Malcolm I. Thomis, *The Luddites: Machine Breaking in Nottinghamshire*, (David & Charles, 1975)

A. R. B. Haldane, *New Ways through the Glens, Highland Road, Bridge and Canal Makers of the Early Nineteenth Century*, (David & Charles, 1973)

Helen & Baron Frederick Duckham, *Great Pit Disasters, Great Britain*, 1700 *to the Present Day*, (David & Charles, 1973)

A. K. Hamilton Jenkin, *Cornish Miner, An Account of his Life Above and Underground from Early Times*, (David & Charles, 1972)

Stanley D. Chapman, *Early Factory Masters, Transition to the Factory System in the Midlands Textile Industry*, 'Industrial History Series', (David & Charles, 1967)

E. G. Power, *A Textile Community in the Industrial Revolution*, 'Then and There Series', (Longman, 1969)
John Addy, *A Coal and Iron Community in the Industrial Revolution*, 'Then and There Series', (Longman, 1970)
Stuart M. Archer, *Josiah Wedgwood and the Potteries*, (Longman, 1974)
John Addy & E. G. Power, *The Industrial Revolution*, 'Then and There Series' source book, (Longman, 1976)
John Pudney, *Brunel and his World*, 'Pictorial Biography Series', (Thames & Hudson, 1974)
R. L. A. Tames, *Isambard Kingdom Brunel, An Illustrated Life*, 'Lifelines Series', (Shire Publications, 1972)
Harold Bode, *James Brindley, An Illustrated Life*, 'Lifelines Series', (Shire Publications, 1973)
R. L. A. Tames, *Josiah Wedgwood, An Illustrated Life*, 'Lifelines Series', (Shire Publications, 1972)
Eric Forster, *No. 6 Death Pit: Story of the West Stanley Pit explosion*, (Frank Graham, 1970)
Edward Smith, *No. 8 A Pitman's Notebook, Diary of the Houghton Colliery Viewer*, 1749-51, T. Robertson (Ed.), (Frank Graham, 1970)
Eric Forster, *No. 9 The Keelmen*, (Frank Graham, 1971)
B. Shurlock, *No. 23 Industrial Pioneers of Tyneside*, (Frank Graham, 1972)
Richard Fynes, *The Miners of Northumberland and Durham*, 1923, (Educational Productions reprint, 1971)

Museum publications for pupils

Useful guide books, posters, information sheets, etc., can be obtained from the following:
Abbeydale Industrial Hamlet, Abbeydale Road South, Sheffield, S7 2QW
Higher Mill Museum, Helmshore, Lancashire
Ironbridge Gorge Museum Trust, Ironbridge, Telford, Salop, TF8 7RE
Mr. A. J. Oldham, Custodian, Nether Alderley Mill, 53 Stoneacre Road, Manchester, M22 6BW
Waterways Museum, Stoke Bruerne, Near Towcester, Northamptonshire
Weald and Downland Open Air Museum, Chichester, Sussex

Slides

Slides of different industrial sites and remains are available from:
Ironbridge Gorge Museum Trust, Ironbridge, Telford, Salop, TF8 7RE
Avoncroft Museum of Building, Stoke Prior, Bromsgrove, Hereford and Worcester
Ulster Folk and Transport Museum, Cultra Manor, Hollywood, BT18 0EU, Co. Down
Abbeydale Industrial Hamlet, Abbeydale Road South, Sheffield, S7 2QW
The Old Industries 1870-1970, Nicholas Hunter Slides — available from Nicholas Hunter filmstrips, see address list in Introduction
The Slide Centre Ltd., sets about:
Windmills
River and Canal Transport
Beamish North of England Open Air Museum
Industrial Archaeology
Weald and Downland Open Air Museum

Filmstrips

Windmills, Mss of the fourteenth to seventeenth centuries, colour, Bodleian Library, 1964
The Industrial Revolution, 'Part 1 Iron Coal and Steam', 'Part 2 Transport', 'Part 3 Textiles', colour, Hugh Baddeley Productions
Introduction to the Industrial Revolution 1740-1840, 'Revolution in Textiles', 'Coal, Metal and Steam', 'Roads, Rivers and Canals', 'Railways, Ships and Trade', (background information to industrial archaeology), black and white, Longman/Common Ground
The Railways; Roads, Bridges and Canals; Iron and Coal, 1770-1870; How People Worked; How People Travelled;
(background information to the industrial revolution), colour, Nicholas Hunter Filmstrips
The Industrial Revolution, 'Then and There Series', Longman

Filmstrips with recorded tape commentaries

Kay, Hargreaves, Arkwright and Crompton, The Slide Centre Ltd.
Darby, Coalbrookdale and Cort, The Slide Centre Ltd.
Isambard Kingdom Brunel: Engineer Extraordinary, The Slide Centre Ltd.
Wind and Water Power, The Slide Centre Ltd.
Canal Transport History, The Slide Centre Ltd.
The Weald and Downland Open Air Museum also has an audio visual kit for schools

Films

The Industrial Revolution — includes scenes at Higher Hill Museum, Ironbridge Gorge Museum, Welsh Folk Museum, 16 mm, colour, 23 mins. Hugh Baddeley Productions
The Industrial Revolution in England, 16 mm, colour, 25 mins. Encyclopaedia Britannica — distributed by Rank

Industrial archaeology

History simulation games

David Birt & Jon Nichol, *Ironmaster*, based on the Darby family at Coalbrookdale, Longmar Resources Unit

B. Barker & R. Boden, *Canals*, Longman Resources Unit

B. Barker & R. Boden, *Railway Mania*, Longman Resources Unit

A derelict barge on the Peak Forest Canal

8 THE MAKING OF THE RURAL LANDSCAPE

Some objectives and outcomes

We hope that by the time pupils finish their study of the rural landscape they will:

1. have sufficient background knowledge to recognise the visible evidence of the various changes made by man in the landscape during the past.

2. have had practice at observing, recording, and interpreting the man-made features of landscapes created in:
Prehistoric times
Roman times
the early Middle Ages 400–1000 A.D.
the later Middle Ages 1000–1500 A.D.
Tudor and Stuart times
eighteenth and nineteenth centuries
twentieth century.

3. have had practice at combining the study of visible evidence and background information to reconstruct the lives and understand the people who changed the landscape in the past.

4. have the knowledge, skills and enthusiasm to explore the man-made landscape and other aspects of their historical environment beyond school.

An approach

Teachers will wish to organise the course to suit the abilities of their pupils and to take account of the visible remains of man's imprint on the landscape in their own area. We hope that the following ideas may prove useful.

1. Introductory lessons

These could make pupils think about the changes made by people in the past on the landscape of their own area. Fieldwork exercises would be combined with the examination and interpretation of 6 inch and 25 inch Ordnance Survey maps. Pupils could go to a suitable vantage point and list:

a. all the features of the landscape which have been made or altered by man in their locality, e.g. roads, villages, railways, field boundaries, coal heaps, spinneys, quarries, forest clearances, drainage, ditches, etc.

b. all the features of the landscapes which have been made or altered by natural forces such as the wind, rock formations, water, etc.

The pupils would then try to work out what the landscape looked like before man made his mark.

In the follow up lesson the teacher and pupils could compare notes. After studying the $2\frac{1}{2}$ inch or 6 inch map of the area, pupils could add to their lists any man-made features which they may have missed, e.g. forest clearance, mill ponds, etc.

Using the same maps as a base, pupils could make their own sketch map or field sketch of the area before man made his imprint.

Finally, the teacher could help the class to draw conclusions from their work by discussing the questions:
Has man or nature made more impression on the landscape?
How many of the man-made landscape features you have noted are:
100 years old?
1000 years old?
2000 years old?
3000 years old?

Pupils may be surprised to see how many of the features of their landscape — lanes, roads, fields, stone walls, drainage channels, etc. are nearly 1000 years old. This will serve to introduce to them W. G. Hoskins' phrase which is a starting point for all landscape studies — "everything is older than we think".

The making of the rural landscape

Ancient field system; Grassington, North Yorkshire

Early settlement around a pond; Ashmore, Dorset

Car Dyke; Potterhanworth, Lincolnshire

Peddars Way, Norfolk; a prehistoric trackway used as a droving road in the 18th century

A deserted mediaeval village; Wharram Percy, North Yorkshire

The making of the rural landscape

A landscaped park; Blenheim Palace, Oxfordshire

Ridge and furrow patterns; Napton, Warwickshire

Church and bridges in the landscape; Skirlaws bridge, Yarm, Cleveland

The making of the rural landscape

An abandoned railway line and station on a branch line in Scotland

Ribbon development; Wistaston, Cheshire

The making of the rural landscape

Reafforestation at Ffawydd, Wales

Quarrying at Ingleton, North Yorkshire

2. Studies in the making of the rural landscape

These could explain man's impact on the landscape at different stages in time. The course could be divided into sections based on particular chronological periods and a sample of the visible remains of each period selected for study. Each section would have its own background lessons, site studies based on maps and fieldwork, and follow up work. The outline scheme below shows one way of planning such a course.

a. Prehistoric man and the landscape

A study of some of the following landscape features either through fieldwork or using slides, diagrams and photographs:
causeway camps, e.g. Windmill Hill, East Sussex
hut circles and corn plots with lynchets, e.g. Dartmoor, Bodmin Moor, Grassington and Malham in North Yorkshire
ridgeways, e.g. Icknield Way, Berkshire, the Ridgeway, Oxfordshire
hill forts, e.g. Maiden Castle
dykes
chamber tombs, long barrows, round barrows, stone circles and standing stones, e.g. Stonehenge, Avebury
deafforestation of some upland areas for farming
Celtic fields, farms and villages, e.g. Chysauster, Cornwall.

b. The Romans and the landscape

Some of the following features could be studied:
Roman roads
boundaries of Roman villas
marching camps
drainage channels, e.g. Car dyke in the fens, Hadrian's wall
signs of industry, e.g. lead mining in the Mendips.

c. The landscape of settlement: Anglo-Saxons, Danes and Vikings, 400-1000 A.D.

Some of the following features could be studied:
position and shape of most of our villages,
e.g. green villages, street villages, fragmented villages
ridge and furrow pattern of open field farming areas
boundary walls and hedges of pastoral farming areas
many hamlets on poor land
some drainage ditches and dykes.

d. The landscape of colonisation: The Normans and English 1000-1500 A.D.

Some of the following features could be studied:
ridge and furrow patterns for open field farming,
hedges and walls for pastoral farming
hunting and game parks,
e.g. Woodstock and the New Forest
hamlets in cleared forest land
reclamation of marsh and fen land: dykes, drainage channels,
e.g. the Wash area
deserted villages,
e.g. Wharram Percy, North Yorkshire
fishing villages on the coast,
e.g. Staithes, North Yorkshire
adulterine castles
moated homesteads
monasteries: their drainage schemes,
e.g. the Somerset levels
their sheepruns and limestone walls,
e.g. Malham in North Yorkshire
droving roads
stone bridges
towns,
e.g. Kings Woodstock, Plymouth, Stratford, Salisbury, Bideford, Richmond in North Yorkshire
signs of early industry: iron workings, mill ponds, flashes, windmills and water-mills.

e. Farmers and landowners in the landscape 1500-1750

Some of the following features could be studied:
early field enclosure for pastoral farming
landed estates — their boundary features and extent
country houses and landscaped parks
resited villages,
e.g. Milton Abbas, Dorset
stone and brick houses in the landscape
quarries
the landscape of the domestic system — weavers' houses scattered up the hillside each with their own piece of land.

f. The landscape of change: farmers, landowners and industrialists 1750-1900

Some of the following features could be studied:
smaller square enclosed fields
hedges of hawthorn and quickset interspersed with ash trees
game cover and fox spinneys
heath lands of East Anglia turned to arable land
farmhouses out in the fields
new straighter roads sometimes 40 feet wide,

joining villages
factories and mills in isolated river valleys
long terraces of workers' cottages in rural areas
new mill towns on the coal field
spoil heaps
turnpike roads and toll keepers' cottages
canals: their construction and decay
railways and their tunnels, viaducts, embankments and stations.

g. The twentieth century and the landscape

Some of the following features could be studied:
ribbon development
conurbations
new towns
motorways and ringroads
disused railways, stations, viaducts, tunnels and embankments
reopened canals
larger fields and grubbed up hedges
airfields and airports
reafforestation of many upland and highland areas with non-native species especially pine, larch, etc.
oil refineries on the coast
national parks
limestone quarries
the flooding of valleys to make reservoirs.

3. Concluding lessons

These could help pupils draw conclusions about the changing face of the landscape in the past, present and future. The following questions could be discussed:
During which period in the past did man make most impact on the landscape of your area? Why?
During which period in the past did man make comparatively little impact on the landscape in your area? Why?
What man-made changes do you foresee taking place in the landscape of the future:
a. in your area?
b. in other parts of the country?

Studying the landscape: some questions and activities

The number, length and frequency of visits will vary from school to school as will the form and amount of help teachers give to pupils during classroom studies or fieldwork. The approach to each section of the course could be as follows:

1. Background lessons

Using film strips, slides, maps, plans and books, pupils could find out background information about:
a. the needs, skills and technology of people in the period being studied
b. the way in which these were reflected in their way of life, e.g. the way people obtained their food, their homes, religion, methods of trade and travel, methods of warfare, etc.

Teacher and pupils could discuss the following questions:
What traces of this way of life may be left in the landscape and why?
What traces of this way of life have disappeared and why?

Pupils could then examine slides, diagrams or photographs of the different visible remains left by these people in different areas of the country.

Finally, they could prepare their own 'clue sheets' for future reference. These would contain brief notes about the people and their way of life together with sketches and plans of their visible traces in the landscape.

2. Site work and visits in the locality

Pupils could search their own locality for traces of these people and their way of life, beginning with modern maps of the area, $2\frac{1}{2}$ inch and 6 inch Ordnance Survey maps and then looking at historical maps such as the Ordnance Survey map of Iron Age Britain.
After locating possible sites, visits can be made to survey and record the remains using notes and photographs or drawings.

3. Follow up work

Pupils could think about the question 'why have so many/so few/ no visible remains of these people survived in the landscape of our area?'
Then, they could make annotated sketch maps marking and explaining the visible evidence remaining in the landscape.
If the landscape of the locality appears to be dominated by one particular feature created at a certain period in the past, e.g. in Somerset and the fenlands this may be mediaeval drainage ditches, in Dorset this may be prehistoric hill forts, then pupils could place this feature in its historical context and relate it to other sites.
This involves an explanation of how and why the feature developed and how it was made. It

could include some information about the people who created it. An annotated map showing and explaining the location of other similar sites in different parts of the country could also be prepared.

Another important man-made feature of the local landscape may be chosen for an imaginative reconstruction. In an area where there are many country houses and parks some pupils could study the work of a famous landscape designer, e.g. Capability Brown.

If many traces of the mediaeval open field system still survive, life in a mediaeval farming community may be studied. A prominent hill fort may be associated with some historical incident, e.g. the Roman attack on Maiden Castle, Dorset — see Chapter 2 for details.

Some background source material

Types of background source material

In order to understand the purpose and significance of many of the visible remains left by man in the landscape, pupils should look at background information from both primary and secondary sources.

The search for background primary source material explaining local landscape features dating from mediaeval times, e.g. estate boundaries, deserted villages and forest parks, could take time. It requires expertise in palaeography and mediaeval latin. Such a specialist subject cannot adequately be discussed within the confines of this book.

Teachers who wish to pursue this further should read W. G. Hoskins, *Fieldwork in Local History*. Chapter 3 explains how to recognise and interpret various surviving features of the mediaeval landscape — parks and forests, moated homesteads, deserted villages, by combining fieldwork with the study of the documents. It includes a list of various kinds of documents and describes their uses in detail, e.g. the Calendars of Miscellaneous Inquisitions, Calendars of Inquisitions Post Mortems, Hundred Rolls, tax assessments, land charters. For an example of a land charter — see Source 1·8.

While teachers are assembling their resource bank of local primary source material they may have to rely on secondary accounts which describe and explain landscape changes. Details of these can be found in the Resources section at the end of this chapter.

Some different types of primary source material which may help to explain man-made changes to the landscape in your area are listed below:

1. Maps

Maps can be invaluable aids for locating and explaining man-made features of the landscape

Ordnance Survey maps
The $2\frac{1}{2}$ inch maps are useful for locating obvious features such as hill forts, forests, tumuli, drove roads, drainage ditches, etc. The scale is small enough to enable any interrelationship between landscape features to be seen, e.g. a chain of hill forts along a valley or a number of interconnecting drove roads.

The 6 inch and 25 inch Ordnance Survey maps are more useful for detailed local investigation. The first edition of these maps — 1840s onwards according to scale and area, may provide useful information about landscape features which have been created in the last 200 years but whose function may no longer be obvious, e.g. earthworks which show where there was once a coal mine or mill pond.

Xerox copies of relevant sections of these maps can usually be obtained from local reference libraries or from record offices. The kind of information to be gained from these maps can be seen by comparing the maps in Chapter 9, Sources 1·9, 2·9, 3·9 and 4·9.

Enclosure maps and awards
These may explain the location of roads and field boundaries and the size and shape of fields. In some areas, the old ridge and furrow marks of the open field system may still survive.
By plotting these marks on a map and consulting the enclosure map, the location and extent of the old open fields can be discovered. Copies of enclosure maps and awards are usually to be found in local record offices.

Tithe maps
Produced for parishes at the time of the 1836 Tithe Commutation Act, they provide a picture of the landscape around 1840 — before many of the great changes which took place during the Victorian era. They show every parcel of land, the size of estates, routes of canals, traces of old earthworks, mediaeval cultivation, names of woods, lanes and commons.
There are three copies of each map: one in the Public Record Office, one in the diocesan registry and one in the parish chest. At least one of the last two copies mentioned above is usually held in the local record office.

2. Place and field names

These sometimes provide information about the origins of particular man-made landscape features such as enclosure walls, clearings, farmsteads. For field and place name dictionaries see the Resources section.

3. Extracts from Roman writers

Caesar, Tacitus and Suetonius have left us some information about Iron Age hill forts and the farming practices of the ancient Britons. For references from the works of these writers see sections on background source material in Chapters 1 and 2.

4. Archaeological reports

The evidence discovered by archaeologists during their excavations can give us invaluable background information about man-made features of the landscape in ancient and mediaeval times, e.g. causeway camps, hill forts, tumuli, deserted villages and other earthworks.

Reports of excavations including maps and plans are usually published in the local archaeological journals. Copies of these can be found in local reference libraries. The text of the reports may be difficult for some pupils, so teachers may need to adapt sections. Where important or large scale excavations have taken place, books and guidebooks are often produced which interpret archaeological evidence for the layman.

For guide books about Prehistoric and Roman remains, castles, churches and industrial sites see the relevant Resources sections.

5. Estate maps, plans and papers

These show the property of a landowner who employed a surveyor to plot the extent of his estate and location of its important features. They were made from the sixteenth century onwards and may show and explain features of the landscape created by the local landowner such as field boundaries, fox spinneys, plantations, roads, mining spoil heaps.

Family papers of landowners may contain documents giving background information about when and why these features were created, e.g. correspondence, accounts, notices of sale.

The estate papers of local families may be deposited in the local record office, if not, the archivist may be able to suggest where relevant papers can be found.

A book which provides helpful suggestions about the use of estate maps is: M. W. Beresford, *History on the Ground*.

6. Travellers' descriptions

These may describe, explain or comment on various features of the man-made landscape at different times, e.g. enclosure boundaries, drove roads, the effects of local industry. Useful references to your locality may be found in the following books:

William Cobbett, *Rural Rides*, (Penguin, 1967), describes the English countryside in the nineteenth century

Daniel Defoe, *A Tour through the Whole Island of Great Britain*, (1722), (Penguin, 1971)

Celia Fiennes, *The Journeys of Celia Fiennes (1685-1703)*, C. Morris (Ed.), (Cresset Press, 1947), describes many country houses and parks

Arthur Young, *A six weeks' tour through the Southern Counties of England and Wales* (1768), *A six months' tour through the North of England* (1771). Xerox copies of relevant pages may be obtained from old editions in the local reference library

J. Aikin, *A description of the country from thirty to forty miles around Manchester*, 1795, (David & Charles reprint, 1968)

William Harrison, *The description of England* (in the time of Elizabeth 1), George Edelen (Ed.), (for the Folger Shakespeare Library, Cornell University Press, 1968)

7. Prints and photographs

These may give background information about the construction of such man-made landscape features as railways and canals. Books of prints showing the construction of two railways were produced in the 1840s:

Edwin Butterworth, *Views on the Manchester and Leeds Railway*, 1845

A. F. Tait, *Views on the London and North Western Railway*, 1848

For details of these and other similar books see the Resources section at the end of Chapter 7.

8. Newspapers

Articles and photographs in past and recent newspapers may give background information about man-made changes in the landscape. A local newspaper may have reported the sinking of an old mine or the building of a canal or railway no longer in use. Newspapers can also reveal disputes over controversial schemes which have affected the landscape such as quarrying, reafforestation schemes, the building of dams and reservoirs, etc.

9. Reminiscences of people in the locality

If a feature of the landscape has been created in the last two hundred years — perhaps connected with a local industry, an estate, or changes in farming, elderly local inhabitants may be able to tell pupils about it.

Some of these reminiscences may have been recorded in manuscript form and deposited in local reference libraries.

Some examples of primary source material

These give background information about visible remains. A selection of material appears on the pages which follow.

Source 1·8 *A tenth century land grant (926 A.D.) describing the ancient boundaries of an estate*

> Therefore I, Athelstan, king of the Anglo Saxons, adorned and elevated with no small dignity, prompted by desire from on high, will grant to my faithful thegn Ealdred the land of five hides which is called Chalgrave and Tebworth, which he bought with sufficient money of his own, namely ten pounds of gold and silver, from the pagans by the order of King Edward and also of Ealdorman Ethelred along with the other ealdormen and thegns; conceding with it the freedom of hereditary right, to have and possess as long as he lives, and to give after his death to whatever heirs, acceptable to himself, he shall wish.
>
> These are the boundaries of the aforesaid land: Where the dyke runs into Watling Street, along Watling Street to the ford, then along the brook to the other ford, then from that ford up to the spring, and thence into the valley, thence from the valley to the dyke, from the dyke to the second dyke, then from that dyke to the brook, then from the brook to Kimberwell, then along the dyke to Eastcote, then thence to the old brook, up from the old brook parallel with the little stream, then straight up to the highway, along the highway to the dyke, along the dyke to Watling Street.
>
> And the donation to the aforesaid land is to be free from every secular burden except military service and the construction of bridges and fortresses, in return for an adequate sum of money which I have received from him, i.e. 150 mancuses of pure gold.

Dorothy Whitelock (Ed.), *English Historical Documents*, VOL. I, (Eyre and Spottiswoode, 1955), pp. 503-4

The making of the rural landscape

Source 2·8 *Extracts from an estate survey carried out for the Duchy of Lancaster in Pontefract, Yorkshire, in June* 1588

This survey describes Pontefract Park — its extent and the use made of it in 1588. In Norman times it had been surrounded by a foss and pale and used as a deer park by the De Lacy family.

1. The said park is distant from Pontefract Castle half a quarter of a mile, but how long the same hath been a park we cannot tell, but so far as we have heard said, it was some time called Pontefract Moor.
2. The whole circuit of the pales include 700 acres, whereof we think there is none may be employed for meadow, 100 acres for arable ground, and all the rest for pasture.
3. We say that every of the 100 acres of arable land, and every acre of pasture, is worth by the year 12d.
4. There is in the pales of the said park, 1370 timber trees whereof we think 400 of the best is worth 10s. a piece; other 400 of the next sort worth 6s. 8d. a piece, and the rest 5s. a piece. In fuel trees 1760, whereof 500 of the best are worth to be sold at 6s. 8d. a piece; of the second sort other 500 at 5s. a piece, and the rest 3s. 4d. a piece. Also 400 saplings are worth 16d. a piece.
5. There are no manner of mines to our knowledge.
7. There was in the said park in anno primo of the queen majesty's reign 300 deer, and at the present 595, viewed by William Mallet, John Tindall and Robert Hippon, keepers there and others.
8. We find that George, Lord Talbot, hath the said park by indenture, under the seal of the Duchy of Lancaster, paying thereof by year £4. 3s. 4d.; and further, that the town and inhabitants of Pontefract and Tanshelf hath, by custom, common in the said park, with their horses and kine yearly, time out of man's mind, from the feast of St. Ellen unto the feast of St. Michael, and so hath at this present, paying yearly therefor to the herbager of the said park, for every cow 12d., and for every horse or mare 2s. for the whole jist, and for a cow if she lie in the park nightly 16d., for a swine in pannage-time 4d.; and further, the queen's majestie's tenants or copyholders of Carleton, Hardwicke and Tanshelf have common in a close called Carleton Close in the said park, with their draught oxen yearly from the said feast of St. Ellen unto the feast of St. Michael, paying yearly therefor, for every beast 4d.
9. There is builded in the said park three lodges or houses, whereof two are in good reparation, and the third partly in decay ... also there is a barn builded in the said park to lye hay in that is gotten for the deer, the reparation whereof is at the queen's charges.
11. The same is a princely park, and meet before another to be preserved.

L. Padgett, *Chronicles of Old Pontefract*, (Oswald Holmes at The Advertiser Office, Pontefract, (1905), pp. 139–141

The making of the rural landscape

Source 3·8 *Extracts from the accounts of the Du Cane family of Braxted Park, Essex*

This extract makes it clear that many of the roads around Braxted Park must have been used as droving roads, perhaps some were even created for this purpose. It also tells us about the type of animals using the roads.

Sept. 9 1761. Expenses attending Gardin Park etc. paid for 10 Welch Calves bought for me by Mr. Griggs at Harlow Bush Fair @ 35s. each — pd. Toll, driving etc. 6s. 3d . . .
Oct. 9. Expenses attending Gardin Park etc. pd. for 5 Welch Calves bought at Brentwood Fair @ 25s. per calf £6. 5. expenses 5s. 8d . . .
Oct. 28. 1800. Expenses of Park etc. paid for 16 High and Scotch Runts bought at Brantree Fair — £72. 5. 0 . . .
Nov. 12. 1803. To cash pd. A. Blackbone for 12 Scotch Runts @ £5 — £60. To do. Toll at the fair, his exps. driving, keep etc. £1. 3. 2 . . .
Oct. 7. 1805. Cost and expenses for 20 Welsh Cattle. 10 @ £48. 6. 6. 10 @ £50. 0. 0 . . .
Oct. 6. 1806. Cost of 20 Scotch runts. £115. 10. 0.
Oct. 20. Cost of 10 Scotch runts, Colchester £62. 10. 0 . . .
Sir John Griffin paid Thomas Richardson £2 for the driving of 8 bullocks from Audley End for sale at Smithfield the proceeds from the sale of these 8 'Scots' amounted to £56.

Essex Record Office: D/DDC A21, f.20, A23 f.9, A28 f.79, K. J. Bonser, *The Drovers*, (Macmillan, 1970) p. 85

Source 4·8 *Arthur Young's description of the area around Matlock in Derbyshire in* 1771

This extract shows how enclosure and new farming techniques had changed the landscape in this area.

I was agreeably surprised to find the country from Derby to Matlock in general enclosed and cultivated. Derbyshire being generally reported as waste a county as any in England, I was led to expect large tracts of uncultivated country in every quarter of it. In the southern part of it are some unenclosed commons, but they bear no proportion to cultivated land. Between Matlock and Chatsworth I went through a country wholly enclosed. From Chatsworth to Tideswell the country is nine tenths of it enclosed and cultivated. Around Tideswell as great improvements have been carried on as any in England. All this country was a black ling but a few years ago, and common land.

Arthur Young, *A six months' tour through the North of England* (1771)

The making of the rural landscape

Source 5·8 *William Harrison's description of the way in which woodland and trees were being affected by man in Elizabethan times*

Ash cometh up everywhere of itself and with every kind of wood. And as we have very great plenty and no less use of these in our husbandry, so are we not without the plane, the yew, the sorfe, the chestnut, the lime, the black cherry, and suchlike. And although that we enjoy them not in so great plenty now in most places as in times past, or the other [trees] afore remembered, yet have we sufficient of them all for our necessary turns and uses, especially of yew, as may be seen betwixt Rotherham and Sheffield, and some steads of Kent also, as I have been informed.

The fir, frankincense, and pine we do not altogether want, especially the fir, whereof we have some store in Chatley Moor in Derbyshire, Shropshire, Amounderness, and a moss near Manchester, not far from Leicester's house, although that in time past not only all Lancashire but a great part of the coast between Chester and the Solve [Solway] were well stored. As for the frankincense and pine, they have been planted only in colleges and cloisters by the clergy and religious heretofore. Wherefore (in mine opinion) we may rather say that we want them altogether, for except they grew naturally and not by force, I see no cause why they should be accounted for parcel of our commodities. We have also the asp whereof our fletchers make their arrows. The several kinds of poplars of our turners have great use for bowls, trays, troughs, dishes etc. Also the alder, whose bark is not unprofitable to dye black withal and therefore much used by our country wives in coloring their knit hosen.

I might here taken occasion to speak of the great sales yearly made of wood, whereby an infinite quantity hath been destroyed without these few years, but I give over to travail in this behalf. Howbeit, thus much I dare affirm, that if woods go so fast to decay in the next hundred year of grace as they have done and are like to do in this, sometimes for increase of sheepwalks and some maintenance of prodigality and pomp (for I have known a well-burnished gentleman that hath borne threescore at once in one pair of galligaskins to show his strength and bravery), it is to be feared that the fenny bote, such as broom, turf, gale, heath, furze, brakes, whins, ling, dies, hassocks, flags, straw, sedge, reed, rush, and also sea coal will be good merchandise even in the city of London, whereunto some of them even now have gotten ready passage and taken up their inns in the greater merchants' parlors. A man would think that our laws were able enough to make sufficient provisions for the redress of this error and enormity likely to ensue. But such is the nature of our countrymen that, as many laws are made, so they will keep none; or, if they be urged to make answer, they will rather seek some crooken construction of them to the increase of their private gain than yield themselves to be guided by the same for a common wealth and profit to their country.

William Harrison, *The Description of England*, George Edelen (Ed.), (Folger Shakespeare Library by Cornell University Press, New York, 1968) pp. 280-1

The making of the rural landscape

Source 6·8 *An article about the effect of quarrying on the landscape from 'The Guardian,' Friday November 29, 1974*

Call to cancel quarry schemes

By PETER HILDREW

Amenity organisations in Yorkshire are pressing for legislation to cancel out planning permissions for minerals extraction which have lain unused for a long time. They argue that many of these permissions would no longer be granted under the criteria now applied to mineral workings, and that technical changes in the quarrying industry have brought much higher rates of extraction than were foreseen in the early postwar years.

Concern has been aroused particularly by the fate of permission for a 10-acre limestone quarry at Ribblehead, in the centre of the Yorkshire Dales National Park, which was bought last year by the Amey Roadstone Corporation. Planning consent dates back to 1952, but very little stone had been quarried by the former owner, and much of the land remains untouched.

Mr David Joy, secretary of the Craven Action Group, a federation of amenity organisations concerned at the impact of quarrying in the area, said yesterday that they were anxious to prevent the creation of a large quarry in an exposed and wild area of a national park, but that under present law the company could proceed to make use of the old permission.

The site is on open moorland on the lower slopes of Ingleborough, in a popular walking and hiking area. A developed quarry would be in the centre of the triangle formed by the famous Three Peaks of the Dales, Ingleborough, Pen-y-ghent, and Whernside. The group believes that it would not only be clearly visible from the hills, but would create noise which could carry a considerable distance in such a wilderness area.

When the site came up for sale, the former West Riding County Council attempted to buy it to preserve the natural state of the area, but was outbid by Amey Roadstone. Members of the new Yorkshire Dales National Park Committee are expected to visit Ribblehead shortly to examine the site for themselves, but for the planning authority to revoke quarrying consent under present legislation would involve paying compensation which could run to millions of pounds.

Mr Joy said: "The best hope we have is for the Government to decide to repeal old planning permissions like this one which have not been taken up, and we have written to the Environment Secretary, Mr Crosland, explaining this point."

The question of old planning permissions for mineral workings is known to be under review by the Government-appointed Stevens committee on minerals planning control, which is due to report shortly, and the Craven amenity groups are hoping that the committee will point to a need for new legislation.

Development of the Ribblehead quarry, which would almost certainly be accompanied by applications for a stone-crushing plant and other associated buildings, is believed to be several years off, and is likely to depend upon developments in the aggregates market.

A spokesman for Amey Roadstone said yesterday that there were "no immediate plans" to begin extraction, but that work already under way close to the Settle-Carlisle railway at Ribblehead was designed to provide a railhead for quarried stone. This would be used to ship out material from the Skirwith quarry several miles away, near Ingleton.

The rock at Ribblehead is believed to be high-grade limestone suitable for use in the steel and chemical industries, but the amenity groups are concerned that much of it would in practice be used as roadstone and concrete, for which alternative sources of supply can be found.

● Opencast quarries should be replaced by mines to save landscapes in national parks and areas of outstanding natural beauty, Mr Fionn Holford-Walker, Secretary of the Council for the Protection of Rural England, said at Sheffield Polytechnic last night. He claimed that national parks and other areas could be saved by mining instead of quarrying in some instances and where this was more expensive the Government should subsidise the cost.

Course work for G.C.E. and C.S.E. assessment

Some history teachers may wish to devise Mode 3 C.S.E. and G.C.E. 'O' level syllabuses which include work on *History Around Us: The making of the rural landscape.*

The following items of course work could be completed by pupils and submitted in a folder as part of their final assessment:

1. Description of a site studied by fieldwork supported by maps, plans, photographs and any records or surveys.

2. Descriptions of sites studied in the classroom supported by maps, plans and sketches.

3. Work setting a site in its historical context and relating it to other sites:
e.g. an illustrated account describing how and why the landscape of an area has changed during a particular period.
e.g. a study of a number of reafforestation schemes explaining why such schemes have become necessary, linking them to past deafforestation and to their impact on the landscape of the future.

4. An imaginative reconstruction of:
either: a specific incident connected with a landscape feature,
e.g. the Roman attack on Maiden Castle, see Chapter 2.
or: life at a particular period on a site,
e.g. the farmer's year in an open field village.
or: a study of the connection between a historical personality or family and a landscape feature,
e.g. Coke of Holkham and the effect of his new farming techniques on the Norfolk heathland,
e.g. Capability Brown and the effect of his parks and gardens on the landscape.

Resources

Lists of resources for the study of the following aspects of the history of the rural landscape have been provided earlier in this book:
the landscape in Prehistoric times
the landscape in Roman times
castles and churches in the landscape
country houses and parks in the landscape
the Industrial Revolution and the landscape.

Some of the books on this list are out of print. You should be able to obtain copies from your local library or from the Schools Library Loan Service.

Resources are listed by order of importance, within each section.

Teachers' books

W. G. Hoskins, *The Making of the English Landscape*, (Penguin, 1970)

W. G. Hoskins, *Local History in England*, (Longman, 1973)

W. G. Hoskins, *Fieldwork in Local History*, (Faber, 1969)

W. G. Hoskins, *English Landscapes*, (BBC, 1973)

M. W. Beresford, *History on the Ground*, (Methuen, 1971)

Eric S. Wood, *Field Guide to Archaeology*, (Collins, 1975)

Christopher Taylor, *Fields in the English Landscape*, (Dent, 1975)

Michael Aston & Trevor Rowley, *Landscape Archaeology*, (David & Charles, 1974)

Ordnance Survey, *Field Archaeology in Great Britain*, (1974)

W. Beresford & J. K. St. Joseph, *Mediaeval England: an Aerial Survey*, (O.U.P., 1958)

K. J. Bonser, *The Drovers*, (Macmillan, 1970)

H. Thorpe, *The Lord and the Landscape*, (O.U.P. 1965)

O. G. S. Crawford, *Archaeology in the Field*, (Phoenix House, 1953)

Christopher Taylor, *Dorset*, 'The Making of the English Landscape Series', (Hodder & Stoughton, 1970)

Robert Newton, *The Northumberland Landscape*, 'The Making of the English Landscape Series', (Hodder & Stoughton, 1972)

Arthur Raistrick, *The West Riding of Yorkshire*, 'The Making of the English Landscape Series', (Hodder & Stoughton, 1970)

Trevor Rowley, *The Shropshire Landscape*, 'The Making of the English Landscape Series', (Hodder & Stoughton, 1972)

Norman Scarfe, *The Suffolk Landscape*, 'The Making of the English Landscape Series', (Hodder & Stoughton, 1973)

John Steane, *The Northamptonshire Landscape*, 'The Making of the English Landscape Series', (Hodder & Stoughton, 1973)

Christopher Taylor, *The Cambridgeshire Landscape*, 'The Making of the English Landscape Series', (Hodder & Stoughton, 1973)

Frank Emery, *The Oxfordshire Landscape*, 'The Making of the English Landscape Series', (Hodder & Stoughton, 1973)

W. G. Hoskins, *Leicestershire: an Illustrated Essay on the History of the Landscape*, (Hodder & Stoughton, 1957)

Margaret Spufford, *A Cambridgeshire Community: Chippenham*, 'English Local History Series', (Leicester University Press, 1965)

K. J. Allison, *The Deserted Villages of Oxfordshire*, (Leicester University Press, 1965)

Edward T. MacDermot, *History of the Forest of Exmoor*, (David & Charles, 1973)

R. Millward & A. Robinson, *The Lake District*, 'Regions of England Series', (Methuen, 1974)

Arthur Raistrick, *Old Yorkshire Dales*, (Pan Books, 1971)

Arthur Raistrick, *The Pennine Dales*, (Arrow Books, 1972)

Reference books for teachers and pupils

John Field (Ed.), *English Field Names: a Dictionary*, (David & Charles, 1972)

Max Hooper *et al.*, *Hedges and Local History*, (National Council of Social Service, 1971)

Eilert Ekwall, *The Concise Oxford Dictionary of English Place Names*, (O.U.P. 1960)

English Place Name Society, various volumes on twenty counties

Books for pupils describing and explaining the visible evidence

W. G. Hoskins, *English Landscapes*, (BBC, 1973)

F. J. Monkhouse & A. V. Hardy, *The Man-made Landscape*, (Cambridge University Press, 1974)

J. D. Chambers, *Laxton, the last English Open Field Village: A guide*, (HMSO, 1970)

Victor E. Neuburg, *The Past We See Today*, (O.U.P. 1972)

Books for pupils

These provide background information about people whose way of life brought changes in the landscape.

Marjorie Reeves, *The Medieval Village*, 'Then and There Series', (Longman, 1954)

Viola Bailey & Ella Wise, *Medieval Life*, 'Focus on History Series', (Longman, 1968)

A. J. Fletcher, *The Elizabethan Village*, 'Then and There Series', (Longman, 1967)

J. West, *The Medieval Forest*, 'Then and There Series', (Longman, 1977)

Paul Fincham, *Tudor Country Life*, 'Focus on History Series', (Longman, 1973)

John Addy, *The Agrarian Revolution*, 'Then and There Series', (Longman, 1964)

Herbert Green, *Village Life in the Eighteenth Century*, 'Then and There Series', (Longman, 1976)

Filmstrips

The Medieval World, 'Then and There Series', colour, Longman

The making of the rural landscape

The Agrarian Revolution, 'Then and There Series', colour, Longman
The Village, 'Medieval Life Series', colour, Longman/Common Ground

Agriculture and the Land, Parts 1 and 2, 'Introduction of the Industrial Revolution Series', black and white, Longman/Common Ground
English Agriculture 1770–1870, colour, Nicholas Hunter Filmstrips

Ribbon development in the rural landscape: North of Saffron Walden, Essex

9 ASPECTS OF THE HISTORY OF THE LOCALITY

Some objectives and outcomes

We hope that by the time pupils finish their study of the history of the locality they will:

1. have sufficient background knowledge to recognise the visible remains relating to aspects of life in their locality at different periods in the past.

2. have had practice at observing and interpreting these visible remains so they can set them in their historical context.

3. have had practice at combining the study of visible remains and background source material so they can reconstruct:
either: a specific incident in the history of the locality
or: a picture of life in the locality at a particular time,
or: a picture of the connections between a historical personality (or family) and the locality.

4. have the knowledge, skills and enthusiasm to explore their own locality and other aspects of their historical environment beyond school.

Approaches

Teachers will wish to organise the course to suit the abilities of their pupils and the nature of the historical remains in their locality.
We hope the following suggestions will prove useful. Both approaches were designed for pupils aged 15-16, studying *History Around Us* as part of G.C.E. and C.S.E. courses.

APPROACH 1
The study of two or three different aspects of the history of the locality

This study uses visible remains from various periods.

The following schemes are examples of this approach.

Glossop and the history around us

This consists of:

A study of four different aspects of the visible remains of the past in the Glossop area of Derbyshire
Melandra Roman fort
roads and tracks from the Bronze Age to the Turnpike Age
houses in Glossop from the sixteenth to twentieth centuries
the Peak Forest Canal.
This work involves visits to sites and the Buxton Museum as well as the study of documentary evidence.

A site study of the pupils' own choice
e.g. a disused cornmill
Buildwas Abbey
a derelict papermill.
Each study includes:
a careful description of the site as it is today
setting the site in its historical context
an imaginative reconstruction
work on primary and secondary source material.

Thame and the history around us

A study of four different aspects of the visible remains of the past in Thame, Oxfordshire:

Aspects of the history of the locality

The vernacular architecture of Thame
This involves the study of plans, maps, photographs and a building survey.

The parish church
This involves visits to the church to survey the monuments and to date and record the main architectural features and a study of background source material such as parish registers and the 1851 religious census returns.

The workhouse
In addition to fieldwork on the plan and measurements of the workhouse, pupils study background source material relating to the Poor Law Amendment Act of 1834, the census enumerator's returns of the workhouse inhabitants for 1851, and workhouse diet in 1836.

Lord William's School, Thame
Pupils study the development of the school between the sixteenth and nineteenth centuries, using visible and documentary evidence.

APPROACH 2
A village study

This approach aims to give pupils background knowledge and skills to help them recognise and interpret a whole range of visible evidence about the history and development of a small area.

A brief study of the development of a village, from its origins to the present using the visible evidence, leads to a more detailed study of village life during one particular period, preferably that for which most visible evidence remains. The following schemes are examples of two village studies.

Aberford, West Yorkshire: a village study

Its origin and site
Pupil activities include:
Map work to investigate the reasons for the origins and siting of a number of different villages, followed by work on various village shapes and the reasons for them.
Map work and fieldwork to relate this background information to the origins and siting of Aberford — studying its place name, location in the valley and fording point on a river.

Its development through time
Pupils make a detailed study of the visible remains of the village, and documentary evidence during the following periods:

Prehistoric and Roman times,
the Middle Ages,
the sixteenth-nineteenth centuries,
the twentieth century.

The village of Aberford in the nineteenth century
Pupils investigate the visible remains relating to:
the coaching trade
other trades and occupations, especially the evidence about milling and coal mining
church and chapel, their role in village life
education
the Gascoignes of Parlington Hall
the Garforth-Aberford Railway and the Garforth collieries.

This work also involves the study of documentary evidence. For a fieldwork work sheet which can be used for some of these topics — see *fig.* 4·9.

Brief comparative study of another village
e.g. Barwick or Micklefield.

Ruddington, Nottinghamshire: a village study

The origins and site
Activities include:
Map work on the site and position of the village.
A history simulation game on the siting of the early Saxon village.

A study of the development of the village:
This includes:
Introductory work about the visible evidence for the development of villages in general, e.g. village shapes and street names.
A study of the visible evidence to explain the development of Ruddington.
Field work visits to:
the remains of a Roman villa
a mediaeval church at Flawford
two Victorian schools
three chapels
a Victorian church
Victorian houses
the railway
a frame-work knitter's workshop and cottage
a hosier's cottage.

Life in Ruddington during the nineteenth century
This involves a study of the frame-work knitters and the development of this industry in the area followed by project work on the following topics:

1. *Either:* domestic architecture
or: the church — a comparative study of Ruddington and Bingham.

Aspects of the history of the locality

Figure 1·9 *Ruddington through the ages — How do we know?*

Here is some information about the way the village has developed through the ages from Iron Age times to twentieth century. This information has been gathered together from different sorts of historical evidence. Read each piece of information and then try to work out carefully how we might have found out each piece of information — What is the evidence?

---

1. There was Iron Age and Roman occupation near to the modern village.

Evidence ....

2. There was probably a small Anglo-Saxon village with a population of 30.

Evidence ....

3. Probably the Danes attacked the area during the late ninth century and later settled.

Evidence ....

4. The village grew during the eleventh century and land was held by Alan Fergant, Earl of Richmond.

Evidence ....

5. In 1487, part of Henry VII's army camped in the area before moving on to fight the Battle of East Stoke.

Evidence ....

6. In 1641, James Peacock founded the first free school in the village — there was a house and garden for the master.

Evidence ....

7. In 1767, changes took place in the shape of the village: the open fields were hedged or "enclosed".

Evidence ....

8. Flawford church was demolished in 1773.

Evidence ....

9. During the nineteenth century Ruddington became an important centre for frame-work knitting and the population increased rapidly.

Evidence ....

10. In 1852, the Girls' & Infants' School was erected by Sir T. G. Parkyns.

Evidence ....

11. The Parkyns built the Manor House and the Pagets the Grange during the mid-nineteenth century.

Evidence ....

12. On March 15th 1899 Ruddington was connected by rail to Loughborough & Leicester.

Evidence ....

Aspects of the history of the locality

> **13.** The old parish church was completely rebuilt in 1887-8.
>
> *Evidence* ....
>
> **14.** Ruddington has developed very rapidly during the last twenty years.
>
> *Evidence* ....

2. Schools, agriculture, the railway, chapels.

3. A historical personality connected with the village:
James Peacock, founder of the first free school
Charles Paget, lived at Ruddington Grange and was involved in "Hay time education for agricultural labourers"
Philo Mills, lived at Ruddington Hall, built many farms and houses
William Parker, a hosier, founded the Liberal Club and Cooperative Society
Thomas Parkyns, lived at South Manor and was connected with schools and houses.
This work involves the study of the visible remains in the village itself and in the village museum supported by background information from primary and secondary source material.

The village today
Pupils review the development of the village in the twentieth century, and then discuss the visible evidence of the history of Ruddington in the past.
For an evidence worksheet on this topic — see *fig.* 1·9.

Studying a village: some questions and activities

The number, length and frequency of visits will vary from school to school, as will the form and amount of help teachers give to pupils studying a village by classroom investigation and fieldwork. We hope the following suggestions may prove useful.

STAGE ONE
The origins and siting of the village

1. Background lessons

These could provide pupils with essential background information about the origins and siting of villages in general so that they can apply this knowledge to the study of their own village. Teachers would introduce pupils to the idea that most of our villages — with the exception of some Industrial Revolution settlements, were already in existence when the Domesday Survey was carried out.

Though many sites were the work of the Anglo-Saxon and Danish invaders, probably half were occupied in Roman times or before.

Few villages were founded on lowland clay sites before the Iron Age. The farmers of the New Stone Age and Bronze Age had to settle in areas of light soil, e.g. the chalk downs of the south and the sandy uplands of East Anglia, which were clear of heavy timber. Then they could cultivate it with primitive tools, bronze axes and wooden ploughshares.

This information emphasises the point, made by W. G. Hoskins, which is an essential element in all landscape studies that "everything is older than we think".

Pupils could be asked to put themselves in the position of these early farmers who had to make themselves self-sufficient by growing all their own food and obtaining all other basic necessities of life.

They could draw up a list of the factors they would consider when choosing the site for their village, e.g. fertile, easily cultivated soil, water and drainage, shelter and aspect, communications, defence.

After deciding on their priorities pupils could be given an outline map of an area showing different geological and geographical features, e.g. highland, lowland, marsh, forest, clay and gravel soils, rivers, valleys, north and south directions, etc. and asked to choose a site for a village.

This work could be conducted as a class exercise or by pupils in groups, or pairs. They would report back at the end of the session.

Finally, the teacher could explain how the original reasons for a village's location and foundation, its physical description and the problems of the early inhabitants, are sometimes reflected in the following visible remains:

The plan of the village
e.g. a street village built along an old routeway, a round or green village where the cattle could be driven into the centre for safety

Aspects of the history of the locality

a haphazard village which grew up piecemeal from clearings made in the forest.

The size of the village and its relationship to other surrounding settlements in the parish
e.g. a nucleated village, the only important settlement in a parish where most of the people lived — before 1750, within one settlement area and went out daily to farm the land

one settlement out of a number in the parish, where the land was too poor or too thickly forested to support one large community

a large settlement in the middle of a parish containing many smaller ones, the main village from which families went out later, perhaps in bad times, to carve other colonies on the fringes.

The name of the village
*Oak*ensham, *Alder*shot — denoting forest
Mansfield *Wood*house — denoting a clearing in the forest
Gilling*ham* — denoting the original settler and his family
*Knight*on — denoting the social status of the early inhabitants.

2. Visits and/or map work

After this introduction pupils could begin to study the site of their own village starting first with maps — the 2½ inch Ordnance Survey map and the geological map of the area and a place name dictionary and then moving on to fieldwork. The following questions could be considered:
Why was the village sited in this precise spot?
What was the original plan of the village? — street, round or haphazard?

3. Follow up work

Using the 2½ inch map as a base, pupils can produce their own annotated sketch map explaining the origins and site of the village and including any information about the early inhabitants.
After looking at the visible evidence, pupils may

A haphazard village; Burton Agnes, Humberside

Aspects of the history of the locality

A street village; Burford, Oxfordshire

Milton Abbas, Dorset; a street village with a difference – it was resited in the 18th century by a local landowner

Aspects of the history of the locality

A pond and green village; Finchingfield, Essex

A pond and green village; Nun Monkton, North Yorkshire

wish to supplement their findings with information from a local history book which incorporates evidence from documentary sources or archaeological reports.

STAGE TWO
A study of the growth and development of the village

This uses the visible evidence to study past development.

1. Background lessons

These could show pupils how to trace the stages in the growth and development of a village by dating the houses according to the architectural style and building materials.

The lessons could be based around slides and filmstrips and would provide pupils not only with background information about the dates when polite styles of architecture were introduced for the houses of the wealthy but also the development of local building styles and materials for vernacular housing.

Teachers and pupils could then cooperate in the production of clue sheets which record in diagrammatic form, information about the architectural styles and building materials of houses in their area for reference during fieldwork — see *figs*. 2·9 and 3·9.

2. Fieldwork

A building survey of the village:
using a plan of the village based on the latest edition of the 25 inch Ordnance Survey plan, (see section on background source material) pupils could make two maps of the village:

Map 1 could show:
the approximate date of each building by using a different shading and a date key, e.g.

pre 1700

1700-1800

1800-1900

its function and type now and in the past, e.g. detached house, terrace of cottages — (the existence of terraces of workers' cottages may be significant since these could be the only visible remains of a vanished village industry).

Map 2 could show:
the different building materials used for the roof, walls, chimneys, etc.

any information known about the name of the owner or builder.

During these surveys pupils could make a special note on their maps of any unusual features, e.g. a bridge, the village lock-up, a pin fold, a market cross and any building whose function is not obvious or appears to have changed e.g. a garage which was once a water-mill.

If the village is large or the time for fieldwork limited, teachers may wish to divide the class into groups or pairs.

Each group could survey a different part of the village. While one member of each pair records the date and function of each building, the other could note the building materials.

3. Follow up work

This could involve the collation of information from different groups so that each pupil has a full picture of the date, function and building materials of all buildings in the village.

Pupils could draw conclusions about the village in the past using the information from these surveys. The following questions could be considered:

What can we tell about the growth of the village from the age of buildings?

Are there any periods in the history of the village for which there is no visible evidence? Why is this? e.g. Why are there no remains of mediaeval houses?

What can we tell from building materials used in different houses about the growth of the village?

What can we tell from our survey about life at different periods in the past? e.g. trades and occupations, religion, education, transport, amusements.

Are there any unusual buildings which cannot be explained?

Do any families or individuals appear to have been important in the history of the village in the past?

Finally, the pupils could look at the first edition 25 inch Ordnance Survey plan of the village — surveyed between the 1860s and 1890s. This may show important buildings which have been demolished. It could also explain the function of any puzzling buildings, e.g. a garage which used to be the water-mill; derelict sheds which used to be the smithy; a house which used to be an inn.

For the information to be gained from these maps compare the 1964 and 1908 edition of the 25 inch Ordnance Survey plans of Aberford, sources 1·9 and 2·9.

Aspects of the history of the locality

Figure 2·9 *Four extracts from a series of clue sheets which help pupils to date houses in the Glossop area of Derbyshire*

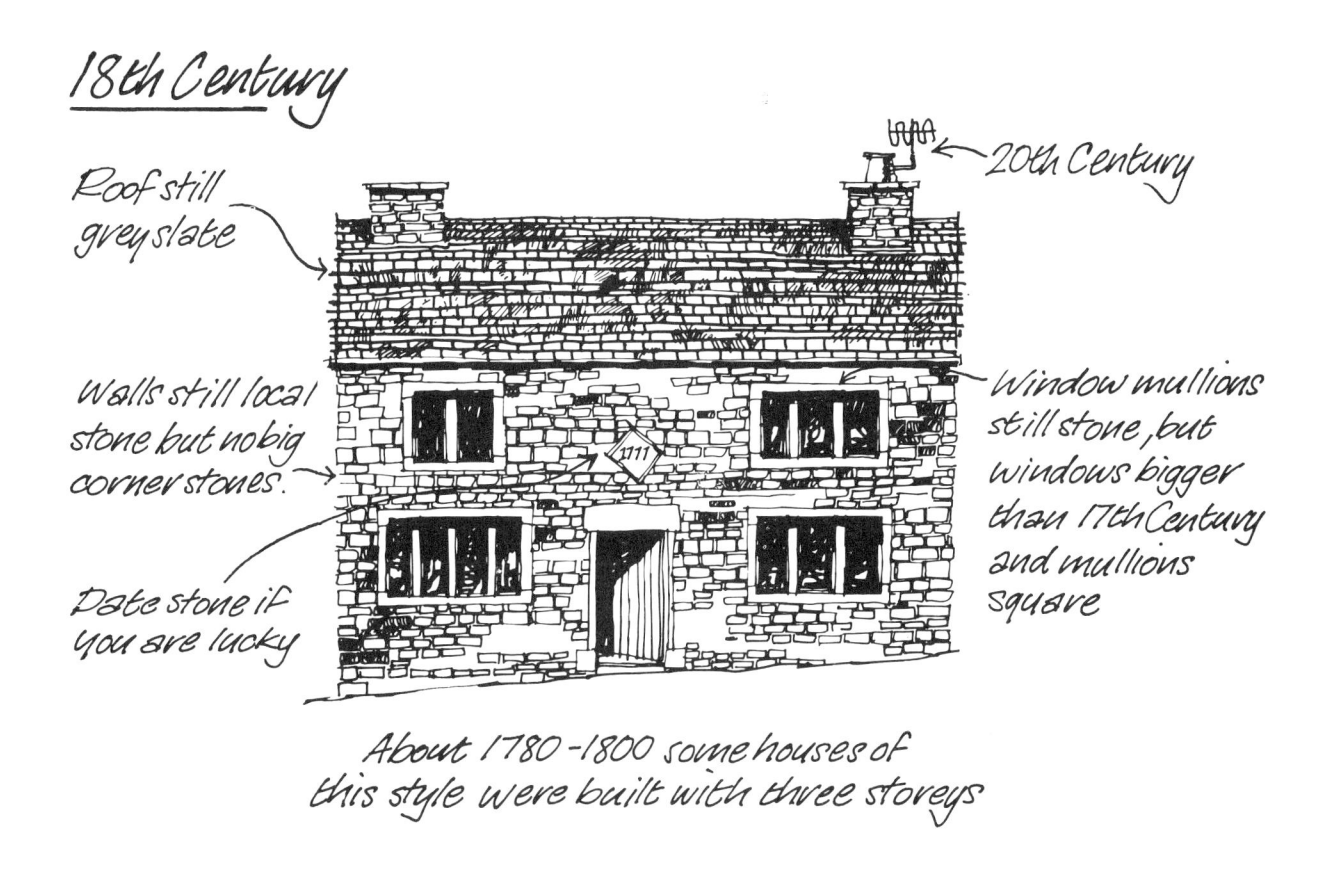

18th Century

- Roof still grey slate
- 20th Century
- Walls still local stone but no big corner stones.
- Date stone if you are lucky
- Window mullions still stone, but windows bigger than 17th Century and mullions square

About 1780-1800 some houses of this style were built with three storeys

Industrial Revolution (about 1800-1850)

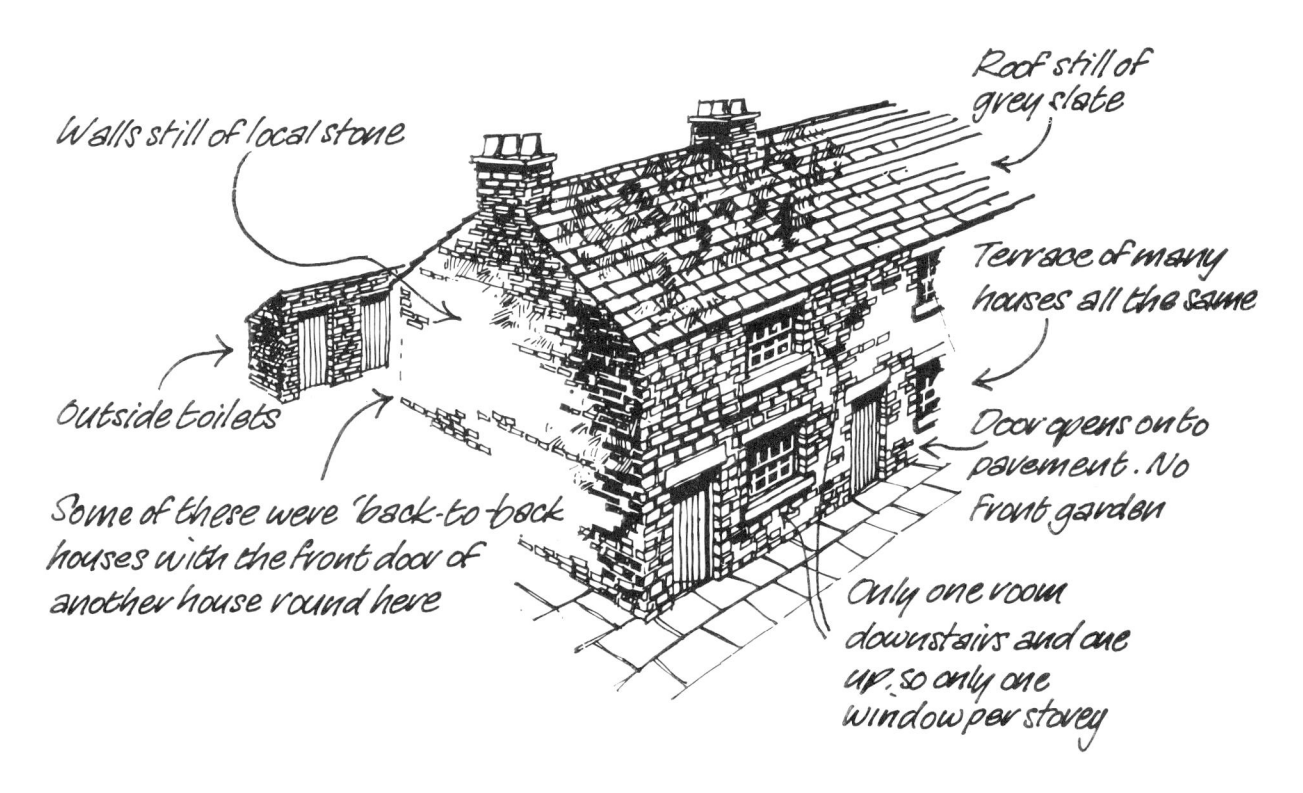

- Walls still of local stone
- Roof still of grey slate
- Terrace of many houses all the same
- Outside toilets
- Some of these were 'back-to-back' houses with the front door of another house round here
- Door opens onto pavement. No front garden
- Only one room downstairs and one up, so only one window per storey

Aspects of the history of the locality

Middle Class Victorian

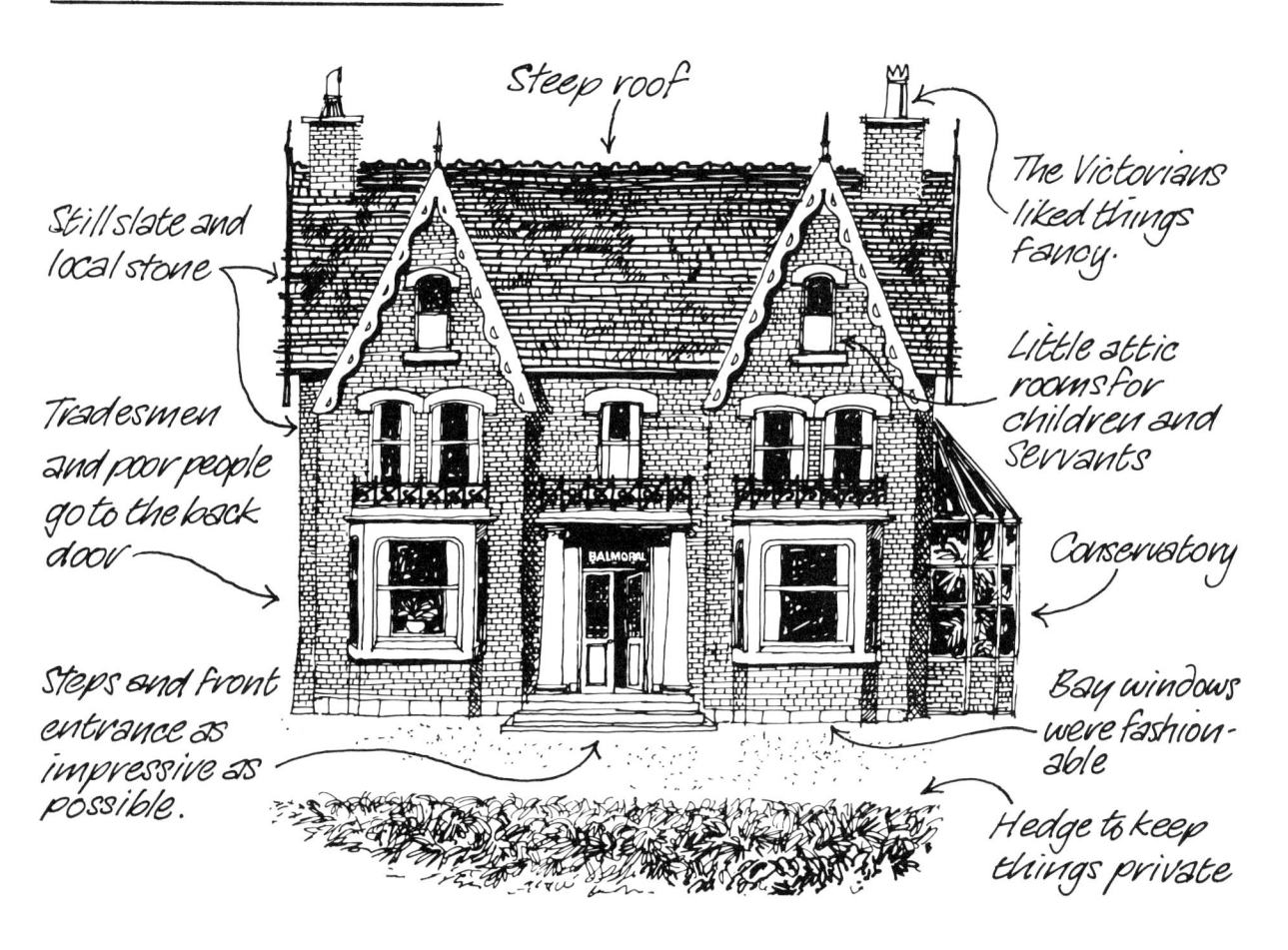

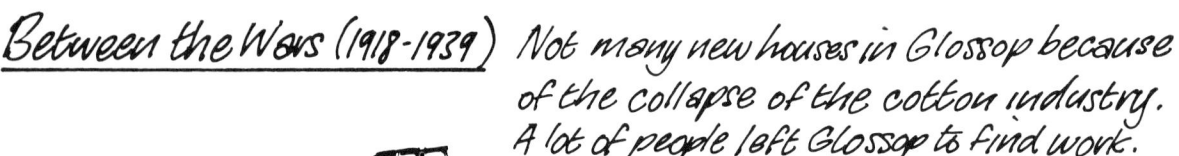

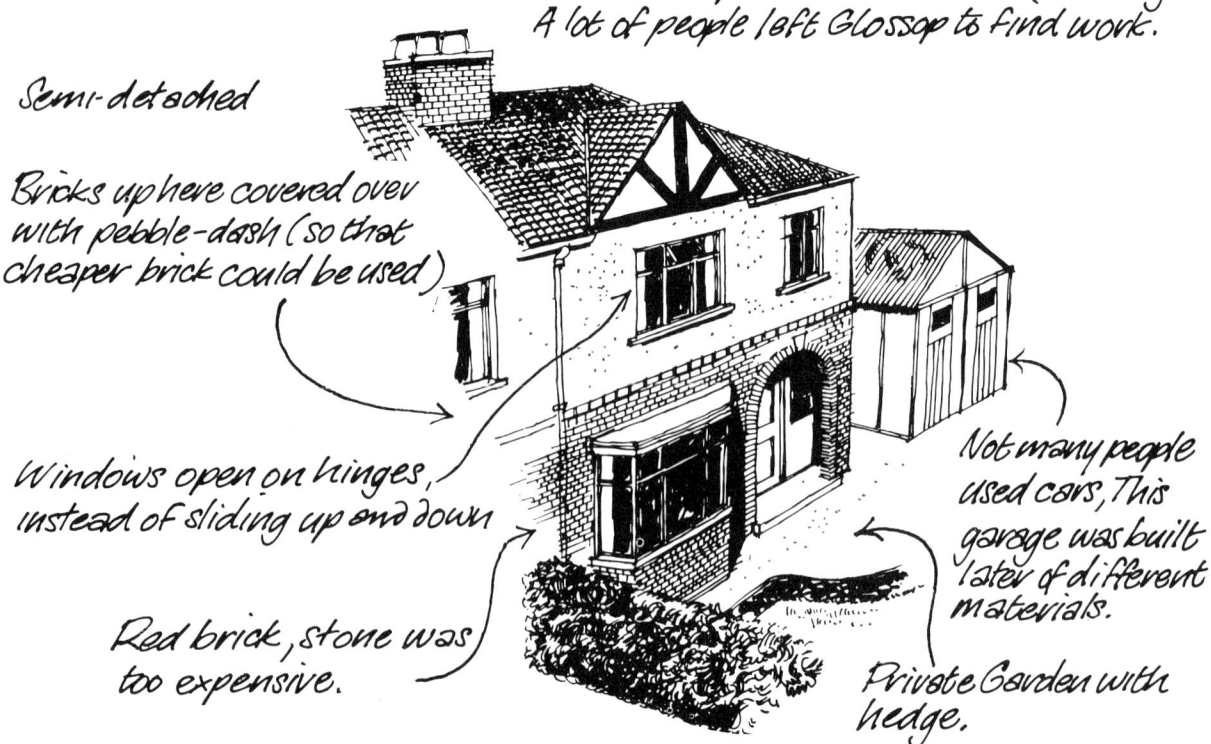

- Steep roof
- Still slate and local stone
- The Victorians liked things fancy.
- Tradesmen and poor people go to the back door
- Little attic rooms for children and servants
- Conservatory
- Steps and front entrance as impressive as possible.
- Bay windows were fashionable
- Hedge to keep things private

Between the Wars (1918-1939)

Not many new houses in Glossop because of the collapse of the cotton industry. A lot of people left Glossop to find work.

- Semi-detached
- Bricks up here covered over with pebble-dash (so that cheaper brick could be used)
- Windows open on hinges, instead of sliding up and down
- Red brick, stone was too expensive.
- Not many people used cars. This garage was built later of different materials.
- Private Garden with hedge.

from drawings by Mr. J. Scott, Glossop School

Aspects of the history of the locality

Figure 3.9 *A chart from R. W. Brunskill's "Illustrated Handbook of Vernacular Architecture" which presents a visual classification of different building materials, roof and window shapes*

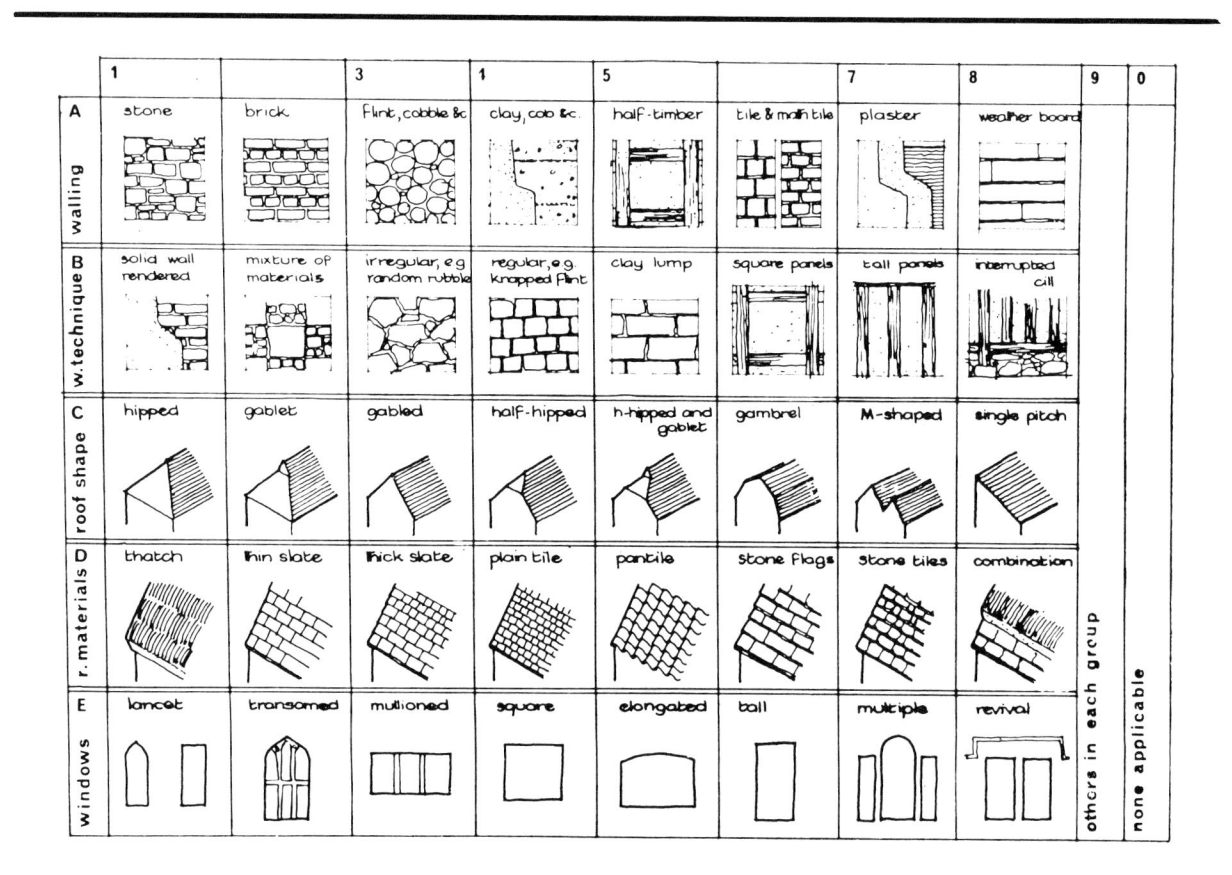

	1	3	1	5		7	8	9	0
A walling	stone	brick	flint, cobble &c	clay, cob &c	half-timber	tile & math tile	plaster	weather board	
B w. technique	solid wall rendered	mixture of materials	irregular, e.g. random rubble	regular, e.g. knapped flint	clay lump	square panels	tall panels	interrupted cill	
C roof shape	hipped	gablet	gabled	half-hipped	h-hipped and gablet	gambrel	M-shaped	single pitch	others in each group / none applicable
D r. materials	thatch	thin slate	thick slate	plain tile	pantile	stone flags	stone tiles	combination	
E windows	lancet	transomed	mullioned	square	elongated	tall	multiple	revival	

STAGE THREE
A study of life in the village at one period in the past

It would be best if this was the period for which most visible evidence remains — this will emerge from the previous survey of the village.

Some villages may retain many signs of life in mediaeval or Elizabethan times, e.g. Laxton in Nottinghamshire and Harwell in Oxfordshire. Others, may be predominately eighteenth century or early nineteenth century in character. Aberford, for instance, has many late eighteenth century houses and shops and also pairs of early nineteenth century estate cottages.

Pupils could choose one or more of the following topics to study:
village trades, crafts and industries
farming and agriculture
religion
education
transport
a local family and its influence on the village
a specific incident which affected the lives of the villagers.

Each topic could involve:
a. further fieldwork to revisit certain features and buildings in the village and gather more information from the visible remains themselves
b. work on primary and secondary source material to find background information explaining the visible remains.

Teachers may wish to prepare a small resource folder for each topic containing some of the following items:
a. an introductory sheet giving a certain amount of background information about the topic
b. an assignment sheet of questions to be answered or information to be discovered by further fieldwork
c. a selection of relevant primary and secondary sources which provide background information to help explain the visible evidence
d. an assignment sheet of questions to be answered by a study of these background sources.

The study of village agriculture would involve fieldwork and map work to locate and draw farms, barns, dovecotes, marlpits, threshing floors, foldyards and drove roads. It could also lead to a combination of map work and surveying to trace the location and extent of the old open fields using visible clues such as ridge and furrow marks and field names.

Pupils investigating village trades and crafts could try to locate the site or remains of the smithy, saw pit, wind and water-mills — see *fig. 4.9*. This in turn may lead to a visit to a museum of folk life to look at the tools used. This fieldwork could be combined with the study of trade directories and contemporary descriptions of the craftsmen at work.

For suggestions about the study of the local castle, church, mill or great house, see the relevant section earlier in this book.

STAGE FOUR
A study of the village today: some conclusions

Teachers and pupils could draw some comparisons between the village as it was at a certain time in the past and the village as it is today. The pupils could list visible evidence of changes which are affecting the face of the village today. This may lead to a discussion of the reasons for these changes and the effects of them on life and the appearance of the village in the future, e.g. the village tradesmen may have benefited or suffered from building of a bypass. Another 'Great Rebuilding' may be in progress with many houses receiving a Neo-Georgian face lift. The village may no longer be a self-sufficient community but a commuter village for a nearby town or city.

A brief comparative study of another village could be made. This may take only one visit but it would provide pupils with points of contrast and give them the opportunity to use their knowledge and skills in a new setting.

Some background source material

Types of primary source material relating to specific features of the locality such as a castle, the parish church, an abbey, a country house and industrial remains have already been described in the appropriate sections elsewhere in this book.

Some types of primary source which may be useful for pupils interpreting visible evidence during their village study are listed below followed by a selection of examples.

1. Maps

Ordnance Survey maps
These are readily available and very useful. Some uses for the first edition 25 inch plan and 6 inch map have already been mentioned.
Xerox copies of the relevant sections can be obtained from the local reference library or record office. Sections of the first edition 1 inch map of the area 1805-1872, according to area, may also be useful. These have been reprinted by David and Charles. Recent editions of the $2\frac{1}{2}$ inch and 25 inch maps can be obtained through local Ordnance Survey agents.

Enclosure maps
These, together with the award papers, could be used to help pupils trace the location and extent of the old open fields in combination with the evidence of ridge and furrow marks and field names.
Xerox copies of these maps may be available from the local record office.

Tithe maps
These were produced for parishes at the time of the Tithe Commutation Act of 1836. They show every parcel of land, road, path, shop, house and stream and provide a detailed picture of many villages around 1840. When used in conjunction with the list of owners, they can show land ownership, state of cultivation, names of occupiers of property, size of estates, traces of old earthworks and mediaeval cultivation, location of farms and houses.
There were three copies of every map, one in the Public Record Office, London, one in the parish chest — now often kept in the local record office, and one in the diocesan registry.

2. Place and field names

They can often tell us something about the origins and development of the village. For your area consult the appropriate volume produced by the English Place Name Society, or Eilert Ekwall, *Concise Oxford Dictionary of English Place Names*.

3. Trade directories and gazetteers

They provide a general description of the village during certain periods together with comments about changes taking place and also a list of tradesmen, clergy and doctors. These are usually available in the local reference library. Information from these books can often explain the original function of puzzling buildings.

4. Local newspapers

They sometimes provide information about specific events or people connected with the village in the past.

Aspects of the history of the locality

Figure 4·9 *Part of a fieldwork assignment sheet for the study of village life and labour in the nineteeth century*

Topic 1 : Farming and village crafts

Can you find visible remains of any of the following?

1. *Farmhouses along the village street together with foldyards, cattle pens and piggeries where cattle were wintered, calves reared, etc.*

If so, note and record:—
— Name of the farm
— Building materials of farmhouse and out buildings
— Shapes of windows and doors of farm house
— No., size and shape of out buildings e.g. stables, cowhouses, piggeries
— Size and shape of foldyard

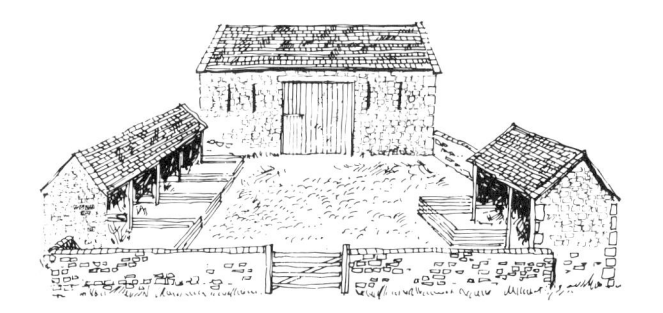

2. *Large corn barns*
If so, note and record:—

— Size and shape of barn
— Building materials
— Large central door for loaded hay or corn wagon
— Door on opposite wall to create through draught for winnowing the chaff from the wheat
— No. of 'bays' inside the barn
— Threshing floor in centre of barn
— Ventilation holes in roof and walls

3. *Water-mills for grinding the farmers' corn*
If so, note and record:—

— Size and shape
— No. of storeys
— Building material
— Size and position of water wheel
— Mill pond supplying water for water wheel
— Position or level at which the water poured on to the wheel
— Tail race for water after it had been used by wheel
— Hoist and trap door for sacks of corn
— Miller's house and barn
— Farm buildings

from drawings by J. Plummer, John Smeaton High School

5. The reminiscences of local inhabitants

They can give useful information about village crafts, the original use of certain buildings and the location of others such as the smithy, mill and saw pit. Some of these reminiscences may even have been recorded in manuscript form and copies of these may be deposited in the local reference library. Some pupils may wish to record conversations with local inhabitants. Teachers may find the published reminiscences of the inhabitants of other nineteenth century villages useful, e.g.
Our Village by Miss Mitford
George Ewart Evans' books which record oral tradition in Suffolk: *The Farm and the Villager; Ask the Fellows who cut the Hay*
The Useful Toil, a collection of autobiographies of working people in the nineteenth century compiled by John Burnett.
For full details of these books see the Resources section.

6. Travellers' descriptions of the area at different times in the past

Many of these have been published and can be found in the local reference library, e.g.
Celia Fiennes, *The Journeys of Celia Fiennes*, (1685-1703), C. Morris (Ed.), (Cresset Press, 1949)
Arthur Young, *A six months' tour through the North of England*, (1771)
Arthur Young, *A Tour in Ireland*, 1776-1779, A. Wollaston Hutton (Ed.), (Bell, 1892)
Arthur Young, *A six weeks' tour through the Southern Counties of England and Wales*, (1768)
Daniel Defoe, *A tour through the whole island of Great Britain* (1722-6), (Penguin, 1971)
John Leland, *Itinerary*, (1535-1543), L. Toulmin Smith (Ed.), (Centaur Press, 1971)

7. Parish records

They provide a picture of village life at different times, e.g. parish registers, accounts of the overseers of the poor. For more detail about these see Chapter 5.

8. Family and estate papers relating to local families

These can give background information about such buildings in the village as the almshouses, the reading room or a disused colliery railway line. They may be in the local record office.

9. Local history books

Many of these were produced by the vicar in the nineteenth century and they sometimes contain line illustrations of buildings which may be derelict — or modernised and unrecognizable, e.g. the windmill, the water-mill, the smithy. They can usually be found in the local reference library together with relevant volumes of the *Victoria History of the Counties of England*.

10. Parliamentary papers

Sections of the famous nineteenth century government reports referring to schools and working conditions in factories and workshops can be found in the local reference library. Two of these which give information about schools are:
Reports of the Charity Commissioners — from 1819
Reports of the Schools Enquiry Commission — 1868-9
For a list of others see:
Percy and Grace Ford, *A select list of British Parliamentary Papers* 1833-99, (Irish University Press, 1970)
W. R. Powell, *Local History from Blue Books: Select list of the Sessional Papers of the House of Commons*, (Historical Association, 1962).

11. School log books and accounts

These give information about changes in the fabric of school buildings in the past, pupils, teachers, curriculum and also other aspects of village life.

12. Census returns

These are useful for pupils who wish to study the inhabitants of a particular street or building in the village such as an inn or almshouse. The enumerators' note books — available only for 1841-71, list the inhabitants of every household, almshouse and inn on the day of the census.
Xerox copies of schedules from the 1851 census note books can be obtained from the Public Record Office. Most county and city reference libraries also have copies on microfilm.

Some examples of useful source material

A selection of source material can be found on the pages which follow.

Aspects of the history of the locality

Source 1·9 *A section from the 1964 edition of the 25 inch Ordnance Survey plan showing the village of Aberford*

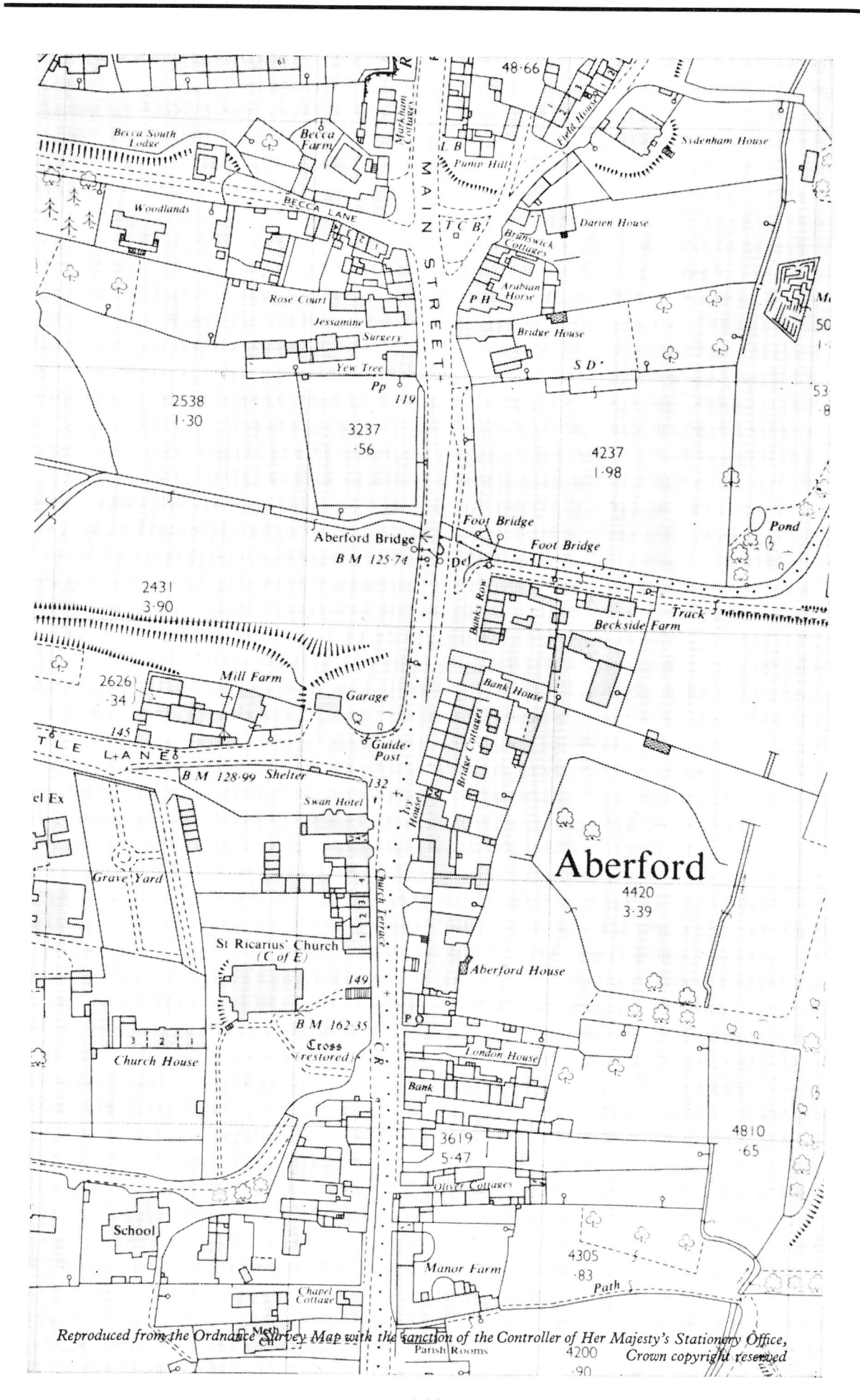

Aspects of the history of the locality

Source 2·9 *A section from the 1908 edition of the 25 inch Ordnance Survey plan showing the village of Aberford*

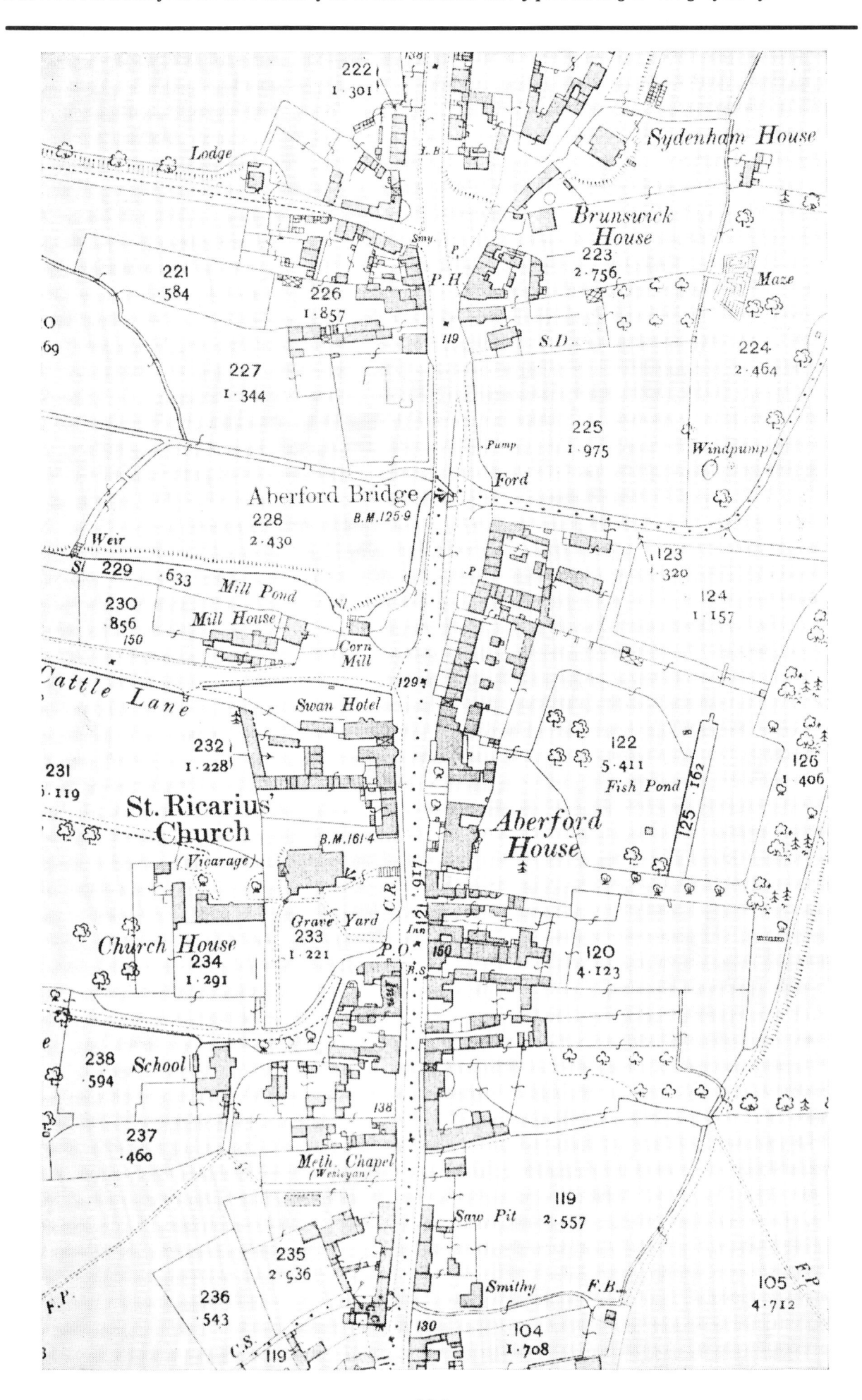

Aspects of the history of the locality

Source 3·9 *A section from the 1849 edition of the 6 inch Ordnance Survey map showing Aberford and the surrounding area*

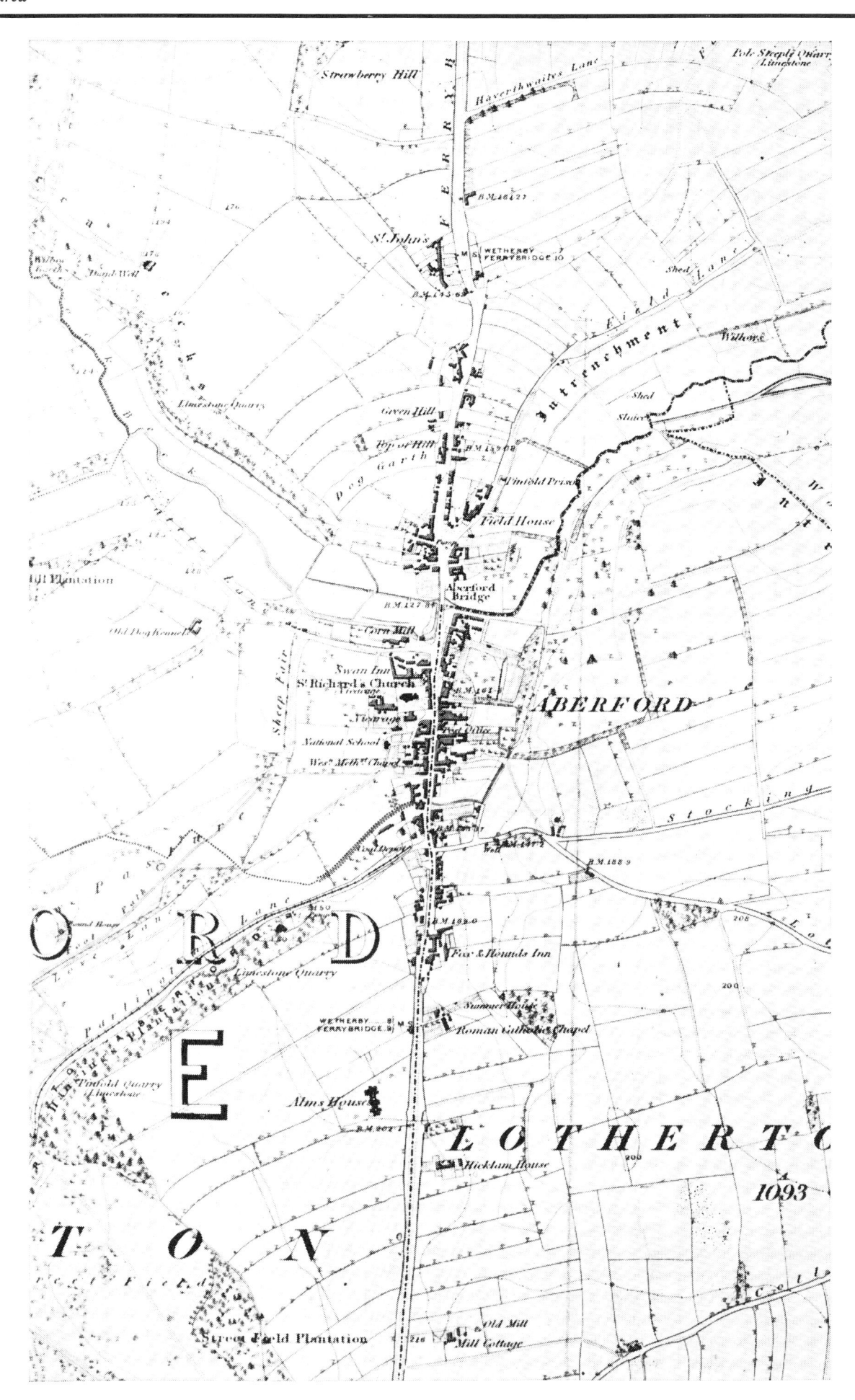

Aspects of the history of the locality

Source 4·9 *A section from the reprint of first edition 1 inch Ordnance Survey map (1858) for the Aberford area*

Aspects of the history of the locality

Source 5·9 *Two extracts from the English Place Name Society's volume for the West Riding of Yorkshire about Aberford*

iv. Aberford

1. ABERFORD (97–4337) [ˈabəfəþ]

Ædburford 1176 P (p), *Ædburgforð* 1177 P (p)

Hedburford c. 1190 Pont, *Edburford* 1218 ib, 1221–4 Dods viii, 215d

Ebberford 13 Skyr, *Ebrefort* 1210 Pont (p), *Eberford* 1267 Kirkst (p)

Aberford 1208 Cur, 1229 Ebor, 1246 *Ass* 32, 1274 *Bodl* 109, 1276 RH *et passim* to 1659 SelbyW, -*forth* 1278 YI, *Abir-*, *Abyrford* 1303 Aid *et freq* to 1488 FF, -*forth* 1413 YI, 1484 Fabr, -*furgh* 1531 Test iv, *Abreford* 1316 Pat, 1428 FA, *Abriford* 1419 YD i, -*forth* 1454 ib

Abberford c. 1216 *RegAlb* iii, 50, 1246 *Ass* 5d, 1251 Ch, 1275 YI, 1280 *Ass*, 1281, 1301 Ebor *et freq* to 1822 Langd, -*furthe* 1562 WillY, 1587 FF

'Ēadburg's ford', from the OE fem. pers.n. *Ēadburg* and **ford**. The ford carried the Great North Road across Cock Beck. On the development of *Ēadburg-* to *Aber-* cf. Phonol. § 19.

FIELD-NAMES

The principal forms in (*a*) are 1848 TA 1. Spellings dated 1536 are MinAcct, 1675, 1764 Glebe, 1685 Thoresby xxvi, 296–7. Others dated without source are YD i.

(*a*) *Aberford Moor* 1825 EnclA 11, *Ash Tree Close*, *Banewells* (v. **bana** 'slayer', **wella**), *Batman Butts*, *Booth Garth*, *Bottom Close* (ib 1685), *Brayfits Garth* 1764, *Britree Acre*, *Five Acre Ing*, *Hall Close*, *Hole garth* 1764, *Humphrey Dale*, *Leg of Mutton*, *Light flats* 1764, *Limekiln Flatt*, *Long Dale*, *Lushpot house* 1764 (cf. *Lush Pott Lane* 79 *supra*), *Maude Garth*, *Mill Dam*, *Near Rifts*, *Pole Steeple*, *School Garth* (*the Vicars close or football now called the School Garth* 1764, *the foot-ball garth* 1675, cf. also *the Parsonage Fould* 1635 BarW, '*the Vicarage fold* commonly called *the School fold* from the Charity school built there in 1716', 1764), *Stack Garth*, *Style Stye Close* (v. **stigel**, **stīg** 'path'), *Sweet Bits*, *High & Low Tofts* (v. **topt**), *Trickets garth* 1764, *Tuff Flatts*, *Warin's bottom close* 1764, *Whinny Close*, *Willow Garth*.

(*b*) *Asgarthcroft* 1523 Rent (the ON fem. pers.n. *Ásgerða*, **croft**), *Bechaghdyke(s)*, -*inges* 1348 (v. *Becca supra*, **dīc**, **eng** 'meadow', the *dīc* may refer to Becca Banks *supra*), *Briggs house* 1685, *Buskett Close* 1685, *Butcher wood* 1675, *the Cockes* 1675, *Cuntelarthayt*, *Kuntelaytwait* 12, 1240 Nost 81d, 89d (v. **þveit**), *Derholmes* 1290 (v. **dēor**, **holmr** 'water-meadow'), *Dobgarth* 1348 (the ME pers.n. *Dobbe*, **garðr**), *the grete feild* 1536, *Hall Garth* 1685, *Kastansike* 1348 (v. **chastaigne** 'chestnut' (with ONFr *c*-), **sīc** 'stream'), *Layndale* 1348 (v. **hlein** 'slope', **dæl**), *Litill croft* 1536, *Murk Lane Intack* 1685 ('dark lane', v. **intak**), *Oxynforth* 1454 (v. **oxa**, **ford**), *Pymusgarth* 1419, *the quarrell' close* 1536 (v. **quarrelle** 'quarry'), *the Rushe Inge* 1685 (v. **risc**, **eng**), *Spittell Fall* 1535 VE (v. **spitel**, (**ge**)**fall**), *Stain-*, *Staynford(e)* 12, 13, (-*gappe*) 1290, 1348, *Est-*, *Westtowford* 1536 ('stone ford', v. **steinn**, **stān** (which often becomes *Stow-* in such compounds), **ford**), *Tentarleas* 1675 (ME *tentour* 'tenter', **lēah**), *the Tutills* 1685 (v. **tōt-hyll** 'look-out hill'), *Wady Close* 1536, *Wood Closes*, -*Inge* 1685 (v. **wudu**, **eng**).

Aspects of the history of the locality

Source 6·9 *Extracts from Baines' "History, Directory and Gazetteer of the county of Yorkshire 1822"*

GENERAL AND COMMERCIAL DIRECTORY

And Gazetteer of the West-Riding.

MARKET TOWNS.

*** For more convenient Reference the Directory of Leeds has been placed at the commencement of the First Volume, as York will take the precedence in the Second Volume. All the other Towns will be arranged in alphabetical order, and the Villages will follow in the same order.

ABERFORD, or ABBERFORD

Is situated on the river Cock, in the wapentakes of Skyrac and Barkston-Ash, in the liberties of Pontefract and St. Peter, in the constableries of Aberford, Lotherton and Parlington, and in the parishes of Aberford and Sherburn. It is 188 miles from London, 7 miles and a half from Wetherby, and 16 miles from the city of York. The population of this place according to the census taken in 1821, amounts to 1235 persons. Formerly there was a market held here on Wednesday, but it is now discontinued. The neighbourhood is rich in coal and lime, and there are many remains of Roman roads and other antiquities. In addition to the Parish Church there is a Catholic chapel, and a Methodist chapel, there is also a Subscription Library and a Charity School, built on the site of the old school house, (endowed by Lady Betty Hastings,) and which is now conducted on the plan of Dr. Bell. This institution is supported by the benevolent contributions of the neighbouring gentry; to which is added an annual benefaction of ten guineas by the trustees of Lady Betty Hastings, and five guineas by Oriel College, Oxford. Huddleston Hall, about 3 miles from Aberford, a building of great antiquity, was formerly the residence of the Hungate family, but is now the property of R. O. Gascoigne, Esq. Near this place there is an extensive quarry, called Huddleston quarry, of excellent white stone, which acquires a fine polish, and is said to have been used both in the erection of St. Stephen's Chapel in Westminster Abbey, and in the tesselated pavement of the choir of York Minster. At Saxton, three miles from Aberford, there was formerly an ancient building, called Saxton Hall, which has been taken down within a few years, and a neat farm house built on the scite, by the late Sir Thomas Gascoigne, Bart. the heir of the Hungate family and the descendant of that ancient house. Near Aberford there is a farm house bearing the name of the Black Horse, which is reputed to have been the occasional retreat of the notorious Nevison the highwayman. The Parish Church which is dedicated to St. Richard, is at present undergoing considerable enlargement, and R. O. Gascoigne, Esq. is erecting catacombs which will contain thirty bodies. Formerly the trade of pin making was carried on to a considerable extent in this place, but it has ceased for some years. In the vicinity there are many rare and curious plants which grow wild, and which afford an ample field for the study of the Botanist.

POST MISTRESS—Jane Frew, office Main street.—Letters from London & the South, arr. at ¼ p. 8 night, and are dispat. at ¼ p. 12 night. Arrival from the North at ¼ p. 12 night, dispatched at ¼ p. 8 night.

Adams William, shopkeeper
Allen Timothy, surgeon
Allen Mrs. Mary
Atkinson William, farmer
Bainbridge Mrs. Mary, Vicarage house
Barker Addiman, joiner & carpenter
Barker Isaac, saddler
Barstow Edward, boot & shoe maker, and hair dresser
Bilton Joseph, grocer
Bloome Mrs. Mary
Bradley Thomas, stone mason
Brown John, carrier
Cant Simon, boot and shoe maker
Carnell William, boot & shoe maker
Chew Rev. William, Roman Catholic priest, Hazlewood
Cockrem Wm. victualler, Fox Inn
Cooper James, maltster; at the White Hart, Cross Parish, Leeds
Dawson Joseph, linen & woollen dpr.
Ellerton Joseph, agent to R. O. Gascoigne, Esq.
Fawcett John, gentleman
Flowett Thos. keeper of the toll bar
Fox G. L. Esq. Bramham park
Frobisher Joseph, surgeon
Gascoigne R. O. Esq. Parlington hall
Groves Joseph, corn miller
Harrison Robert, victualler, New Inn
Hewitt Richard, parish clerk and vagrant officer

132 ABERFORD. [*Towns.*] ALDBOROUGH.

Hick Robert, millwright & thrashing machine maker
Hick Charles, teazle dealer
Hick George, blacksmith
Hick Peter, joiner & wheelwright
Hick John, blacksmith, St. Peter's liberty
Hollings William, wheelwright, pony gig maker and tea dealer
Hutchinson Rhd. Esq. Hicklam house
Hutchinson Mrs. gentlewoman
King William, victualler & surveyor of high ways, Royal Oak
Landon Rev. James, B. D. vicar and magistrate
Layster Elias, stone mason
Lawson Sarah, draper and milliner
Le Jeune Mrs. Ann, gentlewoman
M'William Martha, shopkeeper
Maltus Thos. victualler & blacksmith, Bay Horse
Markham William, Esq. Becca Lodge
Marsh Rev. Rd. Roman catholic priest
Moore James, baker & flour dealer
Morris Edward, victualler, Swan Inn, (post chaise & horses) excise office
Musgrave Sir Philip, Bart. Bramham Biggin
Myers Samuel, wheelwright
Naylor George, stone mason
Naylor Mary, shopkeeper
Nichols John, plumber and glazier; dealer in silver'd glass for mirrors
Pearson Sarah, vict. Fox & Hounds
Penrose William, excise officer
Potter Simon, gent. Cattle ln. Lodge
Prest William, Esq. magistrate, Tolston lodge
Raper John, Esq. banker, Lotherton hall
Richardson John, boot & shoe maker
Sanderson Ephraim, gentleman, St. John's house
Sanderson William, boarding school
Scriven James, butcher
Scriven Joseph, butcher
Seanor Jph. linen draper & flour dlr.
Simpson Chas. baker, flour dealer, &c.
Smyth John, Esq. Bowcliffe
Steel Joseph, corn miller
Steel John, corn miller, Hillam mill
Stones Thomas, patten maker
Thirkill John, flour, (wire) machine maker and wire worker
Thompson Mrs. Mary, day school
Varley John, tailor
Vavasour Sir Thomas, Bart. Hazlewood hall
Webster Mary, corn miller
Wharton Mrs. Sarah
Wheelhouse Robert, saddler & harness maker
Whitehead Thomas, chimney sweeper & smoke jack cleaner
Wilkinson Edw. Esq. Potterton lodge
Wilkinson Joshua, linen and woollen draper & grocer
Wilkinson Joshua, jun. spirit merchant
Wilks John surveyor of the Halton Dial and Tadcaster roads
Wilson Rhd. vict. Gascoigne's Arms
Wood Harrison, solicitor, & agent to the Phœnix Fire office
Wood Sampson, vict. cabinet maker & house carpenter, Rose & Crown
Wood Harrison, vict. Old Red Lion
Wood Thomas, butcher & farmer
Wood Richard, joiner & painter
Wood Christopher, farmer
Wood Richard, farmer

COACHES.—The mails for London and the North pass through the town at the Hours named in the post office account.

The *Lord Nelson*, from Cockrem's, (the Fox) to London, every Tu. Thu. & Sat. at 4 mng. To Carlisle every Mon. Wed. & Fri. at 2 aftr.

The *Prince Blucher*, from Morris's, Swan Inn, to Wakefield, every Fri. mg. at 8. To York the same evg. at ½ p. 7.

CARRIERS—*John Brown* to Leeds every Tu. dep. 5 mng. ret. 10 at ngt. to York every Sat. dep. 3 mng. ret. 10 night

Joseph Seanor, to Leeds on Tus. & every other Fri.; to York every other Sat.

ALDBOROUGH,
Is a parliamentary borough, situated on the river Ouse, in the parish of Aldborough, in the wapentake of Claro, in the liberty of St. Peter; it is 1 mile from Boroughbride, 7 from Ripon, the same distance from Knaresbrough, 10 miles from Harrogate, 16¼ from York, and 208 from London. In ancient British times it was the capital of the Brigantes, and then named Iseur, afterwards altered by the Romans to Isurium, and by the Saxons to Burc, and lastly Aldburgh, i. e. Old Burc. Here are frequently found Roman coins, urns, tesselated pavements, &c. This place is said, by Higden, in his Policronicon, to have been sacked by the Danes, and burnt to the ground, about the year 870. It is now a small village, but returns two members to Parliament; the first return of which was in the year 1542, when John Gascoigne, and John Brown were returned. The present members are, Henry Fynes, Esq. and G. C. Antrobus, Esq. The Newcastle interest is predominant here, and the number of electors

Aspects of the history of the locality

Source 7·9 *Extracts from two newspaper obituary notices commenting on the death of Sir Charles Paget of Ruddington, near Nottingham*

Nottingham Daily Guardian October 15th 1873

Mr. Paget was always a warm friend of education, and the very last occasion that he appeared in public was at the meeting held in the Mechanics' Hall a week or two ago to inaugurate the University classes in Nottingham. At that meeting Mr. Paget mentioned some particulars of a scheme, which he had put into operation for educating the boys on his farm, namely by doubling the number of these youths, and sending them alternative days to school . . . -

. . . Mr. Paget was the author of 2 works — "On the Growth of Mangold Wurtzel" and "Experiments in Half-Time Education in Rural Districts" . . . Mr. Paget's effort in the cause of education at Ruddington were not confined to the Free School there . . . for we believe that he paid the salaries of 3 female teachers in the National School . . .

Nottingham and Midland Counties Daily Express October 15th 1873

Mr. Paget's benevolent concern for the young extended even beyond his ardent desire for their instruction. He had seen the deplorable loss of infantile life in Nottingham arising from the want of suitable and sufficient nutrition and therefore he organized a regular supply of pure and wholesome milk from his own dairies, at extremely moderate rates, in order that the little helpless things struggling for existence in the lowest dens of Nottingham might have some better chance to live than they would have had without such food . . .

On his estate he was a considerable, and we may say, a model landlord; seeking out the diligent and painstaking tenant, whether a farmer or labourer, and assisting him to better his position. Thus the steady and thoughtful labourer was assisted to become a small farmer . . .

Source 8·9 *Extracts from two travellers' descriptions of Aberford showing the growth of the village between 1533 and the early eighteenth century*

Watling Street lyeth straight beyond Castleford bridge. Thence to Aberford is 5 miles partly by low meadow but most by good plain corn land.

To the east of Aberford are 2 or 3 long ditches like the camps of men of war.

I never saw in any part of England so obvious an example as here of the large high ridge of the route of Watling Street, built by man, not naturally formed. Aberford is a poor thoroughfare on Watling Street. Cok Bek rises about a mile west of it and runneth through Aberford, and thence weaves its way to Lead, a hamlet where Skargill had a fine timber manor house.

John Leland, *Itinerary in Search of England's Antiquities*, (1533 - 34)

The great Roman highway goes on to Aberforth, a small Market Town famous for pin-making.

In some places this Roman causeway has been cut into and broken up so that the very great care of the Romans for building firm causeways for the easy passage of traffic and foot travellers can be seen. The layers of different sorts of earth, such as clay at the bottom, chalk upon that, then gravel upon the chalk, then stones . . . upon the gravel, then gravel again.

adapted from Daniel Defoe, *A Tour through the Whole Island of Great Britain*, (1722 - 6)

Aspects of the history of the locality

Source 9·9 *A list of rules for the inhabitants of the Aberford Almshouses, which were built by a local family, the Gascoignes, in the nineteenth century*

1. That all the inmates shall assemble every morning and evening at 8 o'clock when prayers shall be said by the matron.

2. That the bell shall be rung at 5 minutes to 8 both morning and evening.

3. That every inmate shall attend Church every Sunday unless prevented by sickness or other reasonable cause.

4. That the week's supplies of tea, coffee, sugar, soap and candles together with sixpence in money shall be given out by the matron every Monday morning to each inmate.

5. That the bell for dinner shall be rung at 12.30 at which time the inmates shall assemble in the Hall but they shall provide their breakfast and tea in their own rooms.

6. That particular care shall be taken by the inmates for cleanliness and neatness in regard to their rooms, clothing and persons.

7. That any misconduct such as quarrelling, incivility, disregard of the rules or disobedience to matron shall be punished by forfeiture of pocket money in proportion to the offence and shall be reported to the chaplain.

8. That repeated offences or gross misconduct such as swearing or intemperance shall render the offender liable to dismissal from the Almshouses by the Trustees.

9. That no inmate shall go beyond the precincts of the Almshouses without permission from the matron.

10. That no beer or spirits shall be brought into the Almshouses by any of the inmates, who shall on no account enter any house licensed for the sale of intoxicating liquors; but that in the case of necessity spirits shall be supplied by the matron subject to a doctor's certificate; or in case of sudden sickness, at her discretion.

11. That friends or relations of the inmates shall be permitted to visit them occasionally at such times as the matron may appoint, but they shall not remain during the dinner hour nor after 7 p.m.

12. That the men shall cultivate the Almshouse Gardens so that there shall be a proper supply of vegetables for the household; and they shall keep Garden walks and yards in a state of neatness and carry coal and water, and make themselves generally useful.

13. That the women shall do the cleaning of all rooms, corridors, kitchen and offices and wash all the linen of the Establishment including the clothing of all the inmates and of the matron and make themselves generally useful.

14. That all the above arrangements shall be carried out subject to the matron's supervision and direction.

January 1st 1888.

Aspects of the history of the locality

Source 10.9 *Extracts from the 1845 report of the Royal Commission into the Condition of Frame-work knitters*

Two Ruddington Witnesses

Samuel Parker, Frame-work Knitter, Shirt Branch, examined.
2377 Do you work in a wide frame, or a wrought frame?
In a 20-inch wrought frame
2378 Have you any statement of your earnings and outgoings?
I take in my own work
2379 Do you work direct to a warehouse at Nottingham?
Yes
2380 What are you making?
18 inch shirts
2381 What are you getting for them?
14s. a dozen
2382 How many can you do in a week?
Ten shirts
2383 What frame do you work in?
A hosier's frame; I pay 1s. 6d. for the frame
2384 Is it in your own house?
Yes; I have two other frames which my sons work in, in the shirt branch, and I take all the work in. I pay the seaming and winding, and the needles, candles, and such like
2385 Do your sons earn much the same as yourself?
Yes, about the same.

The Rev. Henry Bell examined.
2401 You are the vicar of Ruddington?
I am
2402 How long have you been resident in this parish?
Five years and three quarters
2403 What was the population, according to the last census?
1833.
2404 What proportion of the population are manufacturing, and what proportion agricultural?
I should think about two-thirds are manufacturing, and one-third agricultural.
2405 The manufacturing portion are chiefly engaged in frame-work knitting, are they not?
Chiefly; there is the lace-trade to a small extent, but not to any very great amount.
2406 What are the means of public education now existing in the parish?
There is a free-school for boys and girls, which we have lately made entirely free to all persons living in Ruddington; all that they have to pay is for books . . . there is a very large infant-school, the number of which is 148; and I believe 59 are from the families of 41 frame-work knitters. Then we have a large Sunday-school, of course free, in connexion with the Church, for boys and girls, the number of which are, girls 101, of which 42 are from the families of frame-work knitters; boys 86, of which 46 are of the families of frame-work knitters. In addition, I believe, there are schools connected with the Wesleyan Methodists, the Primitive Methodists, and the Baptists.

Source 11.9 *Extract from the 1851 Census enumerator's returns for Thame workhouse*

Course work for G.C.E. and C.S.E. assessment

Some history teachers may wish to devise Mode 3 C.S.E. and G.C.E. 'O' level syllabuses which include work on *History Around Us: Aspects of the history of the locality*.

The following items of course work could be completed by pupils and submitted in a folder as part of their final assessment:

1. Descriptions of sites studied by fieldwork supported by maps, plans, sketches, photographs and any records or surveys.

2. Descriptions of sites studied by classroom investigation supported by maps, plans, sketches, etc.

3. Work setting a site in its historical context and relating it to other sites:
e.g. an illustrated account describing the origins and growth of a village and comparing other village plans with it.

4. The imaginative reconstruction of:
either: a specific incident in the history of the locality,
e.g. the siege of a local castle,
e.g. a Luddite attack on a local mill.
or: life at a particular period,
e.g. village life in the nineteenth century.
or: a study of the connection between a local historical personality or family and the area,
e.g. the Gascoigne family and Aberford,
e.g. the Arkwright family and Cromford,
e.g. William Parker, a Hosier of Ruddington.

Resources

Lists of resources for the study of certain specific features of the locality — such as a castle, church, country house, industrial relic, Roman or Prehistoric remain, have been provided earlier in this book. Teachers should look at these where they are relevant. This list provides details of material not previously mentioned, especially books relating to the study of a village or small area. Useful book lists about agricultural history are available from: The Keeper, The Museum of English Rural Life, Whiteknights, Reading, RG6 2H6.

Some of the books on this list are out of print. You should be able to obtain copies from your local library or from the Schools Library Loan Service.

Resources are listed by order of importance, within each section.

Teachers' books

Joscelyne Finberg, *Exploring Villages*, (Routledge & Kegan Paul, 1958)
David Iredale, *Discovering Local History*, 'Discovering Books Series', (Shire Publications, 1973)
Maurice Willmore Barley, *The English Farmhouse and Cottage*, (Routledge & Kegan Paul, 1961)
R. W. Brunskill, *An Illustrated Handbook of Vernacular Architecture*, (Faber, 1970)
David Iredale, *Discovering this Old House*, 'Discovering Books Series', (Shire Publications, 1968)
R. W. Brunskill, *The Vernacular Architecture of the Lake Counties: A Field Hand Book*, (Faber, 1974)
J. T. Smith & E. M. Yates, 'On the dating of English Houses, from External Evidence', a reprint from *Field Studies*, Vol. 2, No. 5, 1968 — available from E. W. Classey Ltd., 353 Hanworth Road, Hampton, Middlesex
W. G. Hoskins, *Fieldwork in Local History*, (Faber, 1969)
W. G. Hoskins, *Local History in England*, (Longman, 1973)
Eric S. Wood, *Field Guide to Archaeology in Britain*, (Collins, 1975)
Ordnance Survey, *Field Archaeology in Britain*, (1974)
John West, *Village Records*, (Macmillan, 1962)
Robert Douch, *Local History and the Teacher*, (Routledge & Kegan Paul, 1967)
Michael Aston & Trevor Rowley, *Landscape Archaeology: An Introduction to Fieldwork Techniques on Post-Roman Landscapes*, (David & Charles, 1974)
John Richardson, *The Local Historian's Encyclopaedia*, (Historical Publications, 1974)
F. G. Emmison, *English Local History Handlist: A Select Bibliographical List of Sources for the Study of Local History and Antiquities*, (Historical Association, 1969)
W. R. Powell, *Local History from Blue Books*, 'Helps for Students of History', (Historical Association, 1962)
F. G. Emmison & Irvine Gray, *County Records*, 'Helps for Students of History', (Historical Association, 1973)
Joyce Youings (Ed.), *Local Record Sources in Print and in Progress*, 'Helps for Students of History', (Historical Association, 1972)
Peter Eden, *Small Houses in England 1520 – 1820;*

Towards a Classification, 'Helps for Students of History', (Historical Association, 1969)
Alec Clifton-Taylor, *The Pattern of English Building*, (Faber, 1972)
R. B. Wood-Jones, *Traditional Domestic Architecture in the Banbury Region*, (Manchester University Press, 1964)

Reference books for teachers and pupils

Doreen Yarwood, *English Houses*, (Batsford, 1966)
The Victoria History of the Counties of England, each county series has general volumes covering aspects of the history of the whole county, e.g. agriculture, also 'topographical' volumes dealing with visible evidence relating to each parish, town and city. These are available in the local reference library.
Volumes of the English Place Name Society — twenty or more counties have been covered and relevant volumes are probably in the local reference library
Eilert Ekwall, *Concise Oxford Dictionary of English Place Names*, (O.U.P. 1960)
Royal Commission on Ancient and Historic Monuments and Constructions, *Inventories* of all historic buildings in the following areas: Cambridgeshire, Dorset, Oxford, Peterborough, New Town, Cambridge.

Books for pupils

These explain how to study the history of a village and its houses using visible evidence.

Denis R. Mills, *The English Village*, 'Local Search Series', (Routledge & Kegan Paul, 1968)
C. J. Lines & L. H. Bolwell, *Discovering your Environment: History in a Village*, (Ginn, 1970)
Henry Pluckrose, *Villages*, 'On Location Series', (Mills & Boon, 1975)
Henry Pluckrose, *Houses*, 'On Location Series', (Mills & Boon, 1974)
J. D. Chambers, *Laxton: The Last English Open Field Village, a guide*, (HMSO 1964)

Reference material for pupils

These contain background information and contemporary accounts of village life and occupations in the last 170 years.

George Ewart Evans, *Ask the Fellows who cut the Hay*, (Faber, 1972)
George Ewart Evans, *The Farm and the Village*, (Faber, 1974)
Flora Thompson, *Lark rise to Candleford*, (Penguin, 1973)
Mary Russell Mitford, *Our Village*, Sir J. Squire (Ed.), 'Everyman Library', (Dent, 1936)
Raphael Samuels, *Village Life and Labour*, (Routledge & Kegan Paul, 1975)
John Norman Thatcher Vince, *Carts and Wagons*, 'Discovering Books Series', (Shire Publications, 1974)
Marie Hartley and Joan Ingilby, *Yorkshire Village*, (Dent, 1973)
Marie Hartley and Joan Ingilby, *Life and Tradition in the Yorkshire Dales*, (Dent, 1968)
John Burnett, *The Useful Toil: Autobiographies of Working People from the 1820s to the 1920s*, (Allen Lane, 1974)
Frank E. Huggett, *A Day in the Life of a Victorian Farm Worker* (George Allen & Unwin, 1972)
J. C. Wilkerson, *Two Ears of Barley; the Chronicle of an English Village*, (Priory Press, 1969)
Herbert Green, *Village Life in the Eighteenth Century*, 'Then and There Series', (Longman, 1976)

Slides

The following topics are available from the Slide Centre Ltd:
The English Cottage
The English Village
Villages and Village Life
Exhibits from the Abbots Hall Museum of Rural Life of East Anglia, Stowmarket, Suffolk.

Filmstrips

The Village, 'Medieval Life Series', colour, Longman/Common Ground
The Village, 'English Scene', black and white, Tartan — distributed by John King
Development of the Dwelling House, colour, Hugh Baddeley Productions
Other filmstrips dealing with the development of domestic architecture are listed in the Resources section of Chapter 6.

Films

Medieval Village, 16 mm, black and white, 19 mins, distributed by Rank, 1935

History games

David Birt & Jon Nichol, *The Development of the Medieval Town*, first section useful for village siting, Longman Resources Unit
David Birt & Jon Nichol, *Village Enclosure*, Longman Resources Unit

Aspects of the history of the locality

An aerial view of a fortified manor house; Stokesay, Salop

A typical 1930s suburban house; New Malden, Surrey